THE WHOLE

THE WHOLE
FAMILY OF GOD

KESWICK MINISTRY

Edited by David Porter

OM Publishing
Carlisle, UK

Keswich Convention Council, England

© The Keswick Convention Council 1994

All rights reserved. No part of this publication may be reproduced, stored in a retrieval system, or transmitted, in any form or by any means, electronic, mechanical, photocopying, recording or otherwise, without the prior permission of the publishers or a licence permitting restricted copying. In the U.K. such licences are issued by the Copyright Licensing Agency, 90 Tottenham Court Road, London W1P 9HE.

This book is sold subject to the condition that it shall not, by way of trade or otherwise be lent, re-sold, hired out, or otherwise circulated without the publisher's prior consent in any form of binding or cover other than that in which it is published and without a similar condition including this condition being imposed on the subsequent purchaser.

British Library Cataloguing in Publication Data

A catalogue record for this book
is available from the British Library.

ISBN 1–85078–151–6

OM Publishing is an imprint of Send the Light Ltd
PO Box 300, Carlisle, Cumbria, CA3 0QS, UK

Typeset by Photoprint, Torquay, Devon
and Printed in the UK for
OM Publishing, PO Box 300, Carlisle, Cumbria, CA3 0QS
by Cox and Wyman Ltd, Reading

CONTENTS

'The Whole Family of God'

CHAIRMAN'S INTRODUCTION

Some things, happily, never change at the Keswick Convention! The sheer beauty of the setting of mountains and lakes, some beautifully sunny summer days and crowds upon crowds of eager Christians packing the vast Convention marquee—these were heart-warming aspects once again at Keswick 1994. But times change, and changes there were also at Keswick. An overall theme was set for the speakers to work to, and this helped to sharpen the relevance of the ministry in today's world. 1994 has been 'The International Year of the Family,' so the theme decided itself. As a result we found ourselves confronted and challenged by major issues facing Christian family life, and the family life of the church. The result was a fresh seriousness and relevance. 'We were not playing games', as one Convention-goer put it.

In this volume you can read the two sets of five Bible Readings—yes, five. A change this year was to move the great World View Meeting to an enhanced profile on Wednesday evening, thus giving the Bible Readings an extra morning. You will also read some of the excellent addresses given during the two weeks. In publishing them we are most thankful to the publisher, and most prayerful that in the reading of these pages God will continue to bless the ministry wherever this book reaches.

A further change in 1994 was the hand-over of chairmanship. No doubt many have come to equate the Convention with Philip Hacking, whose nine years as Chairman have been accompanied by much change and much blessing. It was particularly encouraging that this year was again marked by his presence giving the first set of Bible Readings. We thank God for Philip, and his successor would want to thank him, and all those who have been such a support, especially in prayer and encouragement, in the hand-over.

Readers of these pages will, we trust, catch a glimpse of the inspiring meetings at which these addresses were given. To *be* there and to be part of that vast gathering of 'the whole family of God' is a blessing in itself beyond measure. But it is the relevant, reverent exposition of Scripture which draws the thousands, and it is this ministry which is encapsulated in these pages.

May God bless you as you read.

Keith A. A. Weston
Chairman of the Keswick Council

EDITOR'S INTRODUCTION

This section of the annual Keswick volume is rather like the standard speech about life-jackets and escape-drill given just before your plane takes off—essential information, but hardly a highlight of the trip. Yet it is important that readers should know that as usual, the material is an abbreviated transcript of the spoken occasion, which means that this is a different book to that which would have been produced had the speakers created it in the calm of their studies; that most of the speakers have graciously waived the right to scrutinise the edited version before publication; and that a representative of the Keswick Council reads the proofs each year to ensure that the material has not been accidentally altered in the editing. The selection of the material was also by the Keswick Council, and the order in which the addresses are printed reflects the particular emphases with which each successive day of the 'Keswick Week' is associated.

Bible quotations have been checked against the appropriate version except where the speaker is obviously paraphrasing (which is usually clear from context, or by the insertion of 'cf' before the reference); every reference to Scripture has been retained, though the quotations have sometimes been shortened; and the editorial intention has been to preserve all the teaching and as much as possible of the atmosphere of the meetings included.

The expanded contents have made it necessary to prune harder this year, and for the same reason, together with a tighter-than-usual schedule, it has also not been possible to supply as many footnotes as usual. As an ex-librarian I regret this, but I can assure you that attempting to track the quotations down will be as profitable for you as it has been for me; an elusive reference to C. T. Studd (which I never did trace) led to my re-reading Norman Grubb's biography of the great man, and there were other unexpected pleasures too. However, enjoying the full Keswick atmosphere—sharing Philip Hacking's grief at England's deplorable performance in the early Test Matches, and enjoying Jim Graham's wonderfully delivered quotations of poetry and prose, for example—demands that you investigate the Keswick tape and video libraries described on p. 252.

You will get most out of this book, however, if you have an open Bible to hand as you read.

I would like to thank Peter Cousins for being at the end of a telephone with an enviable collection of obscure reference books, and Jeremy Mudditt for continuing the tradition of fun and fellowship that has marked my association with Operation Mobilisation since I began this annual task seventeen years ago. Most of all I would like to thank my wife Tricia for transcribing a great many more words than made it into print, and our daughters Lauren and Eleanor for putting up with yet another summer shared with Keswick.

David Porter

THE BIBLE READINGS

'The Alternative Community': Paul's Letter to the Ephesians

by Rev Philip Hacking

1. True Riches (Ephesians 1:1–2:10)

Some of my congregation told me I must be looking forward to a nice relaxed week at Keswick, now that I'm not Chairman any more. While five Bible Readings don't exactly lead to a nice relaxed week, it's a great joy to be able to expound God's word. I hope you enjoy studying it, as I certainly enjoy the privilege of ministering it. In a way I am partly a victim of my own planning: the Council decided this year to have five Bible Readings instead of four, which in principle is a very good thing till you have to do it yourself! And secondly they decided that for the first time they'd tell the Bible expositor what part of the Scripture they wanted him to expound.

I confess that I doubt whether I would have turned to the Ephesian letter by choice. There are other passages on my heart that I might have wanted to expound and which I have been studying recently. Yet I am glad I've worked through Ephesians. I've certainly benefited from it, and I hope you will too. For I believe this letter to Ephesus is saying something very prophetic to the world of today.

I've chosen the title 'the alternative community', because I believe God is saying through this letter, which is all about the church, what it means to be 'in Christ'. It's telling us that we have the privilege of being the alternative community, in a world that is desperately trying to find a place that makes sense.

The Background (1:1–1:2)

There are people here who have come with a lot of experience of Christian teaching; they've got their Greek New Testaments in front of them and they are ready for deeper truths in Ephesians. I trust they may find some. And there are many young Christians here, who have never studied the Ephesian letter before.

By the grace of God—it will need all the grace of God!—I want to take this letter seriously. We shall try to expound virtually every verse. I hope that those who are senior in the faith will discover something new, but will also be gracious and patient when I say some fairly obvious things to people to whom it may be new. And to those who may be young Christians, at least I hope I shall excite you with a possibility or two.

The recipients

As we look at the letter to the Ephesians, one of the great things about it is this recurring phrase 'in Christ'. It means much more than being 'in the church', but that is included. Now, it's possible that the letter was not addressed just to Ephesus. We're not sure about the little phrase in verse 1, 'to the saints in Ephesus'. Many manuscripts don't have it. Some people think it's peculiar, if the letter is meant for the church in Ephesus alone, that in 1:15 Paul says that he has 'heard about' their faith and your love, when he spent the longest period of his ministry in the church in Ephesus. Also, at the end of the letter there are very few greetings; but you would surely send greetings if you were writing to a church you knew and loved.

What I think is generally agreed is that it was probably a circular letter, sent to a number churches of which Ephesus was one, and that this is the reason for the vagueness. And it fits, this idea of a circular letter, because here we are, representing hundreds of Christian fellowships, and what's here in Paul's circular letter is for all of us.

Yet I do like to keep the Ephesian connection. If that was the main church to which the letter went, remember it was the place where Paul had his longest ministry (cf Acts 19). It was a remarkable ministry which lasted for three years; God did great things. It was a church that had a tremendous heritage: Paul was there, Apollos was, Timothy was, John almost certainly was. What a long tradition! Do you come from a churches with a long history of great clergymen? No church had a greater tradition than Ephesus.

Yet in the book of the Revelation it is the first church to which the risen Lord speaks. He says: 'You are a very sound church, you are a very hard-working church. But I've one thing against you, you've lost your first love' (cf Rev. 2:1–7). And if you've lost your first love, in a sense you've lost everything. So none of us can come today without a sense in which we can learn from this letter.

We shall rise to cosmic heights. There are some truths in the Ephesian letter that go way beyond my understanding, they are great and they are wonderful. And then they become extremely practical. I do hope you stay the course, because the practical bits come towards the end. They stem from the highly spiritual bit—indeed, the practical part is as important as are the great spiritual heights of this letter.

The author

Though doubts exist about the readership, I have no doubts about the author. 'Paul,' he calls himself, 'an apostle of Christ Jesus by the will of God.' That's a wonderful phrase! His calling was 'by the will of God'. His whole ministry was 'by the will of God'. And where was he writing this letter? Check Ephesians 3:1, 4:1, 6:20. He was a prisoner. Not of Rome, he says, but of Christ Jesus, 'an ambassador in chains'.

He writes almost certainly in Rome around AD 60. The letter is the mature reflection of a great thinker, but one who believed that Christianity was to be lived out in the market place. Now, I know that sometimes an in-depth exposition becomes more theologically interesting than spiritually challenging. If this does, I shall have failed. But please, the two do go together. You do not become a Christian by anaesthetising your mind. Occasionally I hear people saying, 'If you really want a blessing from God, shut up your mind

for a while and just feel.' Be careful! This letter will stretch
your mind, but it will call to action.

The saints ... the faithful

Verse 1b: He is writing to 'the saints'. That's all of us; those
who are set apart. 'The faithful' may mean those who have
faith or those in whom people put their faith—the two ought
to go together. What has gone wrong with the church today?
Ministers tell me, 'It's terribly hard to get commitment from
people. They'll believe, they'll praise—but when it comes,
for example, to teaching children or leading young people
week after week, they're not queuing up to do it.' It seems to
me that if I have faith, I ought to be absolutely dependable
and loyal.

The saints ... in Christ Jesus

Eleven times in fourteen verses comes that little phrase or its
equivalent 'in Christ'. It is a wonderful picture: if I'm in
Christ, if I've a living relationship with him, then I'm part of
the body of Christ, which is the doctrine of this great letter.
That's why in this family year we are taking this theme. And
I do trust that you will recognise seriously that we are looking
at the most urgent need of our day.

The greeting

'Grace and peace' (verse 2) is much more than a combination of the Greek and the Hebrew greetings. The word
'grace' comes twelve times, the word 'peace' seven times, in
the letter. We will see, particularly tomorrow, how this letter
tells us that peace and reconciliation—that 'horizontal'
peace, in a world where there is no reconciliation, may only
be had when you have 'vertical' peace with God.

We have something unique to offer. That grace and peace
comes 'from God our Father and the Lord Jesus Christ'.
Lest any doubt, the Scripture is consistently sure that the
Father and the Son are together. This letter consistently
sounds that note. And woe betide any part of the church
when it compromises on the uniqueness of Jesus Christ,
which is a danger to which we are prone. Don't get me
wrong! The alternative community is a community which

stands true to Scripture. It doesn't compromise one iota, it doesn't water truth down to be popular and acceptable, it wants to speak to the culture but it doesn't let the culture dominate. So it doesn't mind being thought different, even old-fashioned, provided we're scriptural. Yet it wants to be attractive . . . But one thing we will hold on to at all cost is that Jesus and God are intimately linked. The Old Testament speaks of God the Father, and the New Testament picks up its verses of praise to Him and uses them in praise to Jesus.

Our theme this morning is what I call 'true riches'. Somebody said at a conference recently, 'The church of today has not learned to live with affluence.' I'm sure they were right. Most of us live in an affluent world.

What we are offering as a church is *true* riches. The verb comes out in verses 7 and 8: 'the riches of God's grace that he lavished on us'. It's a lovely picture. We are meant to be rich Christians, if we are those of whom verse 13 is true—those who heard the word of truth, the gospel of our salvation, believed and were sealed by the Spirit.

Resources Expounded (1:3–14)

These verses are a single sentence in the Greek. One commentator describes it like this: 'It's rather like a snowball running down the hill and picking up more snow as it continues.' Somebody else has compared it to a racehorse running. Another has likened it to an operatic overture that includes all that is going to follow. Or to an eagle in full flight.

It's a remarkable passage, and it's all praise. 'Praise be to the God and Father of our Lord Jesus Christ.' Real praise should be mind-full praise, not mind-less praise. I do want to know why I'm praising God; I think it's very important. I think we've got our music right at Keswick—a lovely sense of praise and worship, but all linked in with the word of God. Please feel that what we do as preachers links in with what the musicians are doing with music. We are living together. The mindfulness of our word should lead to mindful praise.

Have you spotted that the Trinity's very much there?

Verses 3–6, the Father elects; verses 7–12, the Son redeems; verses 13–14, the Spirit seals. All the persons of the Godhead. And all of it (verses 6,12,14) is to the praise of God's glory.

So let's look at these resources. First of all,

Resources in the past (verses 3–6)
This is the doctrine of election. Let's get the doctrine right. It's a glorious doctrine! You see, it means that we have to have got our perspective right (verse 3). The blessings that go back into eternity are those blessings which are, in that lovely phrase, 'in the heavenly realm'. That phrase comes five times in this letter. It's getting your perspective right. I don't accept the old saying, 'He was so heavenly-minded that he was no earthly use'. On the whole, I think, Christians are so earthly-minded that they are neither heavenly use or earthly use. The more I have heaven in my perspective, the more of a Christian on earth I will be.

I was never good at art at school. I couldn't understand perspective. You were supposed to get a pencil and hold it towards the horizon. I never got it right, so I will never be an artist. I married an artist instead. She understands perspective ... she has to, being married to me! I don't understand how to do it.

But Christians, we need the heavenly perspective. Verse 3 does not promise us the riches in this world. Beware of the prosperity cult, beware of those who take part of the Old Testament and say, 'If you believe in Jesus then you can expect to be rich and well-off.' What a selfish way of being a Christian! I don't give to God so that I can get. I get, so that I can give. The promise here is a spiritual promise. At the end of the book of Habakkuk comes that lovely statement that you have heard so often, but let's read a little of it again to thrill you with the blessings of the heavenly realms: 'Though the fig-tree docs not bud and there are no grapes on the vines, though the olive crop fails and the fields produce no food, though there are no sheep in the pen and no cattle in the stalls, yet I will rejoice in the LORD, I will be joyful in God my Saviour' (Hab. 3:17–18).

There's a man who got his perspective right! And when, as

I sometimes do, I meet Christians like that, they humble me
and give me cause to rejoice. Let's get our perspective right.
Don't you see, this is an alternative community? In the world,
if things go wrong my happiness goes, because happiness
goes alongside happenings. But as a believer my joy
continues.

It all began in eternity. Verse 4: we are elected in Christ
before the creation of the world. Peter tells us (1 Peter 2)
that that is true of the church. We're the new Israel, we are
called of God to be a kingdom of priests and to be prophets;
that's our assurance. Jesus said in John 15:16, 'You did not
choose me, but I chose you.' That does not mean they didn't
respond; of course they did. Of course they said 'Yes'. Then
they went back to the assurance that salvation does not
depend upon feelings or actions but on His grace and mercy.

But you will only find assurance and save yourself from
arrogance if you realise why He chose us. Verse 4, 'to be holy
and blameless in his sight'. That is, we are chosen to become
more like Him, so that we might be 'conformed to the
likeness of his Son' (Rom. 8:29).

In verses 5 and 11 the idea of our predestination comes
out again. Those of you who are Anglicans, may I draw your
attention to the Thirty-Nine Articles of Religion? Have you
ever read them? I used to say to my congregation that when
you hear a boring sermon, pick up your Prayer Book and
turn to the Thirty-Nine Articles at the back. Read them; they
are even more boring. You'll come back to the sermon with
great joy!

But let me read to you Article 17—not because it's
Anglican, but because it's good Scripture. The doctrine of
predestination, it explains, is:

> Full of sweet, pleasant and unspeakable comfort to Godly
> persons . . . For curious and carnal persons, lacking the Spirit of
> Christ, to have continually before their eyes the sentence of
> God's Predestination, is a most dangerous downfall.

In other words, we don't fully understand this grace, this
wonder. All I can say is: 'Thank God in His mercy that I am
part of that elect people of God!' I don't carry any merit, I

just thank God for His mercy. And I'm challenged to live a life of holiness to demonstrate to the world that I am part of that church of Jesus, which is the elect people of God called and therefore called in the world to witness. Read 1 Corinthians 1:2, where a 'church' is defined as those 'called to be holy' in the world.

Did you know that the Greek word for 'parish' actually means 'strangers'? It's an interesting word; I often think that whole idea of a parish church, of whatever denomination you are, should be saying to our nation: 'There is another world.' Would that all churches were alive with that message! The church is there to say: 'This is the *parish*; we are strangers, the elect people of God, elected in the past.'

Resources in the present (verses 7–8)

One of the great riches we have is the beauty and the wonder of our salvation in Christ; redemption through His blood, the forgiveness of sins. We are rich in Him.

Please notice the word 'redemption' in verse 7. It's a word often used in Scripture. It implies that we are bought back, just as a slave could buy himself out of slavery into freedom. Jesus said, 'The Son of Man came to give His life a ransom' (cf Mark 10:45), and Peter wrote that we are redeemed not with silver and gold, but with the precious blood of Christ (cf 1 Pet. 1:18–20). So you see, the great message is that in the present we are rich, and the greatness of our riches is the forgiveness the redemption of Christ.

I want to use an illustration from one of the great writers on the Atonement, James Denney, who said—and I'm updating his illustration—'If I were lying on a sun-soaked beach on the Costa del Sol and a friend rushed by saying, "I'm going to prove how much I love you"—and then threw himself into the sea and drowned, I might be very impressed by his amazing self-sacrifice, but I might well think he's a little dotty. But if I were actually swimming in the sea and in trouble, and the same man came rushing by and flung himself in and rescued me and died in the attempt, saying, "I'm doing it because I love you"—then I would understand.'

If the children of the world are not lost without Christ, if at the end of the day we all get to heaven anyway, then why did Christ die? How does the cross demonstrate His love? It's only because I'm in desperate straits and I need to be redeemed, to be rescued, that God's love is manifest in the cross.

I bring that in because, it seems to me, this is where the riches of the gospel lie. Because we don't take sin seriously we don't take the cross seriously, and we keep on wanting something else more exciting. 'Not *that* old story, please!' But if the cross is not the only hope, it is no hope at all. Here is this marvellous picture: the riches of God's grace lavished on us are that He actually took our place on the cross, rescued us, redeemed us. It is, says Paul, 'in accordance with the riches of God's grace that he lavished on us' (verse 7). So there are these riches for us in the present. Please, take it seriously.

There are people who offer a way of salvation which is just one out of many. 'After all,' they say, 'don't all religions say the same thing? Can't we get there by different routes?' A month ago I was driving along a crowded motorway getting more and more frustrated, when suddenly I realised that the other cars had all disappeared. I turned my radio on and started to whistle—a sure sign that I'm at peace and relaxed and all is well. Until suddenly, there was gravel crunching under the car and I realised that I was on a stretch of the motorway that hadn't yet been opened. I had to reverse all the way back and join the bumper-to-bumper crowd.

I was absolutely sincere. There wasn't anybody more sincere on that road. I thought I was right, and I was gloriously happy. But I wasn't getting anywhere. 'There is a way that seems right to a man, but in the end it leads to death' (Prov. 14:12). I wasn't exactly on the way to death, but I wasn't getting anywhere.

The riches we offer are only riches if we believe that He is the only way, that all roads do not lead the same way, and that there is therefore something unique to offer. When people come in desperate need, there is no other gospel; and there we stand with something unique. The sad thing is, the church becomes so dogmatic about things it ought not be dogmatic about and so reticent about things it ought to be dogmatic about. May God help us to enjoy and share our riches.

Resources in the future (verses 9–10)
In the future there is final victory. One day there will come the finality of our salvation; that lovely picture of things that are yet to be.

There is always in the Christian life a 'not yet', there are always things for which we must wait. Verse 10 does not mean that one day everybody will get there—that would make Paul desperately inconsistent. What it does say is that there will be a final day when it will all be added up in Christ. It does not say that everybody will get to heaven. It says that He is sovereign, that every knee will bow. 1 Corinthians 15:24–28, He will offer everything to the Father; Romans 8:18–21, the whole creation which is groaning will then be at peace. What a lovely picture. Why don't we share it?

Link Passage: The Spirit Who Brings Hope (1:11–14)

And now we have a dynamic link, this lovely picture of the Spirit who brings this hope to us all: election, riches, victory.

In verses 11–12, Paul talks about 'we'. He's talking about the Jews who have become Christians (verse 13) and 'you', the Gentiles who have become Christians. That's our theme for tomorrow: All One in Christ. And we have the wonderful cosmic purpose of verses 11 and 12, which is already ours because we have heard the word, the gospel, we believe, we've been sealed.

I want to say two things about those verses. Expert theologians tell us they contain all sorts of problems; I'm inclined to agree. For example, there are those who see the sealing of the Spirit as being a 'second experience'. As I understand the text it's not saying that. It's saying that the sealing is the other side of believing the word of truth. And from God's angle, we convert ourselves: God regenerates us. We listen and believe: God seals us, guaranteeing security.

Then the other, more important thing: 'You heard the word of truth, the gospel of your salvation.' There's a danger today of saying, 'Well I'm involved in evangelism but I wouldn't call myself an evangelical.' Many people are becoming almost ashamed of calling themselves evangelical. I'm proud to be an evangelical! To me it's a very beautiful word. I can't see how you can be consistent in evangelism unless you are actually sure about the *evangel* you are offering—the word of truth. Paul says, 'You must hand on to others what you heard me say in the presence of many witnesses' (cf 2 Tim. 2:2). The evangelical truth is that alone which brings rebirth. So if I am going to be evangelistic, I must hold on to the evangel. Evangelism is what we do with the evangel.

I know some evangelicals who seem terribly uninterested in evangelism, but are very determined to hold on to the word of truth. They will write rude letters about bishops who don't believe the gospel, but they don't seem all that bothered about winning their neighbours. I say to such people: 'You don't really believe the evangel. If you did you'd want to share it.' But then there's the other side of the coin. 'Well of course I don't really believe in Scripture, but I'm concerned to reach out.' But with what? How can you hold out, if you are not sure what you're holding on to?

This kind of regeneration, the work of the Spirit, comes when people hear 'the word of truth, the gospel of your salvation'. If they don't hear they can't believe. And if they don't believe they're not saved—I hope we believe that. And when they are saved, they are sealed with the promised Holy Spirit.

Years ago I thought up the illustration of an engagement ring—a first instalment—for the word 'deposit' in verse 14. And I'm delighted to discover that in modern Greek the same word actually means an engagement ring. When I got engaged I gave my fiancée an engagement ring. It was a promise of what was yet to come. But one ring was not enough: there had to be a second ring, the wedding ring, the final ring. (I was an impoverished student, and was delighted to find that the wedding ring was cheaper than the engagement ring!). Do you see, the one ring said, 'The other ring will follow'? The engagement ring is lovely, but one day there will be a wedding day. Just so in verse 14. The gift of the Spirit tells me that one day there'll be the final redemption; one day we shall be all together as the people of God, in the presence of God guaranteeing our inheritance. The Spirit says, 'Don't worry, one day you will have the full inheritance.' We are being saved, and one day we shall be finally saved. God's people depend upon God's will, live for God's glory, and are God's possession.

Resources Expected (1:15–23)

Paul was always praying. He'd started praying in verse 3, and he picks it up in verses 15–23. Please note he has God in mind in verse 17. The Trinity is there: 'that the God of our Lord Jesus Christ, the glorious Father, may give you the Spirit of wisdom and revelation'—it's probably a capital S, though people argue about it. But Paul brings this awareness of God in verse 17 and the awareness of their need in verse 15, and he prays.

I wonder why we don't pray like we used to? In the days when revival came—genuine revival, the real thing—people agonised in prayer. I don't know why we don't seem to now; maybe that's why we don't see revival. But when I see the needs of that world out there and I realise the greatness of my God, the two should meet, bringing the needs of the world to this great God, focusing God and the needs of the world. Of course He doesn't need me to tell Him. He knows the needs before I tell Him. But He longs for me to be involved. And my prayer, says the book of Revelation, goes up like incense and comes down in blessing and activity.

What should we pray for? Very simply, he tells them to expect these resources.

Pray to know the hope (verses 17–18)

The first thing he prays for is wisdom, revelation, knowledge, enlightening. Is that what you pray for most? It comes so often in Paul's praying. We need wisdom. The Bible says that if I lack wisdom I should pray to God; He loves to give me wisdom. Right at the head of the list of the gifts of the Spirit in 1 Corinthians 12 is the message of wisdom and the message of knowledge. And here Paul prays that they might know the hope. And may I point out that that great phrase 'the riches of his inheritance' recurs in verse 18—'that you may know the hope to which he has called you'?

'Call' refers to what happens to every Christian, not just the special call to those who are going out to be ministers or missionaries. Every Christian has been called to a hope, and we are meant to know the hope—not least in a hopeless world. Woody Allen once remarked, 'The future is not what it used to be.' I believe we live in a world which no longer has a future. I no longer say to young people when they graduate, 'What job are you going to do?' because quite often the answer is they haven't a clue: is there going to be a job at all? In all sorts of ways, the hope, the security, the future seems to have gone.

Now we as Christians have a hope which we know, and we want to say to people there is a hope; and we should know it, so that we can share it.

Pray to experience the power (verses 19–21)
'That power is like the working of his mighty strength' (verse 19). There are four words, all full of power. We have watched the news on television and seen those pictures of bits from space smashing into Jupiter. And I remember reading in the newspaper about the power of those fragments, many times more powerful than all the nuclear weapons in the world combined. Paul is talking about that kind of power. We know that the power of his mighty strength seen in the resurrection of Christ is the power that raised Jesus from the dead—that power is available for us. We are meant to be powerful Christians.

Pray to show the glory (verses 22–23)
Christ is sovereign. He's head over everything, He is Lord, He is risen, He bears the marks of His suffering but He's Lord. Verses 22–3: '[He is] head over everything for the church, which is his body, the fullness of him who fills everything in every way.'

Most commentaries on Ephesians take about twenty pages to explain verse 23. It's one of the most complicated passages. Let me summarise, in just a sentence or two.

It could be (and the Greek word for fullness, *pleroma*, allows it to be) that the church 'fills out' Jesus, that Jesus is filled in His church. Now there is a truth in that: that is to say—how do people see Jesus today? Only through us. I like to juxtapose two verses, John 1:18 and 1 John 4:12, both written, I believe, by the same person. They begin identically: 'No-one has ever seen God.' John 1:18 goes on to say, 'but God the only [Son] . . . has made him known.' 1 John 4:12 says, 'No-one has ever seen God; but if we love each other, God lives in us.' That's a staggering thought. Nobody can see God. Nobody today can see Jesus. But they do see the church. They do see a company of Christians. We're delighted to have some Keswick residents with us today; but the Keswick residents who don't go to church—they see these vast numbers of people flooding their town. What sort of image do they see? But even more, where we live day by day, in our parish, wherever we live, it ought to be true that Christ is, as it were, 'filled out' in us.

I prefer to think, however, that perhaps the meaning is not that Jesus is filled through us, but that we, the church, are filled with Him; and that the church is meant to be the body of Christ filled with Christ. He is our fullness. But we are to show His glory.

We know the hope, we experience the power, we show the glory—we'll come back to this in chapter 3. And you can see as we come to our last Bible Study that in Ephesians 6 all these words come back again together with their promise to us in our lives.

Resources experienced (2:1–10)

Paul has given his readers the great cosmic picture of 1:23, the fullness filling everything and everywhere, and now suddenly he says, 'As for you'. From the broad canvas he focuses on us.

Our own work

Verses 1–3 give a grim picture of what we are all like apart from Christ. In verse 1 'you', in verse 3 'us'. It's all of us, whatever our background. Paul is saying, 'We Jews, all of us are like this—dead in transgressions and sin, dead spiritually, cut off from God.' By what? By transgressions, which means 'going away from', 'falling short of' the path.

David Sheppard used to play cricket for England. He was once stumped twice in the same Test Match. Once he was stumped by a mile, and once by a few inches. He points out that in the newspapers the next day, it didn't say 'stumped, but only just'. He was out, whether it was by a mile or by an inch. He comments, 'Some people miss the kingdom of God by miles. Some miss it by inches. But if you are out, you are out.'

Paul is saying, 'You people, you were dead in your transgressions and sin, you followed the ways of Satan' (cf verse 2). 'And all of us, Jewish people, religious people still fell short.' Look at verse 3: we were all, he says, 'gratifying the cravings of our sinful nature and following its desires and thoughts'. The word 'desires' is the word 'lusts'. If I were to ask you what the word 'lusts' means, you'd probably talk about sexual immorality. You'd be partly right. Did you know that that there are fifteen works of the flesh listed in Galatians 5:5? Three to do with sexual immorality, two to do with the occult, two to do with drunkenness. All evils. That makes seven. The other eight are to do with envy, malice, pride—they are all as guilty as the others.

And Paul is saying that we all stand condemned and because of that we deserve God's wrath (cf verse 3). That's all our own work.

His own work
But thankfully, verses 4–10 are all His own work. How many preachers have pointed out verse 4! 'But God', that's how he starts. Without God's help, this is where we all are—'but God'. Note some lovely words: 'grace' (verses 5 and 8), 'mercy' (verse 4), 'love' (verse 4), 'kindness' (verse 7). And it all leads to salvation.

Salvation is a word we don't use much nowadays. I don't suppose anybody's asked you recently, 'Are you saved?' But it's a lovely word which needs to be reinstated sensibly and sensitively. And if all that's our experience (look at verses 5 and 6), if we've been the result of God's love, mercy and kindness and we've been saved and we're being saved, then (verse 5 and 6) we've been made alive together, raised together and we're sitting together. What a lovely picture of our union with Christ! We share His death, we share His resurrection, we share His victory. And all that (verses 8 and 9) is not of us. 'This not from yourselves, it is the gift of God—not by works, so that no one can boast' (2:8–9).

I want to say two things as I finish. First: *we do have a real part to play.* Don't get the idea that God's work is so sovereign that we are merely passive. Sometimes we try to say that. But there is something we have to do. For example, 'It is by grace you have been saved, through faith—and this not from yourselves' (2:8). The word 'this' does not refer to 'faith'. One is a neuter, the other a feminine word. 'This' refers to the whole act of God. We still have to believe. Faith is what we must do. Verse 10: there are good works that we have 'to do'. We'll come back to that phrase again tomorrow. So we do have a part to play. We don't sit back and let go.

But the real emphasis in verse 10 is, 'We are his workmanship'. The word 'his' is emphatic in the Greek. I finish on that word 'workmanship'. In Greek, it's the word for a poem. God has written something in our lives, and people out there are meant to be able to read that poem.

He's done it in us. What matters in the church is not the building but the people. Not long ago we built an extension to our church. An architect commented, 'What a marvellous conversion job here.' I thought. 'Hello—here's a chance for the gospel!' So I said, 'We specialise in conversion jobs in Fulwood.' He said, 'Can you show me some more?' I said, 'I could, but you wouldn't understand.' It led to a good conversation. But what is a 'conversion job'? What was he looking at? He was looking at an old school building that bore traces of being a school but was now a lounge. You could see the marks of what it had been, but now it was different.

The workmanship of God in the world in which we live means that of course we bear the marks of the old, in the right sense of the word. I don't mean the old way of wickedness; I mean, we still are ourselves. And the world is going to be impressed when they see the alternative community. Yes, we are like them. Yes, we do have the same problems, we get ill like they do, we get made redundant like they do, we have joys like they have too, but there's something different. There is that which is unique. Our riches seem to be inexhaustible. We are His conversion job, His poem, His workmanship. And behind all that there is a revolution, as we shall see—tomorrow.

2: Lasting Reconciliation
(Ephesians 2:11–3:21)

There are several three-letter words in Greek that are often translated by the English 'therefore'. And we shall find that these words form natural divisions for our reading today and the next two days.

Chapter 2:11 starts 'Therefore', and in the Greek it's one three-letter word. There are two kinds of 'therefores' in the New Testament epistles. One, such as tomorrow's, moves from the doctrinal substructure to the practical outworkings. The other, such as today's linking back to yesterday, gives us the other side of the same coin. Yesterday was a reminder to us of those true riches that are ours (2:7ff). That is the wonder of our being reconciled to God. Today we look the other side of the same coin. If we've been reconciled to God and through that vertical reconciliation have peace with God, then by that very token we are reconciled one to another. You cannot say 'Our Father' without saying 'My brother'.

The word 'hermeneutics' is one of today's fashionable words. It has to do with the importance of looking at what the Bible says in its context and of translating it into the context of our own day—I know that the experts will tell me that it's more complicated than that, but that's the essence of it. It's often quite straightforward. Very often when I read Isaiah, he's speaking to the eternal unchanging need of a human heart. I don't need to know when he wrote it or to whom he wrote it, it speaks right to my heart and I understand it perfectly well.

But there are times when it is important to know the culture of a Bible text. We are seeing such an instance in these chapters, where the great issue is the Jew-Gentile divide. Verse 14 speaks of 'the dividing wall of hostility'. It was a visual aid in a temple that's now gone. In the temple in Jerusalem was a point beyond which no Gentile could pass on pain of death. Further on was a point where no woman could pass on pain of death. Further on again, and nobody but the high priest could pass and then only once a year. And so on. There were walls which said 'No further'. And you will know, if you know your Bible, that when Jesus died on the cross the veil—the last wall, if you like—was torn down and the way to God was made clear. The dividing wall, Paul was saying in his day, the Jew/Gentile relationship, is now gone.

That's not the main issue for most of us today, but it's an issue. In our congregation for many years was a gracious gentleman who was a world expert in hermeneutics. He used to sit at my feet when I preached. He was on the staff of Sheffield University. His book, *The Two Horizons*, is the expert's book on hermeneutics. Some years ago one of my curates said at a staff meeting, 'Philip, I think we ought to discuss Tony's book. He's a member of our congregation.' I said 'That's a splendid idea. You read the first two chapters, and when you've understood them we'll meet and discuss it.' That was fourteen years ago and I'm still waiting. But in *The Two Horizons* Tony Thiselton is asking: where does the horizon of today meet the horizon of the Bible?

There is a very important phrase in today's passage. It comes in 2:12, and in the NIV is translated 'excluded from citizenship'. It comes again in 4:18, where it says 'separated from the life of God'. It's the same word in Greek, and it's the word that's used today so often for alienation. It is found only in these two verses and the equivalent verses in Colossians.

Where is there alienation in the world today? Well, it's everywhere, but not so much between Jew and Gentile. Think of the other walls. Sometimes they come down, like for example the Berlin Wall. But you remember how wonderful it all seemed, and yet how sad it is that it hasn't gone quite as we hoped? We rejoice at the end of apartheid in South Africa, we go on praying that that dividing wall might be down permanently. You can think of other alienations. Here Paul speaks of those who are excluded from belonging to the people of God (2:12), and excluded from the life of God Himself because of sin (4:18).

But the message is that once we are brought near to God through Jesus, we are all brought near in the same way—at the foot of the cross. Therefore if we are reconciled to God through Jesus' death on the cross then we are all one in Christ.

Notice how the two halves of chapter 2 are in parallel. Yesterday we saw that verses 1–3 gave a picture of the world without God—a grim picture, a picture, so often, of our day. There's a lot that's good in our world, but there's a lot that's evil. Then in verses 11–12 you get another picture of the world without God. There's the parallel. In verse 4 Paul said, 'but God', and in verse 13 he says, 'but now'. And into the midst of this unreconciled world comes God and His offer of the gospel.

But I want to point out (and keep this in mind as we go through the passage) that we are only reconciled to one another because we have peace with God. There is no other way in which men and women in our torn world will ever find with peace with each other, apart from the cross. And I would have hoped we'd have heard the message by now. I hear all sorts of odd things talked about 'creation-spirituality'—that we are all human beings, that we are all made in the image of God, so can't we all beautifully live together? Do we *need* the cross?

We desperately need the cross.

I led a mission some years ago at Leicester University. The great opponent of the gospel was the Humanist Society. They did us a world of good, they defaced our posters——there's nothing better for bringing posters to people's attention! But you see, even twenty-odd years ago humanism had a following. There were those who did believe that man had come of age. Can't man learn to live together with man without all this gospel business? Can't we be reconciled without any message of the cross? I would have thought that to be a humanist today means that you must be a greater believer than any Christian. And it's blind faith, for there is no evidence for the humanist creed.

And so as I dare to speak this week from Ephesians about this alternative community that we offer to the world, we are not running away from the world, we're not escaping. We're saying to the world, 'It can be.' But there's a big qualification: unless we practise it, proclaim it and pray for it, we will be of all people the most responsible for the mess. And I say it not about them, but about us. The mess our country's in today is without doubt largely the failure of the church. And the church is 'us' not 'them'. If only, if only we had practised, preached and prayed as we should have, things would be different.

Practising it (2:11–22)

We start by practising it. There are three 'Rs' here. First of all,

Remember (2:11–12)

He uses the word twice in two verses. And it's very important that Christians should remember what once we were. You do become holier-than-thou when you forget. It's amazing how often people complain about the behaviour of people today, forgetting that once they too were like that. Remember!

'You Gentiles,' says Paul, 'remember what you once were' (cf verse 11). The Jews called Gentiles 'dogs'. That was the kind of thing that was said—these awful labels in verse 11. 'But,' says Paul, 'what were you? You were Christless, stateless, friendless, hopeless, Godless.' That's the picture of the world without God. It's all true.

Note the word Godless, 'without God in the world'. The Greek word is the one from which we get the English word 'atheist'. There are not all that many genuine atheists in the world. There are some, of course. My concern here is not with those who don't believe in God, but with those who live as if God were not there. And there are plenty of those around. 'And remember,' says Paul, 'that's what once you were, remember.'

Reconciled (2:13:18)

Now secondly, remember what Christ has done to make you what you are.

Verses 13–18—He has brought us, those who were far away and those who were near (verse 17), and He's preached peace and He's brought us together. How? Verse 13; 'In Christ Jesus you who once were far away have been brought near through the blood of Christ.' It is like being a privileged visitor to an old Highland croft, invited as a friend of the family not just to remain in the formal visitors' room but allowed into the inner, family rooms. All of us who are Christians have been brought into the inner presence of God. We are able to draw near; we can 'draw near' (Heb. 10:22), because He has opened the way for us.

Think it through. If *I* can draw near, so can people of different races and backgrounds. We've all come the same way. How? Through the blood of Christ. Do recognise that in verse 13, we're not just drawing near through Jesus: we're drawing near through the blood of Christ. Jew, Gentile, black, white, middle-class, working-class, upper-class if they still exist—all come because Jesus *died*. It's not some vague notion that we're one in Jesus. I'm not one with everybody who talks about Jesus, and I'm a long way removed from some who do. Their Jesus is certainly not mine. But I do draw near through the cross. And the cross, while it divides, also gloriously unites. Only at the cross are we brought near.

But if we are brought near by the cross, the same cross draws others. Verse 14: 'He himself is our peace.' He has reconciled us. Or again, in verse 15, He 'made peace', He is our peace-maker. Or in verse 17, He 'preached peace'; when He came back from the dead Jesus went into the upper room. He said first of all to them 'Peace be with you,' the normal greeting. Then He showed them His hands and His side and said 'Peace be with you.' And when He did that He was saying, 'The peace I offer you is not just an inner feeling, because I've died. I've made peace.'

The word 'peace' is misunderstood. Study it some time. Discover how often the great phrase 'the God of peace' comes in the Bible. It's a very dynamic phrase. For example, 'The God of peace, who . . . brought back from the dead our

Lord Jesus' (Heb. 13:20); 'The God of peace will soon crush Satan under your feet' (Rom. 16:20). It's a very positive phrase. Peace is not woolly placidity.

I want to stress this, because some say, 'Well—if I'm a peace-maker and if I love peace and if I've been drawn in through the blood of Christ—then I ought to always be nice and tolerant and not disturb. Peace for all.'

When I was a curate our lay reader was particularly good at remaining calm in the middle of total uproar during the 'Open Sunday School' sessions we had in the summer. Chaos went on around him and he remained quite placid. I said to my fellow-curate, 'How does he cope?' 'Oh,' he said, 'he doesn't even notice. He lives in a pool of peace.' But should we live in a pool of peace? Should I allow awful things to happen in the world and the church, and because I belong to Jesus just live in my pool of peace—so I might say a few prayers, but I don't ever muddy the waters or stir things up? I don't find that Jesus was like that at all. The message of this peace is a much more dynamic message.

Notice what He's done because of His peace. Verse 14: the dividing wall is down; verse 15: no more can we think we get there specially because we know the law. The moral law still remains, it is not pushed out, He said, 'I came to fulfil the law.' But it's not a matter of some people getting there because they are law-keepers, and some being outside. He's got rid of all that structure. And when the veil was torn in two, it was a symbol of that.

And now—this is the bit I get excited by—do you see it? Verse 14: He has made the two one. Verse 15, making of Himself one new man out of the two. Now Jews didn't become Gentiles and Gentiles didn't become Jews, and men didn't become women, and women didn't become men. But we are one in Christ Jesus and what He's done. We are equal but different. But He's made us, in the family of God, one new glorious thing called the church, His bride, His great creation. And I hope you love the church. You ought to, because it means a great deal. Christ died for the church. He loves the church. So whatever our background, whatever our denomination, whatever small differences we have, we are new man and woman in Christ. A new humanity.

A friend of mine who is bolder than I am was speaking in Northern Ireland to an audience made up almost wholly of Protestants. He thought he'd better stir them up. He began, 'I want you all to know there will be no Catholics in heaven.' And that brought a great many murmurs of assent. His second sentence was, 'There will be no Protestants in heaven.' They weren't quite as enthusiastic about that. His third sentence was, 'There will only be Christians in heaven.' You may say to me that you still have problems with Roman Catholicism; so do I. Of course. But there will be people in heaven who have a Roman Catholic background. There are some here today, and I am sure it will be true of heaven too.

What matters in heaven, what matters on earth, what matters now, is that we are a new humanity. It matters that we should demonstrate that our motto, 'All one in Christ Jesus' (Gal. 3:28)—is a reality. We've been reconciled, Jew or Gentile, whatever our background, at the foot of the cross. And note that verse 18 is a trinitarian reference: through Jesus, we both, Jew and Gentile, have access to the Father in one Spirit. That's the glorious picture. And 'we . . . have access.' That means, we can get there.

A couple of weeks ago I was privileged to have lunch in the House of Lords. How did I get in? Did I say to the man on duty at the door, 'I'm the ex-chairman of the Keswick Convention Council'? It wouldn't have made the slightest impression. No, I was the guest of a bishop who wanted to talk to me. He had to introduce me, I was his guest. So I had access, because there was one person who had a right to be there; and through him and through him alone I was able to enter the House of Lords.

Nobody in the world, whatever their background, has a right of access. Some of us think we have, but we are only there by the grace of Jesus. We are only there through the blood of Christ. So let's cease the boasting in secondary things!

Reformed (2:19–22)

So, to what we are now. Note the phrase 'no longer'. We will come across it again. It's a phrase that should be written across all our lives: 'Things are different now'. Verse 19, we are 'no longer foreigners and aliens, but fellow-citizens'. We are strangers in the world, but not to each other. Remember in Philippians, where Paul says to a church in that city whose citizens were proud to be Roman, 'Our citizenship is in heaven' (Phil. 3:20)—we belong to the people of God, we are members of the family of God, God's household.

The most joyful aspect of travelling for me is discovering the wonder of the Christian family when I am miles away from home. I can step off a plane and meet a man for the first time, whose background is a thousand miles removed from mine and who talks a different language; and I am closer to him than I am to some people who may have my blood going through their veins. I don't really believe that blood is thicker than water. The spiritual renewal that comes to people brings you into a far greater kinship than exists even in the most wonderful human family. We are adopted into that great family of God.

In verses 20–22 he picks up the illustration that we are part of a building. Notice, it was built on the foundation of the apostles and prophets. We'll see tomorrow that there's a uniqueness about that ministry. We are part of the church that started at a certain time with a certain message. If you throw overboard the apostolic message you are no more a church in the biblical sense of that word. What makes the church is that foundation. We belong to the church built on the apostolic truth of the word of God. Our Lord is the chief cornerstone, and we grow together.

Let me remind you of two well-known passages. One comes after the Sermon on the Mount, and tells of those who built on sand and on rock (Matt. 7:24–29). We sometimes misunderstand who these people are. Those on the rock are those who hear the word of God and do it, those on the sand are those who hear the word of God and don't do it (verses 24, 26). That is, the real foundation is the foundation of listening and obeying—having the word of God, and obeying it.

Look now in 1 Peter 2:4–5, where Peter talks about Christians being built as 'living stones' into the building of Christ, the cornerstone. But he goes on to point out that the same Jesus is a stone of stumbling and offence (verse 8). That very same stone on which people will build is the stone which causes other people to trip up. Now, I want to develop that, for Bible studies ought not just to make us better theologians but also better Christians through knowing the Bible and its teaching.

So what is this passage saying? It is saying that the very same person on whom we build is the person over whom some people trip. If you preach Christ crucified and none other, people will come to faith: if you preach Christ crucified and none other, people will leave your church. I say to you what I have been saying to younger ministers for some time: make your minds up. If you decide that you want a gospel that nobody will ever get upset over and leave your church—then you must reckon on nobody getting converted either. For if you want to preach a message by which some are converted, you can be quite sure that some will leave.

Some years ago we had a lady in my congregation who always sat in the same place. So I noticed when she hadn't been in church for a few weeks, and I went and knocked on the door.

'You'll be asking me why I'm not at church, won't you.'

I said, 'Yes, I am.'

'Well, I don't intend to come any more.' At least that was honest!

'Why not?' I asked.

'I've moved around the country,' she said, 'and I've been in half a dozen Church of England churches. You're the first vicar who's told me I need to be converted and born again. How do I know all the others were wrong and you are right?'

So I said, 'Well—it's not a matter of whether I'm right and they're wrong. Let's look at the Bible together.'

But she didn't want to. She didn't come back to our church. She preferred the ones who told her what she wanted to hear.

I don't like people leaving. I'm not thick-skinned, it upsets me. But if I'm going to preach the gospel by which some people are built up, others will leave. And I therefore want to say to you preachers and would-be preachers here, make your mind up! We are in a world of success-madness. Of course you can build up numbers, of course you can be very successful if you've got a particular gift and you don't upset people by preaching something unpopular. And that is the challenge.

Verse 21 is a lovely verse: you are growing together, rising 'to become a holy temple in the LORD. And in him you too are being built together to become a dwelling in which God lives by his Spirit.' How often the Bible speaks of individual Christians and the church as being like a building, a temple of the Spirit. And it's the building of people that counts, not the place in which you meet, as I'm sure you believe.

Christ Church Fulwood is no architectural masterpiece. It's a very nice church and we like it; but we are not usually featured in architectural magazines. Yet we've been in one. Recently a gentleman came to me. 'You're the vicar of Christ Church Fulwood in Sheffield.'

I said 'Yes.'

'Oh! I've heard about your church.'

I adopted a humble attitude, expecting him to say 'You have good numbers'. I prepared the humble smile one uses on these occasions.

'Yes,' he said. 'I've heard a lot about your church. You're the church with the see-through pillars, aren't you.'

I felt somewhat deflated. That was the only thing he knew about it, that he could see through the pillars (which is quite true). So I used the illustration: 'The congregation are see-through as well—you see Christ through us . . .'

That is the main thing. It's not the building, it's the people. And the people should surely be a rich people in the sense of gifts diverse, which will be our theme tomorrow.

Preach it (3:1–13)

These verses are the most difficult verses in Ephesians for me. You will have to concentrate with intensity beyond your normal endurance. But they are great verses. Why are they difficult?

See how he starts. Verse 1 breaks off; suddenly Paul goes off at a tangent and only picks up the thread again in verse 14. He was going to start to pray, but he remembered something. I often do the same when I pray. It's not necessarily a bad thing. You apologise to the Almighty and say, 'I'm sorry, Lord, I've just gone off at a tangent.' It doesn't matter, provided the tangent you go off on is a biblical one. And as Paul is about to pray, remembering the theme, remembering the wonder of this reconciliation, he just marvels at it all and goes off into a very complicated bit of language. I want to draw out the main thread of it for you.

Hold on to the truth (1–6)
Notice how Paul emphasises himself in 3:1: 'I, Paul, the prisoner of Christ Jesus.' The same again in 4:1—'A prisoner for the Lord . . . I' Do you see the strange thing? He wasn't a prisoner of Christ Jesus: he was a prisoner of Nero—or that's what you would have thought. He was in prison because the Roman authorities had put him there. But he didn't see it that way. It was Christ who put him there; he was Christ's prisoner.

But also note (3:1) 'for the sake of you Gentiles'. Do you remember how he got to prison? Because he dared to say to a group of Jews at the end of his testimony, 'God sent me to the Gentiles.' The moment he said the word 'Gentiles', they want to lynch him. That's how much they hated the Gentiles—'How dare you suggest to a Jewish congregation that Gentiles and Jews may now be one!'

Earlier, he had been brought into custody. Why? Theoretically, because somebody had said they had seen him with a Gentile called Trophimus in the temple in the holy place (Acts 21:29). It wasn't true. Paul would have had no problem theologically about taking a Gentile there, but he wouldn't have done it. He didn't want to offend Jews, because he wanted to reach his own people. But the rumour started. How many people have had their reputations killed by rumours passed on by people second, third or fourth hand? Most of us in this tent, including the preacher, need to repent of that. 'Have you heard that . . . It's said that . . .' Paul never did take Trophimus in.

And so he really was in prison because of the Gentiles, because God had called him to minister to the Gentiles. What had happened: verse 2—'the administration of God's grace that was given to me for you'; verse 7—'the gift of God's grace given me through the working of his power'. Verse 2 is the mystery, the message, the secret that he'd been given to reveal. And verse 7, the secret that he had to pass on to others.

What was this great mystery of verse 3? It was revealed by the Spirit (verse 5) and revealed to Paul personally (verse 3). What was it? In verse 6 the word 'together' comes three times—heirs together, members, sharers together. It is this wonderful message, that we are all one in Christ Jesus; this revolutionary message that Paul wanted to pass on, that God had revealed to him.

Two things about it. First, remember that when Paul speaks in Scripture, God speaks. Many don't believe that any more, and we are in all sorts of trouble. I know that there are one or two special occasions where Paul says, 'This is not the Lord, but I', but otherwise when Paul speaks, he speaks as from God. And the moment you say 'This is not God, that's Paul,' all kinds of things begin to collapse. So these words Paul speaks he speaks by revelation. Where he speaks elsewhere of 'my gospel' he means '*the* gospel'. And this is tremendously important.

Second, the great message here is that it was God's plan from the beginning. Didn't God say to Abraham that all the nations of the world were to be blessed through him and his family? It is part of the great message of Isaiah. Constantly this message of the word is going out to all mankind. Hold on to this marvellous truth.

Hold out the truth (verses 7–13)

Now Paul says, 'I'm not worthy—I am less than the least of all God's people' (cf 3:8). When Paul says this, he means it. There is no false humility. 'I am less than the least of all God's people.'

'I am the chief of sinners,' as he says elsewhere, 'because I persecuted the church of Christ' (cf 1 Tim. 1:12–17). Now, says Paul, wonderful! I've been given the privilege 'to preach to the Gentiles the unsearchable riches in Christ' (3:8). I love that phrase. To preach is simply to evangelise. 'The unsearchable' means you can't measure it, it's huge, it's way beyond anything we can say. If we still believe that gospel, and I trust we do, and if this so, then this week God's going to say something to us about sharing it with other people.

Paul believed, when he became a Christian, that he was going to be God's answer to the Jews. It was his own people he wanted to reach. And wasn't he the obvious candidate? After all, a member of the Sanhedrin, probably a Pharisee—a Jew who'd got rid of Stephen and opposed Christianity, now converted—and he wanted to go back to his own people: 'This is my ministry.' But they wouldn't have him. And when he was in Jerusalem feeling downcast, the Lord said to him, 'Your ministry is to the Gentiles.'

Logically it didn't make sense. If I had been working out a strategy, assessing people's gifts and callings and backgrounds, I'd have sent Paul to the Jews. I'd have said, 'You're the man to reach the hierarchy: you are one of them.' But God is so much wiser. Expect the unexpected this week. The Lord might suddenly lay His hands upon you and call you to a ministry that is very different from anything that you thought you were ever likely to do. And it's only in the aftermath that you say, 'Thank you, Lord!'

What a ministry! Paul talks about his pioneer ministry in Romans 15:20. He only preached where nobody else had preached. That's not for all of us, of course, but we do need to think afresh. There are plenty of pioneer areas in this country, let alone in other parts of the world, places in which to preach the unsearchable riches of Christ. So that (verse 9) people who are ignorant might know. We live in a world of utter ignorance of the truth of the gospel of Christ. And even more we rise to the tremendous verse 10, which I think I just about understand. Isn't it good that the Bible has depths which it will take you a long time to understand? There's something worth studying here. Verse 10: 'His intent was that now, through the church, the manifold wisdom of God should be made known to the rulers and authorities in the heavenly realms.'

What does that mean? Partly, I think, it means that even the angels peer into the gospel (1 Pet. 1:12). The angels want to know what's going on. There is an old children's hymn that goes,

There's a song that even angels
can never never sing,
they know not Christ the Saviour
but worship Him as King.

The angels cannot sing our song. When we talk about singing with the angels, we sing better than the angels. They are good singers, but they do not sing like we who have been redeemed. We are saying something to the angelic forces.

But I believe verse 10 goes deeper. When Paul talks about rulers and authorities in the heavenly realms (we'll come back to them at the end of this letter), he's talking about cosmic powers of evil as well. That is, he's talking about that supernatural world that is going to be confronted by the wonder of the church, the bride of Christ: that God could redeem people.

We see in 1 Corinthians that in an evil city like Corinth there could be a church of people who were different, who had been brought out of what they once were to what they now were, and were a living witness to that city. This even goes further; a witness to the devil. Hold on to that thought, that the church demonstrates the wisdom of God, not because it's a group of VIPs—it includes them, but it's a group of ordinary people saved by the blood of Christ, indwelt by the Spirit of God, brought together as no other ever could bring that group of people together.

I once sat in a room in Londonderry with two ex-IRA people who were converted in the Maze prison, two Protestant prisoners who had been converted there, and two others. As we studied the word of God together I thought, 'These people apart from the grace of Christ would not be sitting around the Bible, they'd be killing each other. What a testimony to the power of the gospel! Here is a group of people saying to the devil, "You're not going to win. We have the last word, the victory is going to be ours." '

And because of the great eternal purpose of God (verse 11), we can come with freedom and confidence (verse 12).

Those are two terrific words. The world can't live with freedom. The time that a country needs most prayer is when it becomes free. We still pray for South Africa; they probably need prayer more now than ever before. Freedom can bring its own problems. And in Christian lives, liberation can be liberation into doing what we like and forgetting that my freedom can be somebody else's slavery. How to live with freedom? A church, a group of people who are gloriously free. And 'confidence'—not boasting in ourselves, but not ashamed of the gospel of Christ.

But there's a little note in verse 13: it's only possible because of suffering. It's only possible because of Christ's suffering, but here is Paul also saying, 'My sufferings for you are your glory.' The principle always is, the blood of the martyrs is the seed of the church.

Whenever I sing that great hymn, 'We rest on Thee, our shield and defender', I think about a sound-strip back in the days when we didn't have modern technological helps. It was called 'Mid-Century Martyrs', and told the story of how Jim Elliot and others went to their deaths, murdered by the Auca Indians. Before they went they sang that hymn. I can never sing it even now, thirty-odd years later, without feeling as I felt when I first saw that sound-strip. At the beginning of my ministry, it did something to me. It would have been very easy to think that I was now ordained, I was a curate, I was climbing a ladder in the Church of England; I hadn't got very far up the ladder, but I was on it. It was what we called a vocation. And then one remembered that here were people who for the sake of the same Jesus I was preaching went to their deaths. Years later I read that comment of Jim Elliot's which Elisabeth, his wife, recorded: 'He is no fool who gives what he cannot keep to gain what he cannot lose.'

In the middle of all this Paul says, 'Look: it could not happen apart from suffering. There will be suffering right through it all, we expect to suffer. After all, that's how the church came into being.'

Pray for it (3:14–21)

Verse 21 is so wonderful that in a sense it ought not to be expounded. I've only got three simple things to say about it.

Note the content. He starts praying again, and he says 'I kneel.' A Jew normally stood to pray; only in deep emotion did they kneel. Our Lord knelt in the garden, Stephen knelt when he was martyred. Paul kneels before the Father, and he kneels as it were metaphorically, with a Bible in his hand. He prays remembering what he's talked about—these riches, 'the whole family in heaven and on earth'. That's the context of his prayer; but what is the content? What does he pray for?

It's not unlike the prayer we saw yesterday. It has an element of repetition about it, but it's good repetition. He prays first of all for strength, that God will 'strengthen you with power'; the strength that comes when the Holy Spirit dwells in you and makes Christ real within you, verse 17: 'so that Christ may dwell in your hearts through faith'. That word 'dwell' means He is not a lodger, He's come to stay. He's not in the front room, He's taken over all. That's the great theme of our Keswick Convention, and here we see the strength that comes from it.

Then he prays for love; and that theme will continue for the next few days of our Convention. Notice verse 17b. There are two metaphors: 'rooted' and 'established'. 'Rooted' is horticultural, 'established' is architectural. The first word means 'radical'. The church of Jesus should be radical; we are not a group of people who can only exist so long as we change nothing, are terribly conservative, hold on to what we've got. We should be of all people the most radical. But the second word means 'fundamental'. I am a radical fundamentalist. On the things that are absolutely essential to the foundation of the faith, I will by God's grace not budge an inch. But with peripheral things—let's be radical! Paul wants us to be rooted and grounded in love, love which is both fundamental and radical.

Alongside the strength and the love comes that great image of knowledge: verse 18, 'to grasp how wide and long and high and deep'. That expresses how far the love of Christ goes. Then 'to know that love that surpasses knowledge'; that is, you keep getting more and more and more; and finally, 'filled to the measure of all the fullness of God'.

We saw the word yesterday in 1:23—*pleroma*. It has the idea that the church is filled with Jesus; and Paul prays that we as a Christian community we might be filled with the fullness of God. And I don't think that can happen to anybody on their own, it's only when we are part of the family and we are built together in His holy temple.

Then right in the middle of this letter we get a doxology. Most preachers leave their doxology to the end. Paul loves to be different; he says 'Amen', not to end the letter but to end one section and to move on to another. Verse 20–21: Note the phrase—'to [God] who is able to do immeasurably more than all we ask or imagine'. I hope you ask a lot, I hope you imagine a lot! I hope you plan, and pray, and seek to go forward together and individually. But then say: 'Thank you, Lord; You do immeasurably more, sometimes immeasurably different, but always immeasurably more.'

Last of all, 'to him be the glory in the church and in Jesus Christ.' What a balance; for the church is the body of Christ, the building of Christ, the bride of Christ. And He will get glory when the church is what the church is meant to be.

3: Constant Reformation (Ephesians 4:1-24)

The second word of chapter 4 in the original Greek is 'therefore'. It's a reminder to us that we've moved on from where we were to where we are today. To use that very good division of Ephesians in Watchman Nee's book *Sit, Walk, Stand*, we've come to the end of the sitting bit. The first three chapters are 'Sit, enjoy the riches of God's grace and wallow in them, think them through but enjoy them.' And you've been sitting, fairly comfortably. Eventually we'll get to the 'stand' bit towards the end of Friday morning. But now we've reached the 'walk' bit.

I want to point out how important the word 'walk' is in this letter. The NIV translates it in different ways. For example, in 2:2 it speaks of the way you used to live when you followed the ways of this world: that's the word 'to walk'. It comes again in 5:2, to live a life of love: literally, 'to walk in love'. Again in 5:8, live as children of light: literally 'walk as children of light'. And again in 5:15, be careful how you live, not as unwise but as wise—and the word is 'walk'. I almost wish they'd kept 'walk', though I can see why they changed it to 'live'. It's actually the Greek word to 'walk around', and it's a reminder to us that the Christian life is primarily a walk. And these verses today and tomorrow, and on into Friday, will be a tremendous challenge about how Christians walk.

You remember that great verse Isaiah 40:31—'Those who hope in the Lord will renew their strength. They will soar on wings like eagles, they will run and not grow weary, they will walk and not faint.' I used to think that he'd got it the wrong way round; wouldn't it be better to end with soaring with wings like eagles, going out on a high note? But he was right; it doesn't take too much to soar with wings like eagles; it doesn't take too much spirituality to have a great and exciting and ecstatic moment. It doesn't take all that much to do a job of work, to run, to have a period of service in a particular job. But oh what a challenge to be a consistent Christian, who walks worthy every day!

That's what I believe convinces the world, deep down, of this alternative community. What is the difference between Christians and non-Christians? Not our exciting moments; they have them too. Not because we do a job of work; they do too. But we have something that changes everyday life, and we walk differently.

So Paul says, 'I urge you to live a life [or, to walk] worthy of the calling you have received' (4:1). That sums it all up. May I point out, the calling you have received is for every Christian. In this very tent years ago I stood with my fiancée as she then was, and we dedicated our lives to God's service when we heard the challenge that many will hear again this evening.[1] Eighteen months later, in a church in Oxford, I heard a very clear call to the ordained ministry. I'm thankful for the dramatic moments like that call in my life.

But that's not what he's speaking about. He's speaking about the call that comes to every believer. You were called to be a Christian, you were called into fellowship (cf 1 Cor. 1:9). And if nothing else happens this week at Keswick, every person here ought to go back to his or her local church and fellowship with a sense of commitment and calling. To some people, church is an optional extra. I once came across an obituary in *The Times* of a lady of whom it was said, 'Her chief hobby was religion.' That's what the world thinks very often. But it's a calling, a commitment. And I trust it will become even more so this week.

So we are called to walk worthy, having the kind of life

---

1. A reference to the World View Meeting. Mr Dick Dowsett's address is included in the present volume, p. 229.

that fits this dramatic society that I was talking about yesterday. There is one verse, verse 23, that helps to hold it all together. Paul says we should 'be made new in the attitude of your minds'. It's in the present tense, it means 'keep on being made new'. We shall see tomorrow that the great text of Keswick, 'Be filled with the Spirit', is in the present tense—keep on being filled with the Spirit, keep on being renewed. It's a different word for 'new' than the word in verse 24, to 'put on the new self.' The word in verse 23 has the nuance of being 'renewed', getting younger every day. I commend to you 2 Corinthians 4:16—'Outwardly we are wasting away, yet inwardly we are being renewed day by day.' That's the daily experience.

Perhaps somebody has met you at Keswick whom you haven't seen for thirty years; and, hypocrites that we all are, has looked at you and said, 'You haven't changed a bit.' When people say that to me I say, 'I hope I have! I think I've changed a lot.' We are outwardly wasting away—we are getting older, there's no way you can stop that happening —but inwardly we are being renewed. And isn't that desperately important in a world that's concerned about the outward man and the outward woman—what we look like, what we possess, our health, our strength? We are being renewed.

It's a wonderful word. It has become restricted among Christians to a very narrow meaning, so that only certain people are involved in 'renewal'. But all Christians should be involved in 'renewal'. We are being renewed every day. So there in verse 23 we have that tremendous possibility of being 'made new in the attitude of our minds'.

I want to look with you this morning at two appeals that Paul makes. In verse 1, 'As a prisoner for the Lord, then, I urge you to [walk] worthy': and in verse, 17 equally dogmatically, 'I . . . insist on it in the Lord, that you must no longer [walk] as the Gentiles do, in the futility of their thinking.' In the first half of our passage he's calling them to unity. In the second he's calling them to purity. And we shall see that you must always hold those together: unity, purity, one people, pure people.

Notice also that he makes his appeal with authority: in verse 1 he urges them as a 'prisoner for the Lord', not just as an apostle as he calls himself at the beginning of a letter. He's earned the right to say it. He comes with passion as a man who has suffered much.

Today's title is 'Constant reformation', because I believe that's what we should be. Church history records that a church or movement that is of God can in one generation easily become ordinary or even go against the will of God, unless there is constant renewal. We have cause for constant vigilance.

In our first Bible Reading we considered who this letter was addressed to. If Ephesus was one of the churches to whom it was written, then among those who read this letter would be some who not long before had sat and listened to Paul as he was leaving them for the last time. Read what he said to the Ephesian elders in Acts 20:28–31, a message that will reappear in this letter. 'I know that after I leave, savage wolves will come in among you and will not spare the flock. Even from your own number men will arise and distort the truth in order to draw away disciples after them. So be on your guard! Remember that for three years I never stopped warning each of you night and day with tears.'

Paul had already warned them. Now he writes to them again. And what else happens to Ephesus? They get a letter from the risen Lord in Revelation 2 which tells them that sadly they have lost that first love, they must remember and they must repent. So I suggest to you that wherever you come from today within this great alternative community, there are two commands that come from a man who suffered much, written to a church that he loved much.

Keeping It Up (4:1–16)

First of all, we are meant to live,

A life of charity (4:2)
The great note is love (verses 2 and 15–16). May I say a word about *agape*, 'love'? Many people hide behind the word

'love' when they mean moral weakness and an inability to stand up and be counted. If I dare to suggest that biblically I cannot accept the idea of homosexual people living together and ministering together in the church, that it goes against Scripture, I'm accused of lacking in love. And I find that very hurtful. I would deny it emphatically. If that's all I do and I don't care for people who have problems, then it could be so. But I want to say to you that real love dares to say the truth to people and help them in a situation which the Bible calls sinful. It will not do to say, 'Well of course I love him' —which means, 'I tolerate anything'. That isn't New Testament love. When Jesus said of those who lead little ones to sin, 'It would be better for him to be thrown into the sea with a millstone tied round his neck', would you call that 'loving' by today's standards? If I dared to say it, I would be in trouble. But He said it, the supremely loving Saviour, because He cared for the people who were in danger of eternal loss. Unless we take sin seriously, we shall never take love seriously.

I could go on—I've seen so many pastoral situations where people opt out of facing up to real discipline, because we 'love'. 'You must never rebuke, if you love' say some people today. Of course that's nonsense, and the Old Testament and New insist that love often involves rebuke. Because God loves us He chastens us. And that's important.

But we are meant to share a life of charity. And there are five qualities mentioned in verse 2, ending in love. They start with lowliness or humility, which to the Greek mind was not a virtue. To take a lower position, to demean yourself, was a vice not a virtue. 'Gentleness' is the word that is used of Jesus: 'I am meek and lowly' (Matt. 11:29). It was used of Moses, he was 'very meek, above all the men which were on the face of the earth' (Num. 12:3, AV). It does not mean he would not say 'Boo!' to a goose. It is a word actually used of a person who can control a horse: meek, gentle, not overbearing in himself. Then the two words, 'be patient', and 'bearing with one another in love'. That is what must always be the mark of the alternative community; whatever else we do, this ought to characterise our living.

A life of unity (4:3–6)

The word 'one' is repeated seven times. I have to say, because this is a passage about unity, that the reference in verse 3 to 'the unity of the Spirit' does not refer to the church becoming one great ecumenical organisation. I believe that the Lord is concerned that we should appear to be one, and that our banner here, 'All one in Christ Jesus', should reflect something true. But I do not believe that the Bible insists that we shall become one by forming some great organisation. It is a much contested area.

And there is a recurring appeal that evangelicals should all come together: why have all these denominations? Why not just be 'The Evangelical Church'? I'm not sure that's the will of God either. There is real danger in thinking that so long as we are organised as one, all will be well. You can't get new life by just putting organisations together. Paul is not talking about that kind of unity. Thank God he isn't! We'll come back to that later.

But these seven 'ones' are interesting. They are all linked to the Trinity. There's 'one Spirit', and because there's one Spirit there's 'one body'. That's the joy of it. And I'm delighted in that some of the divisions that did come from the Charismatic movement have been overcome; not all of them, to be honest, but many of them. And that's good and I hope we can grow in that way.

'One Lord', that is, Jesus; and so there's only 'one hope', 'one faith', 'one baptism'. It's associated with new life in Jesus. We have 'one' because we have only one Saviour. And because there's 'one God and Father', there is one family.

I want to say a couple of things about that. First, I think this says a lot to us about the church family in an age when the 'nuclear' family is everywhere breaking up. It's being said now that very soon, if not already, what we think of as a 'normal' family—father, mother, children—will be the exception rather than the rule. It goes further: there are forces around which want deliberately to destroy the idea of the family, and that this is their hell-bent aim. So it's terribly important that we demonstrate that we are a church family.

Second, there's a lot to be said about the word 'father'. The Bible insists on the very real ministry of fatherhood.

God is our Father. He has within Him, says Isaiah, all the qualities of motherly care (cf eg Isa. 66), yes of course; but He is called our Father, as I will always call Him 'our Father'. And I am sure that the women here would want to call Him 'our Father', as I was told to call Him. But I believe it's a challenge to those of us who are male. What kind of fatherhood do we represent? Often our problems come because men are not prepared to face their responsibilities.

So there is in the 'oneness', all these seven attributes. And that leads to the thrust of verse 7: we are to make every effort to keep the unity of the Spirit. You cannot create it, but you are called to maintain it. It's 'given': we are one because we are in Christ. We are God's children, we are in the Spirit, so we are one. But we can spoil it. And so we are meant to hold on to it, both in our local church and in the wider grouping of the people of God. It calls for hard work. The word 'make every effort' (verse 3) literally means, 'sweat it out'.

Note the phrase at the end of verse 3, 'the unity of the Spirit through the bond of peace'. One of my favourite passages on which to preach at weddings includes that lovely verse Colossians 3:15, 'Let the peace of Christ rule in your hearts, since as members of one body you were called to peace.' The word 'rule' means 'umpire': when the umpire's finger goes up you are out. And in a way, though Paul knew nothing about cricket, this word 'rule' has the same note of arbitration. At the end of the day, what has the last word in your church? I hope peace does.

In honesty I must acknowledge that sometimes some of us could be accused of spoiling the peace when we stand for important truths that we think are being neglected. But as I suggested yesterday, there is a peace which is not of God. There is a kind of somnolent solemnity that is not God's. Yet at the end of the day, how many divisions in church could be—should be—avoided, if we let peace have the last word! It's true in the earthly family, too. Of course you don't always agree, why should you? But: does peace have the last word?

A life of diversity (verses 7–12)
Now suddenly we move from the 'all' of the previous verses to the phrase 'each one of us'. We all have a responsibility for

the well-being of the church. The church is ourselves, we are the church, and God gives gifts to each of us. The word 'gifts' is the word also translated 'grace', *charis*, from which we get the word 'charismata', the gifts that God gives to His people.

These verses do have some controversial aspects and different interpretations are possible. But I hope we would agree that these verses say that though we must look for unity, we must not look for uniformity. God save churches from becoming identikit churches in which we are all the same! In one church, we need to be different. And indeed across the churches we need to be different. I think it's healthy that churches worship in different ways. When you attend church while travelling you don't always want to transfer what they do to your church at home; it might not be right to do so. For example, in Korean congregations they pray simultaneously, aloud, every single one of them; at the end the pastor rings a bell and they stop. That's their way, and thank God for it. But I don't need to introduce it into our church, nor to Keswick. We don't all want to be the same.

And within a church God gives different gifts. In Romans when Paul talks about gifts, they are the gifts of the Father (Rom. 11:29). In 1 Corinthians 12 they are the gifts of the Spirit. Here in Ephesians they are the gifts of the ascended Lord: verse 8. He quotes Psalm 68, the psalm that's linked to the idea of the ark going back to Jerusalem, a great triumphant moment. And it links in Paul's mind with our Lord's triumph going to heaven. The Old Testament psalm speaks about God receiving gifts. Here Paul quotes it in the context of gifts given. Both happen on these days of triumph. When a Roman general came home he brought his booty, and he offered gifts to others.

The lovely thought is that the 'gifts' of these verses come from the triumphant ascended Lord. Let me mention in passing that verses 9–10 probably do not refer to Christ's decent into Hades which is mentioned in the Creed and which 1 Peter 3:19 seems to talk about, going to the 'spirits in prison'. It probably means, 'He who was in heaven came down to earth.' I believe it has to with the incarnation.

Paul says that he descended from heaven to the 'lower' parts of the earth (verse 9). I wonder, were any of you at Keswick when we did a Christmas broadcast from here for Trans-World Radio? Every Christmas we are reminded of the incarnation, that He came down from glory to the 'lower, earthly regions'. This was His humility, a pattern for every Christian. The way back to the crown is the way of the cross. He could ascend only because He had descended.

And then comes the list of these gifts. Nothing gets people more excited than the gifts, but can I remind you that people are always involved? In the New Testament there are over twenty gifts mentioned individually. I don't believe they are meant to form an exclusive checklist; they are symbolic of the gifts of God. Five of them are listed here. And whatever else you make of these five, please note that they are all primarily to do with the teaching ministry, with the mind which we have neglected. The weaknesses of the church of today come, I believe, from neglect of the teaching ministry of the church. So let's look at these.

'It was he who gave some to be *apostles*' (verse 11). Now the apostle as defined in Acts 1 is a person who was around in the time of Jesus and was a witness to the resurrection. So that when Judas failed and they had to appoint another, he had to be somebody who had experienced that unique moment, who had known the living Jesus. So in that sense apostleship dies. Have you noticed that Judas was replaced because he let the Lord down, whereas when James, one of the Twelve, was martyred they never replaced him? It was because the day was ended. The apostles were not going to continue—in that sense. It is true that Paul says in 1 Corinthian 9:1 that he is an apostle because he has seen the risen Jesus. He had that unique ministry. And it was also true that the word 'apostle' was used of other, quite ordinary people in the New Testament who had a sending-out, pioneering job.

I would simply make two points. One: if we believe in the uniqueness of Scripture, then what we have died into is the apostle's doctrine. Acts 2:42: the church is built on the 'apostle's teaching'. In one sense, God has finished speaking in that way. Of course he still speaks, or I wouldn't be here today trying to get across what the word of God says to us, but we are tied in to 'the faith once delivered to the saints'. The apostolic message is written. I hear people say, 'But isn't he saying new things today?' No, in one sense he's not. He's actually giving new light on the old things, but that's different. And it's very, very important that we should recognise that. Two: the concept of the apostles has the note of 'going out'. The word 'apostle' means 'sent out', and in that sense the church must always be apostolic.

'He gave ... some to be *prophets*' (verse 11) Again, I believe that this is probably a unique ministry. Once we have the New Testament the word 'prophetic ministry', in that sense, changes. But I would point out too that later on in 1 Corinthians Paul shows that God does enable some to speak prophetically. Read Jeremiah 23: it's a whole chapter on false and true prophets. He says of the false prophets, they have dreams and visions but they are not really close to God, of their ministry that it's like straw, where the real word of God is like a hammer that breaks the rock in pieces. So you can always tell a prophetic word, not by whether dreams and visions are used, but by the effect of that word. Does it hammer the rock to pieces, does it lead to repentance, does it change lives?

For those who are preachers or would-be preachers here, can I point out that in one sense, I hope, everybody who preaches the word of God is prophetic. That is, we take the word of God and we apply it to the world of today. We are not just saying 'This is what it says', and we must avoid the danger of swinging back from experience to the Bible so far that we become so concerned about the minute details of the text that it doesn't relate to the word of today. As John Stott has written, every good sermon is like a bridge; it is earthed in the world of today and it's earthed in the world of Scripture, and it must be firm both ends. Some people are very good on the word of Scripture. They know what Scripture says, they can give you a clear exegesis, but it doesn't relate to the world of today, it's hanging in mid-air. People nod in agreement, but they are not really listening.

The second danger is the person who knows the world of today, he can quote pop-songs, he can quote writers of today, quote novels, he's living in our world—but there isn't very much Scripture in it. But a prophetic minister takes the word of God and says, 'Thus saith the Lord.' And it should be true for every Keswick meeting that it's been like a hammer, doing some breaking in our lives.

Thirdly, *evangelists*. Strangely, the word occurs only three times in Scripture. The word 'evangelise' comes frequently; we are all called in that sense to take out the good news. Sometimes people argue that we are not all called to be evangelists, but we are all called be witnesses. I'm not convinced of that, but I believe that 'to evangelise, to take out the good news' is what we are all called to do. Read the Acts of the Apostles. Churches were founded as much by ordinary people gossiping the good news, as by the great men like Paul.

But only three people are called evangelists. In Acts 21:8 Philip is referred to as an evangelist. In 2 Timothy 4:5 Timothy is told to do the work of an evangelist. Do you prayerfully in your own church fellowship look out for those with special evangelistic gifts and encourage them? I do believe we are lacking here. How many churches are growing in evangelism? So often we grow because people leave one church and come to us. We shuffle the pack around. But when we plan for our future, are we daring enough to give the evangelist in the congregation a real place? Encourage him or her in the ministry.

And the other one, *pastors and teachers*. I want to argue strongly that they are the same. The Greek seems to be saying that. In other words, they are pastoral teachers. One of my great campaigns is for every teacher to be a pastor and every pastor a teacher.

The word 'pastor' means 'to feed'. Now, what are you doing when you are doing pastoral work? You may reply, 'Well, I visit the sick, I look after the newcomers.' And all that's very important. But in the New Testament, pastoring means *feeding*. 'Peter, do you love Me? Feed my sheep . . . feed my lambs . . . feed them.' 1 Peter 5:2: we are to be shepherds. We are to feed people. So pastoring and teaching always go hand in hand.

People sometimes ask me, 'How long does it take you to

prepare a sermon?' And my answer is very simple: 'All week.' Preparing a sermon is not just sitting in a study with the Greek New Testament and my Bible in front of me and every commentary under the sun, extracting what the text means. That's part of it; but it's just as much part of it when I go to visit an old lady in her home, when I meet people going through times of suffering, when I talk with a man who's redundant, when I meet students, when I dare to try and get alongside teenagers—whom I half understand these days. I try, as it were, to be a pastoral teacher. I commend it to you as being a very significant combination. And the charge comes to us from Paul that this is what we need in our churches more than anything. Christians who are fed —not fed-up, but fed; Christians who get fed by pastoral teaching.

It needs to be said: all these lists are not about status or position. Nor are they about whether you have bishops or pastors or whatever. In Acts 20, when Paul talks to these same people who are called 'elders', he calls them overseers, which is the same word for bishops. And he tells them to be shepherds, which is the same word for pastors. So they are bishops, elders, pastors—all meaning the same thing. And I would argue strongly that a bishop and an elder in a sense are the same: the presbyter bishop and the pastor. The Bible doesn't seem bothered about position and status. You don't build a church around the question of whether not you have elders and bishops. Of course it's necessary to sit down and set up an orderly pattern. But that's not what counts. What counts is people in the church with a gifting of God within the family of God. And urgently we must reach them.

Now what, verse 12, are all these people meant to do? I checked the Authorised Version at this point, and I want to point out a problem in its rendering of verse 12: 'For the perfecting of the saints, for the work of the ministry . . .' It's what I call the fatal comma. What I believe verse 12 *should* say, and the NIV says it well enough, is 'to prepare God's people [literally, saints] for works of service.' What's the difference, you may say. A lot, I think. You see, the AV suggests that the pastors and teachers do the job of perfecting the saints, they do the job of the work of ministry.

No. The job of the pastor/teacher is to prepare the people of God so that they may do the works of service. And that spells the end of the one-man band.

There is an opposite danger. Some churches desperately lack leadership and everybody runs them. A church run by everybody is probably going to come into chaos. There is a place for right leadership, I believe that with all my heart; but any leader who thinks he can do the perfecting of all the saints and all the work of ministry is either heading for the collapse of his church, or an ego trip, or a nervous breakdown. No, our job is to help the saints so that they might do the work of ministry.

Let's go a stage further. If anyone asks what 'works of service' are, we all think 'deacons'. And we're partly right. We all do it in our own churches; we make a list of all the jobs that need to be done, and we say to people, 'Do you find that you may have a gift here?' It's valid and reasonable, for we want through our ministry, those of us who are pastor-teachers, to help these people to find their niche in service.

But I think it goes further, and I find this exciting. Any Christian fellowship includes people who out there in the world have some position of influence in their daily work, in their neighbourhood, in politics sometimes, in leisure activities—even those who are not employed; for example, there are people in the neighbourhood who help in all sorts of community work, the kind of thing that all churches should have a lot of people involved in. I believe that's part of what Paul is trying to say, and it's certainly what I believe I've got to say today—that if the alternative community's going to be effective, we must not become a ghetto. I suppose that's why I have been happy with the parish system as an Anglican, because it did say something about the local church. Things are changing, and people's relationships very often are with folks from work or leisure activities rather than with their neighbourhood. But the principle remains the same. We should be in that community, spilling over around us, so that people come and receive blessing.

One surgeon in my congregation came to me with grateful thanks the other day and just simply said, 'You cannot know what it means to me in my desperately busy life to come on

Sunday morning and evening and benefit from the teaching which helps me to keep going.' Now, I can't tell him as a preacher how he should work out his medical ethics. I can't tell people who are MPs how they should vote in the House of Commons. But what I can do is to say to them, 'These are truths of the word of God as I see them in Scripture; now, by God's grace, you go out and practise them.' It's very exciting. Isn't that why 1 Corinthians 12 talks about gifts from another angle, that all the gifts are given for the common good, to build up the body? So we find here (verses 12–13) 'so that the body of Christ might be built up'—that is, edified, strengthened, built up numerically, yes; but first of all spiritually. Lots of people today are very keen on physical fitness. But how much more should we be concerned about building the body of Christ!

A life of maturity (verses 13–16)
These verses reminds us that we are meant to become mature. If there's a unity in verse 3 that we maintain, there's a unity in verse 13 that we attain: 'until we all reach unity'. I hope that yours is a beautiful united church. I do hope that everybody who comes to Keswick is not going through great traumas. There are happy churches. God is doing things, it's not always miserable and defeatist.

But we can go further. There is more to possess. There is a deeper unity, there is a goal to reach. Do you see what the goal is? 'Unity in the faith'. Hold on to the faith which we all should know and rejoice in, and get closer to the knowledge of the Son of God and become mature.

In verse 14 there is another 'no longer'. You see there is a sense in which people sometimes think that because we are called to be child-like, we are meant to be childish. We're not. We are meant to grow up. If we are like infants, says Paul, we shall easily be moved from one thing to another; children never stay long at one thing, they move from one to another; that's childish.

Christians shouldn't always be looking for something new and exciting. We have many childish Christians in Britain today, who are waiting for some new excitement so that they can get caught up in it. It will keep them going for another few months, and then they'll look for something else. It's a lot easier than discipline, repentance, study; we need to take care to be 'no longer infants, tossed back and forth'. The devil loves childish Christians. In 2 Timothy 4:3–4 Paul points out that you will always find teachers to encourage you if you've got itching ears, and they'll tell you what you want to hear. Please, grow up as a Christian.

What is maturity? We find it in verse 15–16. We are to speak the truth in love. That is the mark of the corporate growth described in verse 15–16. In the Greek, the word 'speaking' isn't there. It simply says, 'truthing it in love'—not just speaking truth but being truthful. A life of integrity and of consistency makes for a mature Christian you can depend on. Paul is telling his readers that always, in any ministry, we must balance truth and love together. And then (verses 15–16), we shall 'grow up into [Christ]'. It's not a piece of anatomy, but a lovely picture of the body; we grow up into the Head, we grow up from the Head, who is Christ.

Thinking it out (4:17–24)

From tomorrow, we'll be thinking very much at the individual level: how we do this that and the other. That's a good thing, because a church is made up of individuals. But we are stopping here today on this picture of the great unity of the church. You see, we are meant to have a high view of the church.

I don't mean in the Anglican sense of 'High Church'. But evangelicals ought to have a high view of the church in that they should not only be concerned about personal responsibility. We are a community. The church matters, it's the body of Christ, the bride of Christ. Hold a high view of it. And if unity matters, purity matters. So once more, in verse 17, a solemn word from Paul: 'I ... insist on it in the Lord'—he's using his authority—'You must no longer' —once more—'live as the Gentiles do, in the futility of their thinking.' Now, do you see, he's moving at last from doctrine to behaviour, from creed to conduct, from exposition to exhortation. And tomorrow he will become very practical indeed.

But he wants to start by saying to us, 'Think it out, use your mind.' (Note that reference to the mind in verse 18: warped minds produce warped people.) And you and I need to be reminded that we are all the time, almost unconsciously, taking in the attitudes of the world. Our television sets and newspapers shout it at us. They are moulding us into the ways of the world. So we must win the victory in our minds; and we must not become like the Gentiles, darkened in their understanding.

The life left (4:17–19)

These verses describe what is no longer true of Christians. In his book on Ephesians, *God's New Society*,[1] John Stott makes a telling comparison between these verses and Romans 1. The parallel is very interesting: the move from hardness to darkness, from deadness to recklessness. Look at verse 18–19: 'Darkened ... separated from the life of God ... hardening of their hearts ... having lost all sensitivity ... given over to sensuality ... every kind of impurity ... with a continual lust for more.' There's no end to this. I could easily remind you of some of the depths to which we stoop in our modern civilised society. And I hate to read these things, I get to a point where I just don't want to read newspapers any more because they feed that lower part of one's nature. When you think that some paedophiles (what a word—'lover of children', indeed) are people in positions of quite significant influence in the country ... And so the awful move away from God continues.

That's the life, says Paul, that we've left behind.

The life learned (verses 20–24)

Note the emphatic 'You' in verse 20 ('But you', AV). Notice, too, it's all to do again with the mind. You learned, you 'heard' the truth. You 'were taught'. You see those words? You were taught 'the truth that is in Jesus'. Jesus said 'Come to me and learn from me' (cf Matt. 11: That's what a disciple

---

1. John Stott, *The Message of Ephesians: God's New Society* (The Bible Speaks Today: IVP, 1979).

is, someone who is always learning of Christ, by what He did, by the things He taught, by the person He was.

And eventually, as we'll see tomorrow, it leads to some very practical things. But just note as I conclude, verses 22 and 24 balance out. What happened when you became a Christian? Even if it wasn't a great dramatic moment in your life, it was a radical shift. You changed from that way to this way. 'I didn't do all those things!' No. But if you hadn't been converted you probably would have. You were saved by grace, you were saved from it.

The challenge is that when you became a Christian you put off that old way and (verse 24) you put on a new way: both verbs are in the aorist tense, which means 'decisively'; this is what conversion's about. We are different people. The old way gone, the new way come, we put off the old clothes, we put on the new clothes. And in between, the text with which we almost began: 'Be made new, be renewed in the attitude of your minds.'

And if tomorrow we come to some very telling practical things, so that you almost find the word of God weighing you down, the Lord in the middle puts a lovely reminder: 'But be filled with the Spirit, keep on being filled with the Spirit, leave that life behind, learn a new way of life. Be a disciple' (cf 5:18).

I took a long time learning to drive a car, and had my L-plates on a long time. I want to say to you that when we go out from this meeting, we will be wearing our spiritual L-plates. We'll always be wearing them. I'm still learning. How am I learning? I am learning from God's word, I'm learning from Christ, I'm giving my mind to Him, I'm letting the truths of Scripture take hold of my life and the way I live. If you stop learning, you'll stop living.

Then comes in verse 25 the little three-letter Greek word 'therefore'. And if you want to know what follows, you'll be back tomorrow morning.

4: Moral Revolution
(Ephesians 4:25–5:21)

Well, we are still walking. You will remember we looked at Paul's plea, 'Therefore we must walk worthy of our calling'. And that word 'walking' ('live' in the NIV) keeps coming: 5:2, walk in love; 5:8, walk as children of light: 5:15, we are to walk as wise people. I call this continuing walk 'moral revolution'. And there's some pretty straight words to us in this passage today. The word of God has authority, it is unchanging and it speaks to us still today. Paul becomes very practical, and that will continue in our session tomorrow.

Somebody in our congregation complained that our sermons are far too doctrinal; he wanted a practical sermon. One day I preached on money, it couldn't have been more practical. As he went out afterwards I said, 'Was that practical?' He said, 'It was a bit near the knuckle this morning, Vicar.' So if I seem a bit near the knuckle this morning, I'm not; Paul is, God is.

I did point out yesterday, and I think it needs to be qualified, that when Paul moves from doctrine to ethics, from creed to conduct, he never just moves. Even in the practical section there is always the ethics, in the conduct section he's always reminding us of the theology that lies behind it. That's why we need to study our Bibles. It's not enough to say 'I want the Christian ethics, I like the bits at the end which tell me how to live.' They are based on the truth at the beginning. What we studied in the first two mornings is very important indeed.

But Paul never just commands, he always gives us a reason why. And that I think is very important. You notice in this passage that God is involved. Verse 30: we are told not to 'grieve the Holy Spirit' with our words. That is our motivation: the Holy Spirit who indwells us. And in 4:32 we are told be forgiving 'just as God in Christ forgave you'. We remember His forgiveness and so we learn to forgive. Chapter 5:2, we walk in love [live a life of love, NIV] 'just as Christ loved us'. And in the rest of the passage, 5:3–21, almost every other verse brings in the name of God the Father, Christ, the Spirit.

It's a reminder that all our Christian living is based on what we believe about the Father, Son and Holy Spirit. You'll only live as a Christian consistently if you keep the relationship with God clear. The moment we get out of tune with Him we get out of tune with ourselves, out of tune with others. As I often say, one generation throws overboard Christian doctrine, the next-but-one throws overboard Christian ethics. We are living in the next-but-one. In between there's always a kind of overlap where people say, 'Of course I don't believe all the Bible, but I do think it's good that we should live the Christian ethics.' That day has long since gone.

So our study today is very practical. Indeed, the Keswick Convention has been from its beginning involved with scriptural and practical holiness. It's meant to be a practical Convention. We are meant to go out not just with some blessed thoughts and a lovely sense of fellowship, but with some new directions for practical living.

The Marks of a Holy People (4:25–5:1)

There are six marks of a holy people. First,

Truth (4:25)

Paul's 'therefore' introduces 'each of you must put off falsehood.' The word in Greek is literally 'pseudo'. It's not the real thing, it's a pretence. It's like the Greek idea of a 'hypocrite'—a mask you put on to pretend to be something else. Many of live with masks on, because we want other people to see us as we would like to be seen, not as we are. But we can't wear a mask with God. In Romans 1:25, Paul gives the same word about falsehood, and he says about unregenerate man that he's 'exchanged the truth of God into a lie'.

There are many lies being told in the world today, and many false promises being offered. Do you get those special offers in the post, the ones that are 'only sent to you'? 'Mrs So-and-so, you have been specially chosen'? Some people actually believe that rubbish. We're being conned. We are given special offers, and at the end of the day it isn't there.

Why should we bother about verse 25? Well, here's the motivation. Instead of the pseudo, the untruths, we must 'speak truthfully'—remember yesterday, 'truthing it in love'. We are to speak truthfully with integrity so that people can trust us; to our neighbour because we are neighbours, and because 'we are all members of one body'. Here's the alternative community. A fellowship can never be built on pretence. The moment you don't trust the people in the fellowship, the fellowship dies. There has to be openness, not in some silly artificial way, but in a genuine way, so that we are truthful with one another. We are members of one body, and the limbs have got to work together.

One of the first questions asked in the Bible is 'Am I my brother's keeper?' To which the answer is always a resounding 'Yes.' Nobody lives to himself or herself alone. If we are a holy people, people should be able to depend upon us. We live the truth, we speak the truth, we are truthful.

Temper (4:26–27)

There is a quote from Psalm 4:4 here that can be misunderstood. It's possible to read it as, 'It's a jolly good thing to blow your top.' There are Christians who imagine you should always be doing so. I know myself of a so-called Christian fellowship where they are encouraged to shout what they feel at the beginning of their worship. They're even told that if the words that emerge are swear-words they needn't worry, because God wants to know the real you. A

friend of mine who had taken a youth group with him walked
out. I'd have done more than walked out! It seems to me that
if we descend to that and have used Scripture to defend it,
we are in danger.

Of course the Bible is not saying that it's a mark of
spirituality to blow your top, nor that it doesn't matter what
you say so long as you get it out of your system. So often
Christians use half-baked psychology that may not have been
true in the first place, and becomes even less true when we
pick it up.

What is Paul saying? He is saying that there is a righteous
indignation, but it must never lead to losing your temper.
Verse 31: 'Get rid of bitterness, rage, anger . . . brawling . . .'
A brawling church is not a church of Jesus. We are to have a
righteous anger but it must not lead to sin. Anger is not
wrong. In 5:6 we see 'God's wrath'—it's not quite the same
as 'anger', I know, but God hates sin, there is a kind of
anger. Jesus was angry: you see him angry with the
hypocritical religious leaders in Mark 3:5. They'd set up a
test case to try to catch Him out. 'He looked round at them
in anger.' He was angry, too, when he whipped the traders
out of the Temple.

Nothing in the Bible suggests that it's a mark of spirituality
to appease, to never say anything, to let evil rise, to refrain
from protesting about social evil, racism and such things.
May I point out that in the letter to the Galatians, Paul,
battling for truth had a stand-up row with Peter. It wasn't
pleasant to watch. Eyeball to eyeball they battled it out,
because it was a theological issue that had to be battled out
(Galatians 2).

May I point out two chapters in the New Testament that
we must hold in balance. In Philippians 1 Paul says he knows
that in Rome, from where he is writing, lots of people were
preaching Jesus out of envy and rivalry. Because he was
there, the name of Jesus was being bandied around. Lots of
those who were talking about Jesus didn't like Paul at all.
But, says Paul with great graciousness, 'I don't mind what
their motive is, provided they preach Jesus.' I wish we, I wish
I, had reached that height of spirituality. Paul wasn't getting

angry with them on account of their dislike of him, whatever he felt inside.

But compare Galatians 1. Here Paul says that 'Even if we or an angel from heaven should preach a gospel other than the one we preached to you, let him be eternally condemned!' (Gal. 1:8).

Has Paul flipped? Is this a different Paul? 'On the one hand, I don't mind what they think of me provided they preach Jesus; but on the other hand, if they preach another gospel, curse them.'

If I were discussing someone with whom I had very serious theological differences, being told that he was actually a very nice person would not satisfy me. It's not relevant. There is the place where Christians cannot just give in and say it doesn't matter. There is a place where we stand, and there we must have a righteous indignation. The name of Jesus means everything to me. When I hear it brought down to the dust or being demeaned I'm angry. And when I see things in our world where the church is denying the gospel, I am angry; and when I see society going against the way of Christ I am angry.

But note the challenge. We are all fallen people. How much of my righteous indignation is righteous, and how much is just me wanting my own way? That's the danger. That is why Paul says, 'Do not let the sun go down while you are still angry, and do not give the devil a foothold' (4:26). Be careful, for your 'righteous indignation' could easily be a cloak for you wanting to get your own way, getting your own back.

I commend to you two lovely verses, James 1:19–20. James says, 'Be quick to listen, slow to speak.' He doesn't say you shouldn't speak. He says, 'Be quick to listen', then 'Be slow to speak ... for man's anger does not bring about the righteous life that God desires.' Peter in the Garden of Gethsemane took up his sword and tried to fight for Jesus. It did no good at all, except to give our Lord a chance for His final healing miracle in the Gospel, that's all. But there was no point in it. It didn't forward God's purposes.

So be careful. Some of us need to say, 'That's where I need to repent, and that's where I need God's grace.'

Money (4:28)

This is where it gets near the knuckle. But the Bible talks about money, and I am going to as well.

There is to be no stealing. 'He who has been stealing must steal no longer.' That's straightforward. I was once shown in a shipyard a hut built many years ago in the time of the great Irish preacher W. P. Nicholson. He reached people and they were converted. The hut had been built to hold the stolen goods that converted men brought back when Nicholson told them to. 'You have been converted; you once stole things, now take them back.' The shipyard didn't know what to do with all the stuff that came back.

But I believe it's a much more subtle problem than that. Most of us don't steal, not in that way. But perhaps we are not very honest in our tax returns; and I suspect that's exactly the same thing. It may be we steal time and pretend we are working, when we are not. We steal reputations. There are all kinds of stealing.

But if even if you can confidently say, 'As far as I know I am honest in my tax returns and I haven't stolen,' see here the positive opposite: 'He . . . must steal no longer, but must work, doing something useful with his own hands'. That detail has always rather worried me, because if it means that manual labour is more sanctified than anything else then I am the most unsanctified of all people—my hands are useless! Paul was a manual labourer, he was a tent-maker or leather worker. He went on doing it. Why? He believed that he had a right to earn money preaching the gospel, but in order not to cause offence he worked with his hands. I believe it with all my heart, it's right for Christian workers to be paid for what they do, though I would worry if the joy of voluntary work were to be pushed into the background.

What I do believe very seriously is that what Paul is saying is that instead of stealing, a mark of a holy people is that they earn money to share with those in need. Yesterday Clive Calver mentioned the prosperity cult. It bothers me to hear people saying that if you give to God you'll get back from Him; your motive for giving becomes getting, which seems to me particularly selfish. When John Wesley, who had lived very frugally, began to earn more money as he became better known, he still lived as frugally as he did before. The extra he earned, he gave away. The Bible doesn't say we have to do that. But there are challenges in the Bible about our giving, to which I believe Christians do not listen. One of the greatest needs of our day is for Christians to release money, so that the work of the gospel can be taken forward.

Our church at Fulwood is twinned with a church in the mining community. It's a church where very few people are employed, but I well remember one of the unemployed members testifying to our congregation as to how he was tithing the support he was receiving. And that to me is amazing; many of my congregation who draw fairly good salaries still balk at tithing. If God has blessed you it is so that you may give. A world of need is waiting for Christians to learn to give.

I could quote many verses to you (one of them would be 1 Timothy 6:17), and I could go on a long time. Let me just say that I believe that this is what makes the world sit up and take notice: that Christians give till it hurts. Non-Christians give to causes they like, and there are many attempts to encourage charity with television programmes, red noses and the like. They are very well meant, though I have some doubts about their long-term effectiveness. But Christians should demonstrate that our giving stems out of a sense of our indebtedness to God who has given everything to us.

When Zaccheus was converted (Luke 19), he promised to give half his goods to the poor and to give back four-fold what he'd taken wrongly. As far as I know, nobody told him to; it was a genuine response of a converted conscience. And it may be that some of you will think that this is the most important thing you will have heard in Keswick today, even though we will shortly be looking at things that are very searching indeed.

Talk (4:29–30)

There are many strong words in the Bible about the use of the tongue. For example James calls it 'a small part of the body, but it makes great boasts' (James 3:5), our Lord in Matthew 12:32 said that by our words we shall be forgiven

and by our words we shall be condemned, and when Isaiah
was touched in the temple and was commissioned, the
burning coals touched his lips, because his lips was what he
was going to use (Isa. 6:6–7).

See what Paul says: 'Do not let any unwholesome talk
come out of your mouths.' That word means 'rotten'. And
instead of rotten talk, 'what is helpful for building others
up'—'edifying', in the Authorised Version. It doesn't mean
that Christians should always be talking pious talk; please
don't become that kind of Christian! There is a place for
relaxation, there is a place for chatting. We don't want to
become intense, high-powered people. But there's a danger
that even in our fun we can be destructive. And those of us
who have glib tongues need to ask the Lord to help us to
keep a watch on them, for speaking should be edifying,
helpful and building up rather than the reverse.

It's interesting to me that at this point he brings in the
Spirit: verse 30, 'Do not grieve the Spirit'; don't make the
Spirit sorry that He dwells in you, because the Spirit above
all is the Spirit of truth. We grieve the Spirit when (as we saw
yesterday) we are disunited, we grieve the Spirit when we are
impure, and we grieve the Spirit when He, the Spirit of
truth, is living in our hearts and our language doesn't betray
it.

Attitude (4:31–5:2)
Six attitudes must go, 4:31: bitterness, rage, anger, brawling,
slander, malice. Notice that they all relate in some way to
speaking.

We need to be honest before the Lord about gossip. Often
it's the reverse of what was originally a virtue. Because we
care about people and get involved in their lives, and people
come to us and open themselves to us, we often know more
about people than others do. We do actually care, but it's a
very thin line. A marriage is in trouble, and right round the
church congregation, the lines are buzzing, 'Do pray for Mr
and Mrs So-and-so—you do know their marriage is in
trouble, don't you.' And there is just a little bit in us which is
a gossip, even as we pretend we want to pray for them. We
pass it on. It's a juicy bit that we know first. There are some

times when the best thing you can do with information is to keep it between you and the Lord. I always ask when people come to me in confidentiality, 'Do you mind if I share this with my wife Margaret?', because I find some of these things intolerable to bear on my own. And ninety-nine times out of a hundred they say yes. Beyond that, I hope I do not go. If I do, I need to repent. And we need to be careful too about slander. It's a very common complaint.

The positive alternative comes in verse 32. Instead of what's wrong (you see how the negative and positive go together) here is the positive word 'kind'—*chrestos*; it's only one letter different from the word 'Christ'. What a lovely thing kindness is! Non-Christians ought to look at Christians and say they want to be like us, not just because we are pure and holy, but because we are kind and actually likeable.

Alongside kindness and compassion comes 'forgiving'— 'just as in Christ God forgave you' (verse 32). It doesn't say 'because' but 'just as'. No word in Scripture is unimportant; that's why I believe in the total authority and infallibility of Scripture. It really means, 'just as'.

I can say to you, 'You must forgive because God has forgiven you'. Well, that's not impossibly difficult, though remember Peter's comment when our Lord told him to forgive: he asked Jesus, 'How often shall I forgive my brother if he sins against me?' Peter suggested the biggest figure he could think of: 'Up to seven times?' And when our Lord said, 'Not seven times, but seventy-seven times,' Peter's maths couldn't cope with it (cf Matt. 18:22).

But mathematics aside, *how* do you go on forgiving for ever and ever? Please look how you do it. It's 'as in Christ God forgave you'.

There are two ways in which that always comes home to me. Many people say of forgiveness of others in their fellowship or family, 'Well I will forgive—but I can't forget.' I want to tell you that the joy of God's forgiveness is that He's forgotten. He says 'your sins are in the depths of the sea, I will remember your sins no more.' May I say humbly, God can forget—so can you. Oh, I know, you can't expunge it completely from your memory. But there's all the difference in the world between allowing a thing to remain in the memory and keeping it there to cherish it. Forgive and forget!

And the second way this is brought home to me is when people say, 'Yes, I would forgive them. But after all, they're the ones who went wrong first. They're the ones who spoilt things. It's up to them to make the first move.' It's terribly easy to say that. But try applying that argument to God and to Jesus Christ. Did He wait until we made the first move? No: He came in all His love. 'While we were still sinners, Christ died for us' (Rom. 5:8). And a really practical Keswick could lead some people to the telephone, or to write a letter, to put something right even before you get home.

In 5:1–2 Paul goes on to talk about self-giving love, in the Spirit of Christ, the family likeness. And again we have a 'just as'. When Paul talks about the love of Christ he always goes to the cross. He doesn't talk about gathering children in His arms or touching the leper, though that was love. He talks about Jesus going to the cross, giving Himself. And will you notice, it talks about the cross as being a 'fragrant offering', a sacrifice to God.

That lovely phrase 'fragrant offering' comes several times in Scripture. It comes in Philippians 4:18 about giving, which is a fragrant offering. It comes in 2 Corinthians 2:14 about spreading the gospel, which is a fragrant offering. And in John 12:3 where Mary broke the alabaster box of ointment, the house was filled with a fragrance of the ointment. John always remembered the place by their smell. Every time he got a whiff of that ointment he remembered that room, and the fragrance when Mary broke the alabaster box. And here's the challenge: that our attitude be self-giving love.

Sex (5:3–4)

Some of what we shall say from these verses is very searching, and I'm saying it because I know it needs to be said. I'm just expounding Scripture.

On a train back to Sheffield I sat with a girl who is a medical student and a member of our congregation. I asked how the term had gone. She replied, 'I had a rough time the other week. We had been talking about AIDS and safe sex. Eventually I plucked up the courage to say, "There are some people who are Christians, including me, who actually believe that you should enter marriage still a virgin, that there's no such thing as safe sex. We want to follow the sexual pattern the Bible has given, and we intend to stand by it." ' She told me, 'When I finished, what bothered me wasn't that they were angry with me or laughed at me, but that they looked at me as though I were something out of the ark. They were thinking, "Do people like that still exist?" '

Another member of my congregation who is involved in medicine was at a conference where the same topic was discussed. He too dared to stand up and say, 'I believe there is no such thing as safe sex. There are biblical standards of sex, and if we want to deal with the issue of AIDS we will only begin to deal with them when we actually follow what the Bible teaches us about sex.' He was howled down as intolerant and unloving. How could anybody say such things? 'But,' he told me, 'over coffee it was very interesting to see how many people came to me and whispered in my ear, "Of course you are right. But you can't say that kind of thing nowadays" '.

This is the world we live in, and this is a huge issue of today. It's not the only issue, and it may be that you need to hear the challenge about money and truthfulness. And it is very easy for those for whom this is not the problem to see it a big problem dividing society. But if we are going to be the alternative community, we certainly need to pray for lasses like the one I met on the train. Imagine the pressure on people like that to conform. How much they need encouragement and fellowship, and how little they need people arguing about unimportant things when they are battling for things that are really urgent! For Christians are stuck— happily—with what the Bible teaches about sexual morality.

Verse 3, 'not . . . even a hint of sexual immorality [*porneia*, the general word for it], or of any kind of impurity, or of greed.' That word 'greed' nearly always, in this context in Scripture, refers to 'lust for people', not 'lust for money'. You find it so in 1 Corinthians 6:9. Let me read it to you, because you need to hear it.

Do you not know that the wicked will not inherit the kingdom of

God? Do not be deceived: Neither the sexually immoral nor idolaters nor adulterers nor male prostitutes nor homosexual offenders nor thieves nor the greedy nor drunkards nor slanderers nor swindlers will inherit the kingdom of God.

He adds, 'And that is what some of you were. But . . .' There were going to be lots of these people in heaven, but they would be those who had repented and turned. And when the church ceases to call sin 'sin', then we are no longer the alternative community. We are compromising with that which has always brought civilisations down.

I feel deeply that we need to say quite clearly that the way of Scripture is quite obvious; all heterosexual relationship outside of marriage is sin, and all physical homosexual relationships are sin. Please do not misunderstand me. There is an awful word current today: 'homophobia'. If you dare to say what I have just said to you, it makes you guilty of homophobia. I've had a spate of letters telling me so. I can only say to the writers that I hope they've spent as much time as I have over the last year or two, battling lovingly and prayerfully with people who have been this way, who battle with this problem and have sometimes have fallen into what they acknowledge to be sin. I am not prepared to be called homophobic. But I do want to say to those of you who agree with me, that I hope the way you speak of this matter is not in that insensitive way which encourages people to feel that we are opposed to a certain group of people.

I say all that, because I believe this is one of the urgent issues of our day. All denominations are facing it. And I believe that Christians must stand up, not as an alternative community which is purely negative, merely saying 'All these things are terrible'—but as a community which says, 'This is the only positive answer to that which is shattering our world.' And if the church compromises, there isn't anything left.

'Nor should there be obscenity, foolish talk or coarse joking, which are out of place. . .' How often in television programmes it's assumed that people live together outside marriage; homosexuality is being pushed at us constantly; and we've become so used to these things. What we get used to today, we acknowledge as normal tomorrow, and the church sanctifies the next day. And you and I need to be consciously aware of that.

Martin Luther said, 'You cannot avoid a bird landing on your head, but you can avoid it making a nest there.' The bird landing is an accident, but if you let it stay long enough to build a nest, it's your fault. You cannot avoid evil thoughts entering your mind, you cannot switch off every television programme that has anything in it that may not be absolutely pure—but you can avoid dwelling on it, pondering it, enjoying it.

At the time of the Profumo scandal the great Dr Martin Lloyd-Jones commented on the people who wrote to the newspapers about it. They were indignant at this scandal in high places. But, said Dr Lloyd-Jones, many of them read every word of the scandal and loved every word they read. And, he said, 'These days as people read the Press and watch the media, thousands of people commit adultery by proxy. They read it and they love it.'

Friends, we are an alternative community. And there's one, easily-missed, little word that to me makes sense of the whole thing. It comes at the end of verse 4, 'but rather thanksgiving'. Now, why does he put 'thanksgiving' there?

I am sure he means saying 'Thank you' to God for the gift of sex, for our sexuality.

It may have been that in the past we have been guilty of not speaking of it. Generations ago you would not have heard the things said from this pulpit about sex that I've said today. Perhaps it's because the world was different then and so was the problem. But there was a time when Christians just didn't mention sex. The very word seemed to be tarnished and tainted. Maybe we helped to create the problem. But say 'Thank you'. It's a lovely gift of God. What is the greatest power for ill can be the greatest power for good.

But I need to say one more thing before I come to my final point. We must not, as a Christian community, become accustomed to what is happening in our society. Like every minister, I find that most people who've come to me to get married in church (and I use the word 'most' without hesitation) are already living together. We face enormous

problems. But one thing we must not do is to pretend it does
not matter. I cannot conceive of anybody, even beginning
with Scripture in their hands, believing that it doesn't matter.
I believe that it's the basis of many ills of our day, and we
don't have the courage to say it. I do not know, but it is quite
likely, that in this tent this morning, unknown to me, there
are some people in this situation. And you will get no further
blessing from this Convention until you consciously do
something to put it right.

A girl came to me a year or two ago. She so much wanted
to be a better Christian; she wanted to grow in holiness. She
was living with a partner. I said, 'I've nothing really to say.
Until you are prepared to put that right, I can't offer you
anything. When it is put right, we can talk.' But she didn't
want to hear that.

So—will you pray? Will you courageously stand? Will you
—positively, please—demonstrate to younger people that
there is in sexuality something good and lovely? Will you say
to them that to go this way is not a big negative, it's not being
hugely different, it's not just being awkward, it's not
depriving you of all the joys in life? That it's actually saying
that God's way is the only way for ultimate joy, and certainly
for sanity in the world today?

The Motives of a Holy People (5:5–21)

In these verses we see three motives of a holy people, the
first two of which we will look at only briefly. The first is:

A future judgement in mind (5:5–7)
This repeats the theme of immorality and impurity. I once
heard a preacher say that you don't find Jesus and apostles
talking about sex like we do today. I don't know where he got
that from! They are constantly reminding us of the evil of sex
when misused.

Paul says, 'Let no-one deceive you with empty words'
—there is a judgement coming and it does matter. And the
clear call in verse 7 is, not to be partners with them. We are
to demonstrate our difference. In 1 Corinthians 5:12 Paul
says, 'I'm not saying you can't work with somebody who's

impure, nor that you can't meet them in society. But I am talking about people within the family of God.' You probably read that great hoo-hah in the Press recently, when somebody was taken to task because he had disciplined a couple in his congregation. They had quite openly left their partners and were now living together and wanted still to be treated as normal members of the church. I don't know anything about the pastoral implications; I don't know how it was done, and when you deal with these situations you never deal with them easily and well. But what I do know is that what he did was biblical.

Yet how often you heard it in the Press—'unloving', 'unkind'. Yet in the end he was being terribly loving and terribly kind. The challenge comes: 'Because there is a future judgement in mind,' he was saying to the couple, 'I am telling you that if you won't hear what I have to say, then you must be disciplined.' That's what Jesus said in Matthew 18:15–17. If you can't put matters right between you, then you listen to the church; if you don't listen to the church, then you are outside. And that's a challenge: a future judgement in mind.

A past liberation in mind (5:8–17)

The contrast comes out beautifully. We were once darkness, now we are light. There are two pictures of that light. First, verses 8–14, it's the picture of light meaning morality: and the light of the gospel gets rid of the darkness. We are called in Scripture to be salt and light, we're to let the light shine. And that is that what we're speaking about now. It's attractive, it's not negative. We should be able to say to the world in which we live, 'We have something lovely.' If we believe family life is something beautiful and lovely, with all its imperfections, let's proclaim it; let's live it; let's show it.

Notice in verse 11, 'Have nothing to do with the fruitless deeds of darkness, but rather expose them.' That word 'expose' is the same word used by Jesus in John about the convicting work of the Spirit, who will 'convict the world of guilt in regard to sin and righteousness and judgement' (John 16:8). So what we do to expose them is not to tell them off.

What we do is show, by the quality of our lives, that there is something better.

We have got to such a mess in our society that I long for and hope that some might soon begin to turn back and look for a community that has said something different and lives something different. I wonder what they'll find when they do? The tragedy would be if we tried to become so like the world out there they wouldn't see any difference. Would they ever turn to us then? But if we were so different, if we'd never spoken to them and lived away in a ghetto—would they then ever come to us? They wouldn't know we were there. We must relate, we are the light that shines in a dark place.

But also (verse 15), the light is to be seen in 'enlightenment': light seen as moral purity and as truth. Thus the concept of wisdom and un-wisdom, using the time fully because the days are evil; living a day at a time, buying up the time. That's very important, isn't it. And we shall only understand the Lord's will if we are actually being faithful to Him now.

The will of God generally is in Scripture. The will of God personally comes when I live close to the Lord and close to His word. So, a past liberation in mind: we once were darkness, now we're light; thank God for the transformation.

A present indwelling in mind (5:18–21)
The opposite of the self-indulgence of darkness is the filling of the Holy Spirit. The most preached-on text at Keswick is Ephesians 5:18: 'Keep on being filled with the Spirit.'

Paul begins, 'Do not get drunk on wine, which leads to debauchery. Instead, be filled with the Spirit.' I have heard preachers say, 'It's rather like being drunk.' But it's not at all like being drunk. It's the opposite. Alcohol is not a stimulant, it's a depressant; and the Spirit doesn't depress. Alcohol doesn't make you a better person, it dehumanises you. The only time when there was relationship on the Day of Pentecost, they weren't taking it seriously, it was meant to be rather bad joke, 'These men are full of wine.' And Peter starts his sermon, 'It can't be; it isn't opening time.' So we don't get drunk with wine, we keep on being filled with the Spirit. And it leads to three things.

One, *fellowship and worship*. That lovely picture of enjoying our singing, in our hearts to the Lord. Whether we are 'musical' or not, it's there. And when we are filled with the Spirit, or when the word of God dwells in us richly (cf Colossians 3:16), we want to sing. That's one of the joys of Keswick. I dare to say that our singing's improved, the music's improved and it's great. I believe that God is at work in our midst. People are writing hymns again in our world of today, thank God they are (keep the old as well, because we need them all).

Two, *gratitude*, verse 20: 'always giving thanks ... for everything'. Now, we must not be foolish. Of course it doesn't mean that if you suddenly discover you've got an incurable disease, you say, 'Thank you Lord.' It doesn't mean at all that if you fall into sin you say 'Thank you Lord.' What it does mean is that even if you do discover you've got an incurable disease, by the grace of God you are able to say, 'Thank you'—not for the disease, but for the hope you have for the future. Thank God for the resources you have.

And even though by the grace of God you can never say 'Thank you' for sin, we can all look back at our lives, where we've discovered God's mercy in time; when we've repented and been forgiven, and then can be a help for other people. But we don't say 'Thank you that I fell into sin,' we say 'Thank you Lord for your grace, thank you that I can use that example to help others.' And certainly being able to say 'Thank you' for everything is a mark of the Spirit. When you know the reality of the infilling of the Spirit, even when like the apostles you are pushed into prison, you can sing praises at midnight. And Paul in prison could say, 'What has happened to me has really served to advance the gospel'.

Three, and less easy, is *submission*. Tomorrow we'll hear this expanded in a particular context. Here, note the general statement. It is a mark of being filled with the Spirit, that all of us submit ourselves to one another because of our reverence and fear of Christ. All of what we'll say tomorrow stems from that fact, and in fact there's no further verb in verse 22: 'Wives submit to your husbands'. We are stopping today at 'Submit to one another out of reverence for Christ', which means that we are stopping half-way through a sentence.

But the general statement is for all of us. It will make all the difference for you tomorrow morning if you get hold of that. This is the general mark of Christian living. There's nothing *infra dig* about submitting to one another. It is a mark of Jesus who came from heaven's glory and submitted Himself willingly to His Father's will. He came down from glory and He was obedient even unto death. On Sunday I shall be preaching on Hebrews 5 in my own church, and I've been getting to grips with the passage. 'He learned obedience from what he suffered' (Heb. 5:8). He submitted Himself. So please don't think submission is something wrong. It's a mark of the fullness of the Spirit, and Christians can say 'We can do it gladly because of Christ.'

And it all follows from that great statement with which I end: 'Be filled with the Spirit'. Three words in the Greek. It's in the plural form, the imperative mood, the passive voice and the present tense.

You should go away thrilled with the prospect!

It's in the *plural form*—that means it's for all Christians. The things about the Spirit I most love to preach about are those that are for everybody. The Spirit does different things for different people, but He wants to fill all of us. 'In one Spirit,' says Paul elsewhere, 'we are all baptised into one body.' 'We all,' says 2 Corinthians 3 'are being changed into the image of Christ from glory to glory by the Spirit.' It's in the plural form for everybody.

It's in the *imperative mood*. It's a command, 'Be filled.' I remember John Stott saying once, I think from this platform, that you *must* obey every command about the Spirit, and you *can* claim every promise about the Spirit; but you don't expect the Spirit to work today exactly as He did then. He doesn't say He will. But every command about the Spirit we can obey, and the command is 'Be filled.'

It's in the *passive* voice. You don't work it up. It isn't a matter of emotional manipulation. It's God's work, and we are open to Him to work in our hearts.

And it's in the *present tense*. 'Keep on being filled.' The same disciples in Act 2 were filled on the Day of Pentecost; in Acts 4, when they met opposition, they were filled again. So it only lasted two chapters. We think in those terms because we think of it rather like a substance coming into an empty vessel. But it's not that. It's a relationship with a person, who comes and He fills us and He goes on filling us. There's a group today that call themselves 'open evangelicals'. I want to know, to whom are they open? I am open, I hope, to the Spirit of God. I hope that you are in that sense an 'open Christian'—that is, constantly opening yourselves to the infilling of the Spirit.

Tonight Keith White will be taking us on into John 7, where John talks in similar words about the Spirit infilling and flowing through us.[1] It's purely by coincidence, so far as I know, that I have reached today the theme that we traditionally speak of on this day of the Keswick week. But there are no coincidences in God's plan. And in some remarkable way he wanted Ephesians 5 this morning as preparation for our gathering this evening.

We need to care about this holy life, because one day we'll stand before the judgement seat of Christ. We need to prepare for this, because we've been changed and want to show it. We need to care, because we have within us the indwelling Spirit.

What does the world believe about the Spirit of God if He doesn't make any difference in our lives? And do you see, the motivation becomes the enabling? If we are convicted about money, if we are convicted about the tongue, if we are convicted about our sexuality, maybe something needs to be done. Even, today.

---

1. Rev Keith White's address is included in the present volume, p. 202.

5: Transformed Relationships
(Ephesians 5:22–6:24)

This is a wonderful passage to come to on the last day. It balances, in the way that only Scripture does, something extremely down-to-earth and practical—all about husbands, wives, children, parents and so on—and the great cosmic battle that comes at the end, the fight against principalities and powers. You blend the two: as Christians we are meant to be down-to-earth, we are meant to be practical and it ought to be true that this week's Bible Readings have affected the way we live at home. But we must be always mindful there's a battle on.

Ultimately the 'alternative community' of which we've been speaking is not just one great big family, like we are in the 'Keswick family'. We are also a family of families. And we are meant in our ordinary relationships to live it out. There's a lovely balance between these meditations in our passage today on how you live at home. Isn't that why Paul, having talked about all these things, finishes with a challenge about the battle? It is not just a matter of enjoying the riches with which were called to sit, it's not even just a matter of walking in newness of life because we have been changed, there's a fight on and there always will be a fight on: thus the title of the book I mentioned earlier, *Sit, Walk, Stand*.

The 'stand' section comes only at the end from 6:10 onwards, that well-known passage. But four times in just three verses we find 'stand, stand, stand.' And never more were Christians called to stand firm, to stand up and be counted than today. When I say that, some people think I'm defeatist. The exact opposite is the case. We have an opportunity to stand up for something wonderful. And the silent majority had better stop being a silent majority, and speak up and stand up for what we believe.

A cynic might suggest that the word about fighting comes after all the injunctions about home life because that's where most of the fights happen. And this is sadly often true. If, as many of you do, you stand where I stand and you receive people coming with stories of sad experiences, you will realise how much in these days Satan has infiltrated Christian homes and is doing untold damage. So the fight is on, God give us grace to stand.

Let's look, then, at these three transformed relationships: at home, at work, in the battle.

At Home (5:22–6:4)

Notice that Paul talks about responsibilities and duties, rather than rights. And I hope that as you listen wives won't be nudging husbands and husbands nudging wives, to make sure they're listening properly. I'm speaking, as Paul does, as the Holy Spirit does, to you.

A word to wives (5:22–24)

You will only understand this passage if you notice that there is no verb in verse 22. 'Submit to one another out of reverence for Christ' leads straight on to 'wives, submit to your husbands.' The wife-husband relationship is just one illustration of a total submission to each other. When we understand that, we shall realise that there's nothing demeaning about the command of verse 22, since indeed we should all be submitting to one another, and we are doing it out of reverence for Christ.

It also needs to be said that there is a difference between 'Wives, submit to your husbands' (5:22), 'Children, obey your parents' (6:1) and 'Slaves, obey your earthly masters' (6:5). There is a difference between submission and obedience. I have to say, I cannot find in Scripture a command for wives to obey their husbands. In 1 Peter 3:6 it speaks of

'Sarah, who obeyed Abraham and called him her master', but I don't know what husband here would believe it if his wife came to him tonight and called him 'Master'. You'd think there was some malicious plot afoot, wouldn't you? And therefore I have no desire to be obeyed as lord (AV) and master.

So I don't believe that when my dear wife Margaret did promise to obey me, thirty-odd years ago, it was the right word. In the old Prayer Book you had no choice. Nor is 'submit' quite the same. And I don't see any conflict in putting this discussion alongside Galatians 3:28, which says that we are all one in Christ Jesus, 'there is neither . . . male nor female'. We may not take one bit of Scripture and say, 'That's the important bit, therefore we must make it fit in with that other bit'—they are both equally important. Equality of status does not necessarily mean identity of role. Male and female are different, and I want to say thank God they are. But they are equal in the sight of God. And when you think what has actually happened in Christian history in terms of liberation of womanhood, you would have to be deliberately blinkered not to say 'Thank you' to God for a remarkable revolution, and compare it with what's happened in many other religions.

Again, think about children. Of course these verses are important, but how we thank God that in Christianity children are part of the community. Jesus welcomed children. They were amazed; the big rabbi, the great teacher, actually let children clamber into His arms. It wasn't the thing to do, but He did it. And our Lord wasn't a rabbi with a certificate of theology, He was a carpenter. So He brought dignity into that kind of manual work. And nothing that I say and nothing Paul says here must ever diminish the truth of the dignity of all individuals before God, of the equality of all people in the family of God. So I insist: equality of worth does not necessarily mean identity of role.

Notice too that Christ is central in every relationship. 'Submit to your husbands as to the Lord' (5:22). 'Children, obey your parents in the Lord' (6:1). I don't think it means 'your Christian parents', that if they aren't Christian parents you don't obey them; it doesn't mean 'parents in the Lord', it means 'obey in the Lord your parents.' Or again, 'Slaves, obey your earthly masters ... just as you would obey Christ' (6:5). So all these are illustrations of submission out of reverence for Christ.

And again in context (all of this is terribly important, and people must listen to it all and not just to a little bit of it), within the total spectrum, notice that responsibilities are reciprocal. Paul doesn't just tell the wife what she must do, he tells the husband; not just the child but the parent; not just the slave but the master. And have you seen what the reciprocal responsibility is? It's very interesting: 'Wives submit.' So—'Husbands, have authority, lord it over them'? No. 'Husbands, love.' What is the opposite of children obeying parents? 'Parents, make sure you keep a firm hand on them'? No. 'Bring them up in the training and instruction of the Lord.' What a different matter that is! And with slaves and masters, of course the master is told that he should treat them with justice and fairness, the way he expects them to treat him. So that gives us the context.

It is clear, if you compare this letter with other writings of Paul, that for him the relationship of husband and wife was part of the creation ordinance. It wasn't just Paul's idea. It wasn't just because of the culture of the day. Our Lord Himself in Matthew 19, when asked about divorce, referred back to the original creation. 'God meant it like this,' He says, quoting Genesis 2. 'From the beginning that's how it should have been—one man, one woman for life.' Certainly, He acknowledges the reality of divorce because of man's sin; but He goes back to the creation ordinance.

But (and we need to say this) we cannot ignore Genesis 3:16.It tells what happened after the Fall. God says to the woman: 'I will greatly increase your pains in childbearing; with pain you will give birth to children. Your desire will be for your husband and he will rule over you.' Sex was the first casualty of the Fall. What did Adam and Eve discover when they sinned? First of all, that they were naked. And that lovely reality, the beauty of sex, was suddenly changed because men and women had fallen. And the relationship which was beautiful in creation, of wife and husband in a right relationship, here being reinstated, was vitiated by the

Fall. The tragedy is today that if anybody today dares even to breathe that they actually believe that this is true, they are simply accused of male chauvinism.

We do not get anywhere as Christians if we just throw shibboleths at people. I would dare to say that one mark of the alternative community is that sometimes we stand against the trend, we dare to swim against the tide, we even run the risk of being thought old-fashioned. If you are a male, you run that risk of being called a 'male chauvinist'. I assure you I've been called that a great number of times.

But I want to suggest to you that the male chauvinism, the rule of men over women, is the result of the Fall. And for that of course we have no mandate whatsoever. Submission in 5:22 is not subjugation, it's a willing self-giving of a person voluntarily to a husband who is a lover. That's what it says. Even more in verses 23–24 it is seen as a relationship: not just a creation ordinance, but a redemption ordinance. It goes not only back to the beginning, it goes back to Jesus, the great theme of 5:23—'The husband is the head of the wife as Christ is the head of the Church.'

If you don't believe the first bit, I should like to know what you make of the second. If you say, 'Of course I do believe in Christ as the head of the church, but I don't believe in husbands as the head of their wives', I have to say that what you're doing is twisting Scripture, and I don't know where you will end up.

But then how is Christ the head of the church? Paul goes on at the end of the verse to add, 'of which he is the Saviour'. So the headship of which these verses speak, and which I believe is still in the economy and plan of God, is to the husband a headship, not of lordship but of saviourhood; not of rule but of responsibility. It is a mirror of how Jesus was head and servant at the same time.

Let me go one stage further. I meet people who say, 'Paul speaks like that because he was a person of his age. He speaks like that to Ephesus, and again when he writes to Timothy who was in Ephesus. It's because in Ephesus there was Diana worship, woman religious prostitutes, broken marriages and social disorder. That's why Paul writes as he does.' I find this disturbing. If that is so, why on earth doesn't he say so? I don't find one verse in Ephesians that makes any reference to that kind of thing. Surely, if Paul was doing it simply because he wanted to relate to a specific situation, he would have said so.

It's a total commitment for all Christians. If I want to believe the New Testament I am left with this. And I hope that most, indeed all, Christian women would accept this as being God's plan and purpose, and a beautiful thing indeed. Because Paul goes on to point out, 'As the church submits to Christ, so also wives should submit to their husbands in everything' (5:24). That relationship of love and submission —which is not subjugation or forced obedience—is a lovely pattern of Christ and the church. And therefore we are meant in the world today to be saying something to society out of our home.

I know there are many single people here, and this passage does not in its context speak to single people. And I know I speak to a number whose marriages sadly have fallen, and you've been hurt; and I hope nothing I say will make you feel even more hurt. But I am saying that where there are Christian families, they ought to be a living radiating witness of the gospel. It's a gospel issue, it's all to do with Christ and His church. And we are being attacked from many libertarian angles who want as it were to destroy this. And I submit that if you destroy this, you are destroying parts of the witness of the church.

A word to husbands (5:25–33)

The husband is called to love. Paul uses the Greek word *agape*. He could have used others. He could have used the word for a sexual relationship or the word for friendship, both of which would not have been inappropriate; but he used *agape*, the love word that's used of Christ's self-giving.

If I had time I could point out how the Bible often portrays God as a bridegroom: for example, Isaiah 54, Jeremiah 2, Mark 2, Revelation 21. In the last of these the picture of the church that is used is that of the bridal feast of the Lamb. In Ephesians 5:25–27 there are five verbs used to describe what Christ did for the church. He loved her, He gave Himself for her, He made her holy, He cleansed her and one day He will present her as a radiant church. Friends, if the church in all its imperfections can be radiant, then we have real hope. The bride will one day be perfect.

It's very difficult to see how far this relates to a husband. I don't think a husband normally helps to present his bride on a wedding day as perfect: it's not his job to make sure that all the bride's preparations—the dress, make-up and all the rest—are done properly. But the picture here is of Christ working in His church, and the marriage relationship is meant to mirror it. The bridegroom says 'I will' and the bride responds with her 'I will'; and then, in the Church of England service, comes that lovely point when the right hand of the bridegroom grasps the right hand of the bride and the groom turns to the bride and says, 'I John take you Sally' or whatever their names may be. And the Prayer Book instructs that when he has said that, 'Then they shall loose their hands.' Then the bride grasps the groom's right hand with her own, and she says the same words.

I always say to the bride when we are preparing for the wedding, 'Do remember that up to that point you are not yet married.' She could turn round and walk out of the church if she wanted to. The groom has said, 'I take you', but until she of her own volition has taken his hand and said, 'I Sally take you John', they are not married. Once, in the days when marriages could only legally be solemnised before four o'clock in the afternoon, we had seven or eight weddings on the same Saturday, and the last bride was very late; she didn't arrive at the church until ten to four. I was a curate at that time, and I said to the vicar, 'What shall we do?'

'Have all the hymns at the end,' he said. And by four o'clock she'd said 'I take you', and we were able to relax and sing the hymns. Because when she said those words, the couple were married.

Do you see the parallel? Christ says 'I will' on the cross; we say 'I will', and so we belong to Him. Christ takes hold of our hand, we take hold of His. That's why we say, surely, in the modern service, that they shall give themselves to each other in love throughout their lives. Woe betide the couple who depend upon their love on their wedding day to keep them for ever! It won't. Woe betide the Christian who depends upon the joy of his conversion day to keep him or her going for ever! It won't. There must be a continual response of love. How often couples have said to me, 'We've never seen a happy marriage, we don't know what it's like.' Both of them come from broken homes; both of them come from situations where they don't know what it's like to live together in love throughout their lives. It makes you realise what an important responsibility it is for those of us who claim to be Christians. Often in the mission field they've said, 'We want to see Christian homes set up'. And I want to say that in Britain we want to see more Christian homes set up, to be seen, and to radiate continuing love in this relationship.

Doesn't verse 28 seem an anti-climax? 'Husbands ought to love their wives as their own bodies. He who loves his wife loves himself.' That seems an awfully selfish way of looking at it. But don't you see what he's saying? The bride/bridegroom analogy merges into the other analogy of the body. I want to hammer home the links with yesterday's Bible Reading: for a Christian, extra-marital relationship is always sin, and it cannot be anything else. We need to keep saying it. To live together in a sexual relationship outside marriage is to deny the whole meaning.

Genesis 2:24, 'Therefore shall a man leave his father and his mother, and shall cleave unto his wife: and they shall be one flesh' (AV). 'No cleaving without leaving'—that is to say, it is a commitment. It is not just a sexual pleasurable activity, it's the self-commitment of one person to another, by the grace of God, for life. And I fear deeply that even in this Keswick tent, people don't take that seriously. The Bible takes it desperately seriously. So the relationship of two bodies together is a sealing of a relationship; and to do that without the commitment of marriage is to deny the gospel. I want you to take that seriously. When Christians are indulging in that, their witness becomes impossible.

So it's all summed up in verse 33: 'This is a profound mystery—but I am talking about Christ and the church.' So, the husband must love and the wife must respect. I would suggest to you, that is a lovely relationship and I see nothing demeaning in it. And I hope that husbands and wives can battle against so much that's being assumed in our day, and argue loud and clear against the danger of what they call 'role-reversal'. Of course things like who goes out to work and so on can be reversed. Sometimes they need to be. But there are some roles that the Bible doesn't allow us to reverse. A wife is a wife and a husband is a husband, and the pattern is set.

A word to children (6:1–2)

It's interesting that Paul, writing to the church at Ephesus and to the other churches, expects children to be around and listening. Whatever your practice is with family services, it's important that children be part of the church family. I don't like the idea of different churches for different ages—youth churches, children's churches—they're surely part of the whole church.

Paul speaks to the children and calls them to 'obey', which is a different word from 'submit'. Why do they obey? Verse 1, because it's 'right'; it's natural. Secondly, why *should* they obey? Note the word 'honour', which makes it applicable even to those of us who are getting on in years. Some of us my age and even older have parents still alive; we still have a responsibility of respect, and some of the issues that crop up can be just as painful for older people. How do we, what do we, do about an elderly parent who can't cope any more? And there are not always simple answers. But respect is very important, and we don't have a very good track record in our country of respect for old age. So whatever age you are, you're still included here. We are not all married here, but we are all children and many of us still have parents alive.

We honour them, says Paul, because of the promise of the fifth commandment, which for the Jew was part of duty to God, not duty to your neighbour. It's interesting that parents were seen in the place of God; God had given them that responsibility. And the commandment says (6:3) 'that you may enjoy long life on the earth.' Of course that does not mean if you are good to your parents you'll live until you're 120. The oldest member of my congregation is a lady of 102. She lives on her own, gets to church quite often and is a very independent soul. I visited her before Christmas, and she said to me, 'I think, Philip, that at last, at 102, I'm giving up Christmas shopping.' I told my wife, 'I think when I get to 102 I'll give up Christmas shopping too.' To which came the answer, from this disobedient wife, 'You've not done Christmas shopping for years, Dear.' Which is also true . . .

But if you were to go to that dear lady and say, 'Have you lived to be 102 because you were good to your parents?' she wouldn't understand what you were talking about. Of course Paul is not saying, 'Honour your parents and you'll have a healthy and long life.' What he *is* saying, because this commandment was given to the Jews going into the promised land (I want to hammer this home) is this: 'If you want society to continue healthily, you need these relationships right.'

I believe we could be witnessing the collapse of what we have known as civilised society in our Western world, because the mess that marriage has got into and the relationships that result are so terribly great. Read history. Read about the collapse of empires, see how often they began to collapse because family life disappeared and sexual perversion, immorality, and the decline of relationships increased. We need to take this seriously. And if we want society to continue, we as what the Bible calls the 'salt of the earth' have a very big responsibility.

'Obey your parents in the Lord.' I think that suggests two things. One, our Lord Himself was obedient to His parents (Luke 2:51). That's a lovely picture: the Son of God came down from heaven and He was subject to His parents. Even when after that remarkable incident when He was twelve years old, when His parents were worried that they had lost Him, and He gently rebuked His mother, 'Didn't you know I had to be in my Father's house?' (Luke 2:49). He went back and was subject to them. And that's the challenge to Christians. It's not easy for those of us who have known Christian homes, and some of us are teenagers whose parents dissuade them from the things of God. It's not easy, but it's part of our Christian responsibility in the Lord.

But there's a second implication in that phrase 'in the Lord'. Our Lord Himself says (and I know this very well) that even this unique relationship of parent and child must come second to Him. If we love parents or children more than Him, we are not worthy of Him. Parents, I do hope that if your children decide that God has called them to Mongolia, Egypt or wherever, you don't say, 'What about me? I'm going to miss you, I'm not going to see my grandchildren . . .' You see what the call of Jesus can mean? Even Christian parents, and I'm not condemning them, can think like that. I hope you would not put unnecessary obstacles in the way of your children doing the will of God.

Last year a couple were here from Mongolia who have been missionaries for thirty years. They are members of my congregation. When they went out to Mongolia after working for thirty years in Japan, we had a very touching valedictory service for them. They knew that the chance of seeing their aged parents again was remote, and the aged parents knew that they might well not see their children again. I can always remember when father and son were saying 'Goodbye'. We're good Yorkshire people in our church; they didn't fling their arms around each other's necks. But there was a lovely moment in front of the church when the father and son shook hands warmly and the father said to his son, 'See you again, Bill.'

The father's wife died some months ago. The lovely thing is that they were always willing to see their children go back. There was never any attempt to pressurise them. And I like to say that there were two aspects to missionary work in that family: the ones at home were as much missionaries as the ones who went out, because they went out with their blessing. That's a cost. The Bible insists that there may come a time when some must say, 'Is it what Jesus says—or is it what my parents say?' Those two can sometimes clash. And surely obeying your parents in the Lord means there could come a moment when you have to put Christ first, and that's sad.

And, because this relationship of parent and child is so precious, woe betide organisations, sects and cults that divide families unnecessarily, who actually ask children to make decisions about leaving families unnecessarily. We have had experience of this with some of the more extreme religious groups in Sheffield.

A word to parents (6:4)

Technically the word is 'fathers', and that's appropriate. Fatherhood, like being a husband, if it's to be done properly must have a real responsibility. See the responsibilities of fathers: they must not discourage their children, nor make unnecessary demands; discipline is right but it must be a discipline that has some reasoning behind it (cf 6:4). Not 'Do it because I say so.' Don't discourage your children.

And the positive note: nurture them and instruct them. The word 'training' involves discipline. Proverbs 13:24—'He who spares the rod hates his son, but he who loves him is careful to discipline him.' I know that some will say that much corporal punishment goes over the top, that it can be wrong; and all that I agree with. But the Bible is very clear that there should be discipline, and it does not say that it is necessarily wrong that discipline should include sometimes punishment, even corporal punishment. If you as a family don't need it and your children love you so much and are so beautifully behaved that a word is enough, then God bless you!—but you are as rare as a dodo, I suspect. All I can say—and I know some of you will get cross with me—is that I believe we are in danger of being conned, and that the European Court of Human Rights is not always right. As Christians we see the importance of discipline.

Even more, verse 4, 'Bring them up in the training and instruction of the Lord.' Obviously, that's even more important. Psalm 78 gives a list of the generations and shows us how we are meant to pass on to our children, so they may pass on to their children, to the generation beyond them, so that they should hear the things of God. I wonder how much the things of God are talked about in your home? I don't think we ought to make Christian homes super-pious ones. Sometimes as a visiting preacher I've sat in homes at breakfast time, and sensed the kids' resentment as family prayers proceeded. When I was asked to join in, I sensed the resentment being transferred to me. I longed to say something rather naughty in order to ease the tension!

There's a danger of being super-pious. It is important is that parents should be happy to talk about the things of God, to discuss them with the children, to talk about what happens in Sunday School and church and so on; to share some of these things, to open up and as they become teenagers to still have a relationship in which they can talk in a natural way about some of the things that deeply disturb teenagers today. We are to bring them up in the nurture of the Lord.

At Work (6:5–9)

A word to employees (6:5–8)

Of course the relationship between slaves and masters cannot simply be applied to the modern workplace. There are thousands of differences. But there are some principles that still apply.

It is said that there were roughly 60,000 slaves in the Roman Empire of Paul's day. Many were in positions of considerable responsibility. Many were well treated, but all of them were slaves. In other words, they were what Aristotle called 'living tools'. They had no rights, they were not regarded as proper individuals. What is surprising is that Paul even addresses them. It is quite revolutionary that he actually gives them some responsibilities, but at the same time, by giving them responsibilities he was also underlining their rights. They were clearly part of the church. There were slaves in that church at Ephesus, as well as masters.

People will say, 'Surely slavery can never be right.' That's true; but can you imagine what would have happened if Paul had said, 'All slaves should join in some great campaign and get rid of slavery'? The whole fabric of society depended upon them. What Paul did do, and this is very important, was to say certain things that would inevitably undermine the whole institution of slavery. For example, the fact that he gave them rights, through this passage; the fact that in Galatians 3:28 he says that they were equal before God, there was 'neither slave nor free'; the fact that he actually says here and in Colossians 4:1 even more so, that masters should treat slaves with justice. And then there is that phrase in Philemon, remarkable because slaves had no rights at all in law, where Paul urges Philemon to welcome his slave Onesimus back, 'no longer as a slave, but better than a slave, as a dear brother . . . in the Lord' (Phil. 15–16). He wasn't saying that Onesimus wouldn't come back to his slave position. What he was saying was, 'He's now your brother; and don't you see that's inevitably going to undermine this relationship?'

It must be added that there is no suggestion that Paul thought the same about the husband/wife relationship. People sometimes argue, 'Since Paul wanted the relationship of slavery to go, wouldn't he also want the husband/wife relationship of submission and headship to go?' Well—no, because Paul refers the husband/wife relationship back to the creation. He acts as if it's always been there. It's part of God's order. Clearly he didn't mean that to go. But slavery never was part of God's order. Let us see what Paul says, and discover the principle that still applies to us at work today.

Each of the four verses addressed to slaves contains the name of Christ. Verse 5—'Obey your earthly masters . . . just as you would obey Christ'; verse 6—'slaves of Christ'; verse 7—'serving the Lord'; verse 8—'the Lord will reward everyone for whatever good he does'. They were doing it as for Christ. And however mean the task, if I do it as for Christ it gives a new dimension.

Notice, too, the qualities Paul expects of slaves. They should be respectful, verse 5; they should be sincere, verse 5b; they should be conscientious, verse 6, not just working hard when the boss is looking, but all the time. And they should be willing and cheerful, verse 7. All these are how we are meant to be. I am fascinated by the fact that Paul says to slaves in his letter to Titus that they must adorn the doctrine, 'make the teaching about God our Saviour attractive' (Tit. 2:10)—and he's writing to slaves.

A word to masters (6:9)
Put simply, verse 9 simply says: 'Treat your slaves as you would wish them to treat you.' It's a lovely thought. You expect them to be conscientious and so on; what about your responsibility to them?

Notice too the end of the verse, 'He who is both their Master and yours is in heaven, and there is no favouritism with him.' It means, He doesn't recognise a face, which means He doesn't give one person a special place and another a lower one. There are no VIPs in the kingdom of God.

I don't think the church always believes that. We need to treat everybody alike, and the worst that you could ever say to me would be that I treat some people in my congregation different from others because they happen to be important people. If that were true, I would have failed in my ministry. All people are to be treated alike: slaves, masters, bosses, employers, whatever. The important titled person and the very unimportant (so it seems) little lady round the corner —they are all the same.

What an alternative position that is! The world is full of status, whatever the politics may be. We are full of status. It's hard sometimes not to become cynical about politicians, I try not to be: as we've been reminded by Clive Calver[1], we must pray for our politicians and care very much for them. But whatever label you may have, status still seems to matter. Thank God, in the family of God it matters not at all.

In the Battle (6:10–24)

In the midst of all we've been talking about—'Sit, walk, stand'—there's always a fight on our hands. In 6:10 Paul says, 'Finally'. You preachers know preachers well enough that the word 'finally' has no place whatsoever in the preaching vocabulary! It simply means that we are moving towards the appointed goal, we are nearer than when we first believed, we've got a bit further on than when we started. Philippians 4 says 'finally' half way through!

Paul actually is near the end. But the word 'finally' could be translated 'for the rest of your life', not 'I am finally finishing.' I am sure he is saying that there will always be a battle. If you heard a gospel preached that said that if certain things happen, then from now on there is no struggle, don't believe it; it's not biblical. Always the Bible insists, 'Yes there

---

1. Rev Clive Calver's address is included in the present volume, p. 186.

is peace, yes there is joy; but yes, also, there is a battle. The two are always together. There's a fight on our hands.'

So three quick points.

Know your enemy (6:10–12)

The enemy is called in verse 12 'principalities and powers', and elsewhere is described in all those phrases which speak of cosmic forces, sometimes working through political, social, even (in the words of Jesus) ecclesiastical channels. They can dress up in sheep's clothing and are ravenous wolves. So we need to be very careful and very subtle.

It is interesting, if Paul as seems probable is writing primarily to Ephesus, that in Ephesus he had had a battle against the forces that worshipped Diana: occult forces. That was part of the battle. He says in 2 Corinthians 1:9 that when he was in Ephesus he felt the sentence of death on him. He felt depressed—yes, the apostle Paul felt depressed; he even despaired of life itself. The enemy was very subtle.

And Paul can say of the enemy that he has great power. 'The powers of this dark world' in verse 12 is one word in the Greek. Interestingly enough, it is linked with astrology: and I still meet Christians who dabble in astrology. Keep away from it! And what we are told to do is to take our stand against the devil's schemes (verse 11: the Greek word means 'methods'). If you know your New Testament you'll know that the devil has many methods.

Paul writes elsewhere we are not ignorant of his devices. Sometimes he comes like a roaring lion, sometimes like a subtle serpent insinuating his mind. The devil's greatest weapons are not demonic forces, though such forces exist. The devil's best weapons are much more subtle than that. He's no fool, and he loves to insinuate ideas into people's minds, he loves to destroy the marriages of decent respectable people. He loves the unguarded moment when he can come like a roaring lion. He loves to get dressed up in ecclesiastical garb and start insinuating false teaching. And he loves (Eph. 4:14) to find childish Christians who desperately want something new. He says, 'Have you tried this? There's a religious note to it.'

Against such an enemy we need to be 'strong in the Lord' (6:10). Notice in that verse three words to do with strength. Those same three words came also in 1:19 about the power of God who raised Jesus from the dead.

Know your weapons (6:13–18)

These weapons have to be considered together. It is 'the full armour of God'. And commentators differ about what was at the back of Paul's mind. Some suggest Isaiah 59:17, which talks about the armour of God. Others would say, and I think I agree with them, that as Paul was in prison and had Roman soldiers coming in day by day, he had the visual aid always in front of him. Can you imagine it, by the way? Those poor soldiers come in. It's their job to stand guard over Paul that day.

'Good morning,' Paul would say. 'Nice to see you, I haven't seen you before.'

'No,' says the soldier.

'Do you know who I am?'

'Yes,' says the soldier.

'Do you know what I'm here for?'

'No,' says the soldier.

'You will . . .'

And the poor Roman soldier was chained to Paul and Paul gave his testimony. That's what they call a captive audience! And no doubt, while he had his captive audience chained to him Paul, was looking at the armour. I think it may be so.

But wherever he takes the image from, note what the weapons are. The belt of truth, that's the inner garment that keeps it together; we'll never fight properly if we aren't truthful people. Second, the breast-plate of righteousness, which John Bunyan suggests in *Pilgrims Progress* only covered the front because Christian soldiers should never run away, and therefore the enemy can never get your back. What we have to protect ourselves with is righteousness, the fact that we are right with God. Three, the boots on our feet ready to go out with the gospel of peace. Four, the shield of faith against all the accusations of the enemy.

Sometimes it's when an accusation is largely true that it

hurts. But we need to remember we live in an age when the devil will want to get false accusations. He would love to bring down people of God. He would certainly love to bring down any people who are in a position of influence. That's why we need to pray for Christian politicians. The devil would love to bring them down, he would love to accuse them. Nowadays the newspaper stories don't even need to have much truth in them; there's no smoke without fire, somebody's going to say.

How can we stand?

We've got the shield of faith, which is going to go on trusting God, trusting Him to keep us from those accusations; the helmet of salvation covering our mind, and the sword of the Spirit—the one positive weapon, which Hebrews calls a double-edged sword. And the word of God is what we take out to the fight.

I do hope you know your weapons. I hope you can give a reason for the hope that's in you. I am useless in practical matters, and when something goes wrong with my car I'm in trouble. In the back of the car are all the tools and gadgets you need to do the repair—but I've no idea what to do with them (if you have the same problem, buy yourself a clerical collar; people stop to help you if you're wearing one). Now, it doesn't matter that I don't know how to deal with car repairs, but it does matter that we should know what to do with the weapons for our defence against the devil's attacks. What did Jesus use when He was being tempted? The word of God. What do you use when you are being tempted? The word of God. And how can you use it unless you know it? Get down to the Bible! Not just picking a few verses in case certain things happen (though that can be useful too); but getting to know it; and to win people for Christ, give a reason for the hope that's in us.

Alongside the sword of the Spirit we have verse 18, praying in the Spirit; prayer and the word together. Go back to your church determined to get praying again. Note the four 'alls' in verse 18—all occasions, all kinds of prayer, always, all the saints.

And finally,

Know yourself (6:19–20).

There is a lovely balance. Paul asks 'Pray also for me.' He was never too big to ask for prayer, was he. He was always humble: 'I need your prayer.' What did he ask prayer for? Are we as big as this? He was in prison and he did not say, 'Pray that I may get out of prison.' He said, 'Pray that while I'm here, I may speak the words fearlessly.'

And we know that at the end of the Acts of the Apostles, when Paul was in prison at Rome, the last two words of the Greek text of the Acts of the Apostles say that he spoke openly and boldly. He was able to do it. The prayer was answered. Please pray for your preachers, pray for yourself if you are a preacher; but pray for all our witness, that it may have both clarity and courage—two of the things that we need most in our day.

And dear old Tychicus—I'm looking forward to meeting Tychicus in heaven. He was an interesting man. Poor Tychicus, whenever he gets mentioned, is always being sent off on a journey somewhere. Paul always calls him 'my dear brother and faithful servant,' but he's sending him off somewhere. He's always ready.

We're not always Pauls, but we've got to be ready to be Tychicuses. Has the Lord put His hand upon you this day, this week, and called you, and you don't know where it's all going to end? Well, that's exciting! When I stood in this tent, I don't know how many years ago, I'd no idea where it was going to end or even continue, but God does and He wants you to be a Tychicus.

And what is our strength? Just note all the lovely virtues at the end—peace, love, faith, grace. May I end with those words with which the letter ends? 'Grace to all who love our Lord Jesus Christ with an undying love.' Please use your own thoughts to link that with all the things I've been trying to say, with lots of words, during these busy mornings; that it's only as we love Him with an undying love that we shall sit and walk and stand, and our homes be changed and the whole of our lives be different. And we will be an alternative community that commends the gospel.

Let me add just this. When you take Communion here tonight (and I hope you do; I believe it's the only fitting climax, for it reminds us, as we take the bread and the wine, of His undying love), we shall never meet again this side of heaven as exactly this gathering of people. But the alternative community is an eternal community. Several times this week I've been reminded of the death, during this last year, of our dear friend John Caiger. I used to say often that it was worth coming to Keswick just to listen to John Caiger pray. He was a man who was close to the Lord. And I am reminded of all the saints of the past and of the present and of the future.

His love is undying. The community of Christ is undying. We owe it to them, like the John Caigers who battled in the past, not to let go; but to keep going, and to thank God that in Christ we have an eternal community. His love is undying, may ours be also.

'Homesick For God':
The Psalms of Ascents

by Rev Jim Graham

1. God is my Protector
(Psalms 120–122)

When the Spirit and the word come together we have the stuff of miracles; and our concern this morning is to explore the word of God and to ask the Spirit of God to be among us to enable us—for He is our teacher—to understand what God is saying to us and what the Lord requires of us.

The subject of these Bible Readings was chosen by the Convention Council. I began my preparation with some apprehension, but as I went on and allowed the Lord to speak into my heart, I began to sense the Lord's blessing. And if nobody else is blessed during these Bible Readings, I've been blessed already!

I have chosen the title, 'Homesick for God'. I imagine most of us here at Keswick have been homesick at some time or other. God has called me to travel a little, and, though I would never have admitted it when I was younger, I get desperately homesick when I'm travelling. So I come to Psalms 120–135 with a feeling for the atmosphere they possess. A friend of mine, Dave Fellingham, wrote a lovely song six years ago. In it, he summed up something of the climate and the atmosphere of these psalms:

> My soul longs for you.
> Oh my God I seek you with all my heart.
> In this dry and thirsty land my soul,
> My voice cries out to you.

Travelling with my wife here to Keswick on Saturday, we listened to a tape of it in the car, and there came upon my soul such a longing for God.

I don't know how you've come to Keswick, whether it's your first visit or whether you've been before. I've come with a longing, which I believe God wants to meet and to satisfy. It's not that I'm not walking with Jesus; it's not that I don't love God; it's not that I'm no longer serving Him with all the enthusiasm of my heart. But I sense that there's something more, something greater that God wants to lead me into, though I've no idea what it is. I'm looking to Him during these days to meet me and to satisfy that longing. And it's in that frame of mind and with that testimony from my heart that I come to this morning's Bible Reading, sensing very much my own weakness, aware of my own inadequacy but at the same time so overwhelmed by the greatness of my Lord and Saviour and the love of my Heavenly Father.

I was preparing for another Christian festival earlier this year. I'd been asked to give Bible Readings on Paul's letter to the Philippians. And in the very first chapter of Philippians, I read of an amazing indecision in the heart of Paul. He says there, 'I am torn between the two: I desire to depart and to be with Christ, which is better by far; but it is more necessary for you that I remain in the body' (Phil. 1:23–24). There is a cry for God out of the heart of the apostle. And why wouldn't there be? He was looking forward to the time when he would see Jesus and would know Him and would be with Him in heaven; where there's service without weariness, life without death, joy without sorrow, light without darkness, joy without suffering, satisfaction without want, beauty without infirmity, living without sinning, presence without absence! No wonder the man says he is torn between the two.

But Paul's homesickness is focused in heaven. In these psalms, the homesickness of the psalmist is focused on earth. David saw Jerusalem not only as the capital city of God's people Israel, but also as the place where God dwelt: He had a house there in Jerusalem. It was left to his son Solomon, of course, to build that magnificent temple for God.

In our church we've been exploring together something of the meaning and the impact and the teaching of the

tabernacle in the later chapters of Exodus. What struck me in
all that teaching was that the main thrust, the substance and
essence of the teaching of the tabernacle is that God wants to
be among His people. It is very wonderful to me that not only
do we want to be with Him, but He wants to be with us. And
He's among us; that's why we've gathered, why we're waiting
with our hearts prepared. God is here; not necessarily
because we feel it, but because we know the heart-beat of
God: 'I want to be with you.'

And so we make our response this morning: 'Oh God we
want to be with You—not then but now, not there but
here—my heart is homesick for God.' I have given the three
psalms we are looking at this morning the title, 'God is my
Protector'. The first, Psalm 120, begins with the psalmist's
prayer: 'I call on the LORD in my distress ... Save me, O
Lord, from lying lips and from deceitful tongues.'

Psalm 120: The Psalmist's Prayer

Many of the psalms that we will be looking at during these
mornings come from David's heart. David was a most
remarkable person. The Bible's account of his life is the
fullest of all the biblical biographies. For example, only
fourteen chapters are devoted to Abraham, but sixty-two to
David. We see him as the poet, the warrior, the champion,
the outlaw, the builder, the administrator, the shepherd and
the king. This complex and fascinating character was, the
Bible tells us, a man after God's own heart (1 Sam. 13:14).
Paul in the synagogue in Pisidian Antioch picked up the Old
Testament record; 'I have found in David son of Jesse a man
after my heart; he will do everything I want him to do' (Acts
13:22).

Why, with all his weakness and humanity, all his frailty and
his failure, was David 'a man after God's heart'? There are
two reasons, I think. First of all, he had learned how to
receive God's *forgiveness*. He knew his need and he received
God's answer to that need. He knew how to receive God's
forgiveness, and live in the freedom, joy and vigour of that
reality.

The second reason, I believe, is that David had learned

how to receive God's *faithfulness* and to rely upon it. I think that God wants to minister that into our hearts this morning, whatever our circumstances might be.

The theme for this day in the Keswick week is: 'Sin in the life of the believer'. We need not go another day into the future without knowing the reality of the cleansing of the precious blood of the Lord Jesus. The blood of Jesus, God's Son goes on cleansing from all sin (cf 1 John 1:7). We need to receive the reality of what God has provided in His grace and mercy. We need to receive His forgiveness. But as we face the future, we also need to rely on His faithfulness: that God is God, and that God will not fail because God is God. We need the Spirit of God to minister these two realities into our hearts this morning.

The pressure he feels (verses 1–5)

And so we begin Psalm 120 with the prayer that the psalmist cries out in the first two verses. I imagine that for a congregation like this it's quite unnecessary to remind you that prayer is God's idea. 'This is what the Lord says, he who made the earth, the LORD who formed it and established it—the LORD is his name: "Call to me and I will answer you and tell you great and unsearchable things you not know"' (Jer. 33:2–3). Prayer is not the result of a conference or a council, or a consensus of opinion. Prayer is God's idea! God says 'Call to me and I will answer you.' And that is precisely what the psalmist is doing here in Psalm 120.

George Muller of Bristol told the story of a transatlantic sea captain who, after twenty-two hours on the bridge in dense fog off the Newfoundland coast, was startled to receive a tap on the shoulder. It was his passenger Muller, then in his seventies. 'Captain,' he said, 'I must be in Quebec on Saturday afternoon.' It was Wednesday. The captain said it was impossible. Muller replied, 'If your boat can't take me, God will find some other way.' That's the way to talk to a sea captain! 'I have never broken an engagement,' added Muller, 'in fifty-seven years.'

'I'd like to help,' responded the captain. 'But what can I do?'

'Let's go below and pray,' George Muller suggested.

That's just what a captain wanted to hear! 'But Mr Muller,' he argued, 'you don't know how dense the fog is.'

'My eye is not on the fog,' said George Muller, 'but on God who controls the fog and every circumstance of my life.' He knelt and prayed the simplest prayer the captain had ever heard; he said later that in his opinion it was 'fit for a child of nine'. 'O Lord, if thou wilt, move this fog in five minutes. Thou dost know the engagement made for me in Quebec for Saturday.'

Putting his hand on the captain's shoulder, Muller restrained him from praying. 'First of all,' he said, 'you don't believe God will do it. And secondly, I believe he has done it; so there's no need for you to pray. Open the door, Captain, and you'll find the fog is gone.' And so it was, and George Muller kept his Saturday engagement in Quebec. Don't you long to pray like that? I do.

George Muller is a hero of mine. Here are some of his prayer principles. First of all, he satisfied himself that he was doing God's will before he started a project. Secondly, resting on the promises of the Bible he came boldly to the throne in prayer. Thirdly, he pleaded his case argumentatively, giving God reasons why God should answer. Fourthly, he said, 'No delay ever discouraged me'; once he was persuaded a thing was right he went on praying for it until the answer came. 'I never give up,' he said. 'Tens of thousands of times my prayers have been answered.' A stickler for detail, he kept a complete record of his prayers. It covered 3,000 pages, contained nearly 1,000,000 words and chronicled over 50,000 specific answers. When you take prayer that seriously, you can put your hand on a ship's captain's shoulder and say, 'There is no need for you to pray, for God has already done it. Open the door, Captain, and you'll find the fog has gone.'

But we need to make new beginnings in prayer. And I believe God wants to give us the opportunity to do just that during these days that we are together.

'I call on the LORD in my distress and he answers me.' The psalmist is obviously under great pressure. 'Woe to me that I dwell in Meshech, that I live among the tents of Kedar!'

(verse 5). Meshech was one of the sons of Japheth, from whom the Gentile nations came, and Kedar was one of the sons of Ishmael. So the psalmist was living in a climate of hostility and disruption. Life was confusing and pressurised, and his daily existence continually burdened. He didn't live in a very good neighbourhood. Untrue rumours were circulating about him. He was being maligned, persecuted, misrepresented. 'Save me, O LORD, from lying lips and from deceitful tongues' (verse 2). That's the pressure that he feels; the pressure of injustice and misrepresentation. Shakespeare in *Othello* gives these words to Iago:

> Who steals my purse, steals trash . . .
> But he that filches from me my good name,
> Robs me of that which not enriches him,
> And makes me poor indeed. (III.iii)

An almost intolerable pressure is being created. 'I call on the Lord in my distress, and he answers me.' Do we know that experience?

In verses 3 and 4, God clearly has answered him. Those of you who were with us last night will remember that I was saying that the apostle Paul knew that God had lips as well as ears.[1] Sometimes, the way we pray you wouldn't think so. We are so concerned to pour out all that's in our hearts before Him (and that's right and necessary); but sometimes, even regularly, we need to be quiet, to hear what God is saying into our hearts.

Isn't it marvellous that we have a God who speaks as well as listens? Actually, that is good news and bad news. It's good news because it ensures that we can have a relationship with God. You can't have a relationship with somebody who doesn't communicate, who doesn't react to what you are saying. But the fact that God listens and responds ensures that we can have a living, vibrant relationship with Him. And

---

1. This address is not included in the present volume, but can be obtained from the Keswick tape library (see p. 252)

we need to give Him the opportunity to express the reality of that relationship. But it's bad news too, because sometimes God says things we don't want to hear.

Here in Psalm 120 God has spoken. He has spoken into his heart: 'What will he do to you, and what more besides, O deceitful tongue? He will punish you with a warrior's sharp arrows, with burning coals of the broom tree.' The pressure that the psalmist feels drives him to cry out to a God who listens and responds. What a God! No wonder this man's heart was homesick for God in a deeper and more significant way in his life.

The peace he longs for (verses 6 and 7)

It's been a difficult and turbulent time for him. Peace has long been the desire of the human heart but very often war has been the reality, the psalmist is saying as he concludes this psalm.

Think of the time when Jesus was born. That first Christmas night, the skies were shot through with the glory of God; the angelic hosts had come. They begin to sing, 'Glory to God in the highest, and on earth peace.' I have come to the conclusion that people seek for peace in vain because they've mistaken the source of peace. The glory of God needs to be seen, to be received and understood, before peace can become a reality. There is no peace without righteousness, and when we seek peace in an unrighteous way or among unrighteous people, we never find it.

But when our concern is to touch the heart of God, we find it. The best definition of peace I know is this: peace comes when I stop resisting the will of God in my life. Age is not the issue; obedience is the issue. I believe that God has been speaking to many of you, before you came to Keswick and since you arrived; He has brought you here so that he can get you to Himself. He is waiting for a response from you.

Psalm 121: His Protector

These are pilgrim psalms. They are called 'The Songs of Ascents'. As you go up to Jerusalem from any direction, there are hills to be climbed or bypassed, whether you come from the east over the Jordan valley, from the even hillier western approach from Tel Aviv and the Mediterranean, or from the north or the south. Jerusalem is set in a circle of hills. And those are the hills to which the psalmist refers.

As the pilgrim approaches Jerusalem he sees the hills of Judea. 'I lift up my eyes to the hills—where does my help come from?' You see, on the hilltops there were altars of pagan worship. As Jeremiah says, 'Surely the idolatrous commotion on the hills and mountains is a deception; surely in the LORD our God is the salvation of Israel' (Jer. 3:23).

Pagan worship was very public. It seemed very impressive and spectacular. But it was deceptive, and that's what the psalmist is referring to here. 'Although the hills seem so eternal, changeless and secure, my help doesn't come from there.' So in verse 2 the psalmist speaks of his Creator: 'My help comes from the LORD, the Maker of heaven and earth.' Franklin D. Roosevelt and a friend used regularly to stand out of doors looking up into the night sky and identifying the lower left-hand corner of the great Square of Pegasus. And one of them would recite the psalmist's words, looking up at Pegasus. Pegasus is a spiral galaxy of Andromeda, as large as our Milky Way. It's one of 100,000,000 galaxies. It's 750,000 light years away. It consists of a hundred billion suns, each of them larger than our own.

After a pause, Roosevelt would say, 'Now I think we feel small enough. Let's go to bed.'

God's creativity (verses 1–4)

Read what the psalmist is saying here, brothers and sisters. This is the source of our help! The God who brings something out of nothing, the God who brings order out of chaos. A God who brings light out of darkness, a God who controls that ebb and flow of the tide, a God who set the stars in their courses, a God who gives summer and winter and springtime and harvest without fail—He is our protector! That's what the psalmist is saying. No wonder his heart is homesick for God.

J. B. Phillips, the well-known Bible translator, wrote a

book entitled *Your God is too Small*, in which he said that nobody is ever really at ease when facing what we call life and death without a religious faith. The trouble with many people today is that they haven't found a God big enough for modern needs. While life has gone in a score of directions and their mental horizons have been expanded to the point of bewilderment by world events and by scientific discoveries, their ideas of God have remained largely static. It's obviously impossible for an adult to worship God, if his image of God is as restricted as that of a tiny child, unless he's prepared to deny his own experience of life. If by a great effort of will he does so, he will always be secretly afraid that some new truth might expose the juvenility of his faith. And it will always be by such an effort that he either worships or serves a God who is really too small to command his adult loyalty and co-operation.

It often appears to those outside the churches, says J. B. Phillips, that this is precisely the attitude of Christian people. If they are not strenuously defending an outgrown conception of God they are cherishing a hot-house God. For them, to join in the worship of a church would be to become a party to a piece of mass hypocrisy, to buy a sense of security at the price of a sense of truth. Many people of good will won't consent to such a transaction. Many men and women today, says Phillips, live with inner dissatisfaction, without any faith in God at all—not because they are particularly wicked or selfish, or, as the old-fashioned would say, Godless; but because they haven't found with their adult minds a God big enough to account for life, big enough to fit in with the new scientific age, big enough to command their highest aspiration and respect and consequently their willing co-operation. God wants to expand our concept of Him, so that we can abandon the limited categories by which we have described Him in the past.

This Convention affirms the eternal, infinite God of the Bible, the God and Father of our Lord Jesus Christ; the one who never changes because He's changeless, who is the same today as He was yesterday and as He will be tomorrow. We worship Him this morning. May the Spirit of God take the reality and character of God, and minister that reality into our hearts at the beginning of this week, so that when we leave this place we will go back with an expanded view of the greatness of God!

God's constancy (verses 5–8)
In the rest of the psalm the psalmist speaks of God's constancy. 'He will not let your foot slip.' Let me change it and make it personal. 'He will not let *my* foot slip—He who watches over *me* will not slumber; indeed, He who watches over Israel will neither slumber nor sleep.'

God is not unaware of where you are this morning, nor of what your circumstances are and what problems challenge and confront you. Neither is He unaware of what is happening nationally. That is what he is saying in verses 5–8. Isn't it wonderful? That's our God; neither sleeping or waking, neither night or day, neither sun or moon, neither light or shade, neither coming or going, neither now or always—God never changes. What a word! Receive it, let the breath of God breathe it into your being beyond your mind, beyond your emotions, right into the very depths of your being.

Edinburgh Castle stands on a great volcanic outcrop on the far side of Princes Street, like a great sentinel overlooking the capital city of Scotland. I am told that only twice has it been conquered by an enemy. On both occasions the enemy overran the castle because the sentry was asleep. But you never catch God unawares. God is not only panic-proof, He is surprise-proof, our protector.

Psalm 122: David's Praise

There is in our third psalm this morning such an anticipation, such an enthusiasm, such eagerness to get there! Do you remember? This is the heart of a man who is homesick for God. He sees Jerusalem not simply as the capital city, but as the place where God has a house. And already in his mind and in his heart he's there, pouring out his heart in worship. Verse 3: he is so aware that there's a pattern that runs through Israel's history. Rebellion is followed by retribution, but repentance is followed by restoration. He remembers this and he recognises that this is the God whom his heart longs to worship (verses 6–9). There's a prophetic edge. There's a future dream in his heart as he journeys towards Jerusalem.

I've called this psalm 'his praise'. I am sure you know that there's all the difference in the world between worshipping God and singing hymns. As I travel around the country I am introduced to 'worship leaders'. And often I discover that they are not worship leaders at all. They're song leaders. But worship is not about musical instruments, overhead projectors, hymn books, anthems, vestments or spiritual songs. It is not about raising hands or closing eyes or bending knees or prostrating bodies. There's nothing wrong with any of these things, but worship, fundamentally, is about two things: a relationship with God, and a response to God.

The best definition of worship that I've ever come across was given by a former Archbishop of Canterbury, William Temple:

> Worship is the submission of all our nature to God. It's the quickening of conscience by His holiness. The nourishment of mind with His truth, the purifying of the imagination by His beauty, the opening of the heart to His love, the surrender of the will to His purpose. And all this is gathered up in adoration, the most selfless emotion of which our nature is capable.

There are five ingredients in that definition of worship. Our *conscience*, because in worship we become aware of the presence and the holiness of God. Our *mind*, because as we confront God in worship we are aware that He is the God of truth, not the God of error, who will condemn and confront what is wrong, and so our minds are captivated with truth. Our *imagination*, because as we worship there is a mystery which we can't fully grasp and hold; we are in the presence of a mighty and magnificent God, and our imagination is purified by His beauty. Our *emotions*, because our hearts are touched in worship; we become aware that God loves me, Jesus died for me, the Holy Spirit has come to enable me and—'I love you Lord.' And, fifthly, our *will*. Most of our spiritual life as Christians is lived in the area of the will and of decision, not in the area of feelings. Romans 12:1—'I beseech you therefore brethren by the mercies of God that you will present your bodies as a living sacrifice, holy acceptable to God, for this is your true spiritual worship.'

And something of that is encapsulated in this psalm. 'Let us go—' to where God is, where we can stand in His presence, where we can absorb the reality of His being, where we can affirm that we have a relationship with Him through grace as a result of the shed blood of the Saviour. We can stand with confidence in His presence, for now we have access. We can make our response.

Praise because of restoration from the past (verses 3–5)
I have already indicated that David is taking a backward look and seeing this holy city where God lives, the place to which the people of God came and found Him again after their restoration. And he worships Him. For our God is a God who takes lives that are shattered and broken and spoiled and marred.

The first time I ever met my friend Brian he had long fair hair and was wearing a denim shirt and jeans and big boots. Brian met Jesus in Dartmoor Prison. Somebody had given him the book *Run Baby Run*, by Nicky Cruz. 'I couldn't put it down until I reached the part of the story where his life was like mine was now,' he told me. 'We were both in a deep pit with no hope and no future and tired of running. Nicky had been told he needed love; but where, he asked could he find real love in a pit?'

'I was in a pit,' said Brian. 'The cell was a pit, my life was one big pit. I read on in a crowded hall. A skinny preacher named Wilkerson was telling Nicky that God loved him. And suddenly in front of his mates and rival gangs this Puerto Rican double of me dropped to his knees crying "O God, if you love me, come into my life, I'm tired of running. Please change me." And as I read how God did change him, I broke down. Tears of despair and tears of hope poured down my face. The pages in front of me went blurred. Where could I find this God of love? Where could I find this Jesus who came so suddenly into Nicky's life that night taking away the nightmares and allowing him to sleep soundly again? I had no preacher to show me. Then I remembered the yellow book lying beside me, the Living Bible. The advert promised this book would tell me all I needed to know about God and Jesus. I didn't know one end of it from the other; I simply opened it and read. And as I lay in my bed facing the door, I knew that Jesus had His arms opened out towards me. He was saying "All you've got to do is ask Me and I will change your life." I wanted it more than anything I had ever wanted and out loud I asked Him to do for me what He had done for Nicky, to change my life taking away all that was rotten and making it worth living. And Hallelujah!—at that instant I began to feel all that pus and poison in me drain away through my feet. All the frustration and anger that had held me a prisoner for most of my life just flowed away. At the same time it was as though a hole opened up in my head and God's love began pouring in. For the first time ever I was experiencing real love, it was God's pure love. Weeping tears of joy, I cracked up,' said Brian, 'and I fell to my knees on the floor.'

What did he do? He worshipped God. He told me, 'I thanked God for bringing us together'—relationship and response!—'and after that I slept a dreamless sleep at peace with God.'

The source of his praise is an awareness of the restoration that came from the past, of a God who takes broken lives and mends them, a God who takes wasted spoiled lives and transforms them.

Praise because of reassurance for the future (verses 6–9)
Finally in the last three verses he looks forward into the future, in a truly prophetic way. And his praise is drawn out, not only because of the restoration from the past but because of reassurance for the future.

> Then I saw a new heaven and a new earth, for the first heaven and the first earth had passed away, and there was no longer any sea. I saw the Holy City, the new Jerusalem, coming down out of heaven from God, prepared as a bride beautifully dressed for her husband. And I heard a loud voice from the throne saying, 'Now the dwelling of God is with men, and he will live with them. They will be his people, and God himself will be with them and be their God. He will wipe every tear from their eyes.

There will be no more death or mourning or crying or pain. For the old order of things has passed away.'

He who was seated on the throne said, 'I am making everything new!' Then he said, 'Write this down, for these words are trustworthy and true. (Rev. 21:1–5)'

May God touch us as we go on to respond to His word this morning, as we have listened to the cry of a man's heart, as we have become aware of the faith of a man's spirit, and as we've acknowledged the outpouring of a man's love for a God who deals with the past and gives us hope for the future.

2: God is my Security
(Psalms 123–125)

Throughout the years of my life so far, I've discovered that often I don't really mind living by faith—until God asks me to do it. I've discovered, too, that from time to time I'm not really living by faith, I'm living by sight. And I believe that the challenge and the call of God upon all of us is that we should live by faith and have our security in Him. I think that's true personally; it's also true corporately. For many years now I've often been in meetings of church leaders, committees and so on; vision begins to emerge and is stimulated, until somebody says: 'Where's the money coming from? Can we afford to do this?' Again and again I've found that to be the death-knell to vision and faith.

That's what we are considering this morning. God calls us to trust Him. The big issue is not whether we can afford it or not, or whether this will affect our lifestyle. The big issue is: Is this what God wants in my life, either as an individual, or corporately as a church? I know there's a very fine line between faith and foolishness. God does not call us to be irresponsible, but He does call us to be faithful. God doesn't call us to be foolish, but He does call us to be men and women of faith.

I was recently in Korea speaking at three pastors' conferences, at the invitation of the Presbyterian Church. Two of the conferences were held in Seoul at a Presbyterian church called Onuri. It began only began nine years ago with twelve families. When I was there this time (it was my fourth visit) their membership was now 9,464. God put a vision into the heart of the senior pastor, that before the year 2000 there would be 2,000 missionaries called out from their church. I was excited to have the opportunity to be part of that and ministering into it. I was thrilled to hear of their plans (already approved) to build a mission centre on a waste plot alongside the church. It will have ten storeys, five below ground and five above. The logic is that if you are going to have 2,000 missionaries called out from your church you need a place to train them and prepare them. And that church began with a bank balance of zero. You see? Its security is in God.

I am concerned when the Bible is expounded simply to instruct our minds. God doesn't give us His word so that we can discuss it and decide whether we agree with it or not. He gives us His word so that we'll do what He says. And that's the issue of this morning's Bible reading.

What are we going to do, if God is our security? Many of you are really committed in your heart to the fact that God is your security. But what is the consequence of that commitment?

Our church building is about a mile and a half away from the headquarters of the World-wide Evangelisation Crusade, now called WEC International. Its founder and visionary was C. T. Studd, whose motto was: 'If Jesus Christ be God and died for me, there is no sacrifice too great for me to make for Him.' He wrote:

The committee I work under is a conveniently small committee, a very wealthy committee, a wonderfully generous committee and it's always sitting in session: the committee of the Father and the Son and the Holy Ghost. We have a multi-millionaire to back us up, out and away the wealthiest person in the world. I had an interview with Him. He gave me a cheque book free and He urged me to draw upon Him. He assured me that His firm clothes the grass of the field, preserves the sparrows, counts the hairs of children's heads. He said the head of the firm promised to supply all our need and to make sure one of the partners, or rather two, were to go along with each member of our parties and would never leave us or fail us. He even showed me some testimonials from former clients. A tough old chap with a long

beard and a hard-bitten face said that on one occasion supplies
had arrived and been delivered by black ravens. And another, by
a white-winged angel. Another little old man that seemed
scarred and marked all over like a walnut shell, he said he had
been saved from death times untold, for he was determined to
put to proof the assurance that he who would lose his life for the
firm's sake should find it.

I don't know if you believe that—but it's the truth. We are
thinking today about the theme 'God is my security'. To help
us to move into this magnificent subject, I've listed a number
of scriptures.

Psalm 41:1—You will be delivered in the time of trouble;
Proverbs 3:10—Your barns will be filled with plenty, there
will be enough not only for your needs but also for the needs
of others; Proverbs 11:24—You will increase your giving
when God is your security; Proverbs 11:25—You will be
prosperous (I don't think that's a foundation for crass
prosperity teaching); Proverbs 19:17—If you give to the poor
it's like making a loan to God, God is not unaware of your
response to the cry of His heart; Proverbs 22:9—The
promise is that when God is your security and you are
responding out of His richness rather than your poverty, you
will be blessed; Proverbs 28:27—You will not lack; Isaiah
58:10—The same thought; Jeremiah 22:16—You will know
the Lord; Matthew 6:4—'Your Father, who sees what is
done in secret, will reward you'; Matthew 19:21—You will
have treasure in heaven; Philippians 4:19—The apostle says
all your needs will be supplied when God is your security.
There's a whole lot of teaching in the New Testament about
the rewards of God for faithful responding, for ministry and
service out of the richness that He makes available to us.

Isn't that good? There isn't time now to explore the
contexts of all of these passages, but if you feel the hand of
the Spirit of God upon you this morning you might want to
read their context and feel their climate for yourself.

Jesus never did feed the five thousand; it was actually the
disciples who fed them, who actually handed out the food.
They did so because they received what God the Father
made available to them through His Son, Jesus Christ. They
had enough to meet the need of the great multitude, and

there was plenty left over. I sometimes think that we often try to minister to others out of our poverty. But God has brought us to this place so thatHhe might bless us and pour the abundance of the richness of His grace, love and providence into our hearts. Not so that we become self-indulgent, but so that we can be effective; so that we can go back to the familiar places from which we've come with something to share and to give, with which to bless and enrich the lives of others.

Let me quote to you something.

In many lands it is customary for a married woman to take the name of her husband. Legally she is placed under his care and authority. For the sake of illustration let us suppose the bride is very poor in every way. She has no money in the bank or the building society, she has no property, she has no borrowing or earning power. She has no financial record of any worth at all. Let us suppose that her husband has and is all that she hasn't and isn't. The moment she becomes 'Mrs', she moves out of the past poverty and powerlessness into all that the name of her husband means. She no longer acts in her name but in his name. She can spend money from his bank, live securely in any property he owns, operate comfortably on his borrowing power, enjoy his earnings and live in the splendour of all that he is worth. It's a transformed life.

Now think about how the church is betrothed to become Mrs Jesus, the bride of Christ. She is totally authorised to operate in the name of Jesus, because God is our security. Isn't that good?

Alexander the Great used to sit in the square near his royal residence so that he could be available to his subjects. Anybody could come without an appointment and talk to him. One day a man came and asked him for three things: 'A farm for myself, an education for my son and a dowry for my daughter.' A government official was standing beside Alexander the Great, and remonstrated with the king when he ordered that the man should receive all three. In the end Alexander said, 'I am tired of those who come asking me for half a piece of gold. That man came and treated me like a king.'

Thou art coming to a king.
Large petitions with you bring.
For His grace and power are such,
None can ever ask too much.[1]

Psalm 123:　The Condition He Abhors

The psalmist's heart-cry in Psalm 123 is that he is living in a climate where the name of God is being brought into disrepute by those who are hostile to God and make things difficult for God's servants (verses 3 and 4). And many of us come out of a similar context, in which people look and say God does not keep His promises.

I have a very dear friend, a well-known servant of the Lord, whose eldest daughter, the same age as our eldest daughter, died of leukaemia. My friend's daughter had herself a seven-year old daughter who is now left alone, for her father left her mother three months after the little girl was born. My friend is the only father that this seven-year old has really ever known; but now the child's natural father has the legal right to take the little girl into a new environment. I was sharing this at our church Communion Service. A woman visitor said to me afterwards, 'I was impressed with what you shared about this girl and the pressures on your friend.' And she said, 'How can you believe in a God of love when that kind of thing can happen?' You see, the name of God was being brought into disrepute.

There are those who say that if God is a God of love then He's not a God of power, or vice-versa. Because of what we see around us and what we hear through the media, it looks to us as if God is not interested and involved among His people, that He doesn't provide for His people. Over more than a generation I've heard people say all of these things and more. And that's the climate of verses 3 and 4.

God's Power
Now, look at verse 1. What is the first thing that the psalmist says as he confronts this condition which he abhors? He

---

1. John Newton (1725–1807), 'Come my Soul, thy suit prepare'.

speaks about God's power. 'I lift my eyes to you, to you whose throne is in heaven.'

> Jesus is king and I will extol Him,
> Give Him the glory and honour His name.
> He reigns on high enthroned in the heavens,
> Word of the Father exalted for us.

A vicar told me of a couple in his congregation who longed to have a baby. A little child was born to them. But after a few months, the baby died in a cot death. The vicar said, 'What really challenged me and stirred me up was the singing of the hymn at the church, "Ascribe greatness to our God, the Rock".' I saw the woman with her husband. Their little child had died, just forty-eight hours earlier. She was standing with the tears streaming down her face, but with her face aglow and lifted up to God. And she was singing,

> Ascribe greatness to our God the Rock,
> His work is perfect and all His ways are just.
> A God of faithfulness, and without injustice,
> Good and upright is He.

That's verse 2: God is reigning, God is sovereign. In the midst of all the mysteries and all that is turbulent and confusing in our lives, all that can create such uncertainties within us, that psalmist out of his longing heart says: 'I lift up my eyes to you, to you whose throne is in heaven.'

Our perseverance

When the Huguenots were besieged at St Quentin by the Spaniards, the Spaniards shot an arrow into the market place carrying a scornful demand for surrender. The Huguenot leader Coligny took the piece of paper on which the demand for surrender was written, and wrote two words on it: *Regem habemus*, 'We have a king'. He shot the arrow right back to where it came from. That is precisely the climate of Psalm 123; in the midst of a situation that horrifies him, the psalmist is aware of God's power. And on the basis of that he declares his perseverance. 'Our eyes look to the LORD our God, till he shows us his mercy.' Whatever happens, whatever the problems and however heavy the burden and however great the confusion, we will not give up.

I was once asked to do some teaching on the prophecy of Habakkuk. It was an enriching experience for me, nowhere more than when I came to 3:17–18:

> Though the fig-tree does not bud
> and there are no grapes on the vines,
> though the olive crop fails
> and the fields produce no food,
> though there are no sheep in the pen
> and no cattle in the stalls,
> yet I will rejoice in the LORD,
> I will be joyful in God my Saviour.

That's the consequence of knowing the reality that God is my security.

> I will not doubt, though all my ships at sea
> Come drifting home with broken masts and sails.
> I will believe that hand that never fails
> from seeming evil, worketh good for me.
> Though I weep because those sails are tattered,
> Still will I cry, though my best hopes lie shattered,
> 'I trust in Thee.'

The heart-cry of my own heart is that during this week I will enter, along with you, into the ministry and reality of Psalm 123.

Psalm 124: The Concern He Addresses

The Psalmist's concern in this psalm is that there would have been complete destruction unless God had intervened. Apart from God acting and being involved, there is only helplessness and despair, darkness and disintegration.

Because of complete destruction
Three hundred years before Jesus was born, a philosopher called Aristotle said, 'When I look at the younger generation I despair of the future of civilisation.' That was over 2,000

years ago. So what has changed? About 200 years ago, the politician William Pitt said, 'There is nothing around us but ruin and despair.' That was in 1806. Then about 100 years ago the Duke of Wellington said, 'I thank God I shall be spared the consummation of ruin that is gathering around us.' That's the heartland of Psalm 124. Unless God has intervened and got involved there's nothing but darkness and despair and disintegration and hopelessness. That has always been the view of man without God.

Let me read to you a very cynical piece called 'Creation in Reverse'.

In the end man destroyed the heaven that had been called earth, for the earth had been beautiful and happy until the destructive spirit of man had moved upon it.

This was the seventh day before the end.

For man said, 'Let me have power in the earth.' And he saw that the power seemed good and he called those who sought power great leaders; and those who sought to serve others and bring reconciliation, weaklings, compromisers, appeasers. And this was the sixth day before the end.

And man said, 'Let there be a division among all the people and divide the nations which are for me from the nations which are against me.' And this was the fifth day before the end.

And man said, 'Let us gather our resources in one place and create more instruments of power and defend ourselves. The radio to control men's minds, conscription to control men's bodies, uniforms and symbols of power to win men's souls. And this was the fourth day before the end.

And man said, 'Let there be censorship to divide the propaganda from the truth.' And he made two great censorship bureaux to control the thoughts of men; one to tell only the truth he wished to know at home, the other to tell only the truth he wished to know abroad. And this was the third day before the end.

And man said, 'Let us create weapons which can kill vast numbers, even millions and hundreds of millions at a distance.' And so he perfected germ warfare and deadly underwater arsenals, guided missiles, great fleets of war planes and destructive power to the extent of tens of thousands of millions of tons of TNT.

And it was the second day before the end.

And man said, 'Let us make God in our own image. Let us

say God does as we do, thinks as we think, wills as we will and kills as we kill.' And so man found ways to kill with atomic power and dust even those as yet unborn, and he said, 'This is necessary, there is no alternative, this is God's will.'

And on the last day there was a big noise upon the face of the earth. And man and all his doings were no more.

And the ravished earth rested on the seventh day.

My brothers and sisters, that's an awesome picture of darkness and despair without God! And that's the climate of Psalm 124.

There would have been constant danger, says the psalmist, if the Lord had not been on our side when people attacked us, when their anger flared against us. Verses 3–5: there would have been complete destruction.

Because of constant danger
In verses 6–7 he addresses the horrendous situation. He abhors it because of the potential for complete destruction and because of the reality of constant danger. We may not be in a position this morning of facing military might and all its consequences, in places like Rwanda and in the thirty-seven other areas where there is war. But we are in a battle. On Thursday morning we will be looking at spiritual warfare. We have an enemy whose desire is to damage us and ultimately destroy us. William Law wrote,

> He never slumbers, never is weary, never relents, never abandons hope. He deals his blows alike at childhood's weakness, youth's inexperience, manhood's strength, the totterings of age—he watches to ensnare the morning's thought, he departs not with the shades of night. By his legions he is everywhere. At all times he enters the palace, the hut, the fortress, the camp, the fleet. He invades every chamber of every dwelling, every pew of every sanctuary. He is busy with the busy, he hurries about with the active, he sits at each bed of sickness and whispers into each dying ear. And as the spirit quits the tenement of clay he still draws his bow with unrelenting rage.

Oh yes: there is a devil, an opponent who is real and active. He attacks viciously, he takes advantage of weakness, he

blinds spiritual vision, he counterfeits, he deceives, he
hinders the gospel, he steals the truth, he afflicts and
destroys, he indwells the physical frame, he tells lies, he
opposes the angels of God, and he tempts God's children to
sin.

And so the psalmist speaks of the condition in which he
finds his life cast, and the concern that he is determined to
address.

Psalm 125: The Confidence He Affirms

But with Psalm 125 comes a glorious confidence. God is the
security of the people of God.

As we saw yesterday, pilgrims came to Jerusalem from all
over the land and beyond it; and as they came towards
Jerusalem, they became aware of the hills and the mountains
of Judea. And as they made further progress they could see
Mount Zion settled and strong and secure. That was a great
encouragement to them, for they saw there a symbol of the
nature of God Himself: strong and settled and secure. That's
what verse 1 is saying. The very strength and security and
stability of God is ministered as a result of trusting in the one
who gives us security.

Because of God's care
Martin Luther wrote:

> A mighty fortress is our God, a bulwark never failing.
> Our helper He amid the flood of mortal ills prevailing.
> For still our ancient foe doth seek to work us woe.
> His craft and power are great and armed with cruel hate.
> On earth is not his equal.

It is the battle hymn of the Reformation; actually, a free
adaptation of Psalm 46. But it could have been Psalm 125.

> Did we in our own strength confide, our striving would be
>   losing.
> Were not the right man on our side, the man of God's own
>   choosing.
> Dost ask who that may be? Christ Jesus, it is He;

Lord Sabaoth is His name, from age to age the same.
And He must win the battle.[1]

The confidence that this man affirms, the confidence that God wants to minister into our hearts and our lives this morning—because of God's care. God cares for you. Could you allow the Spirit to put that into your heart? However fragile and wounded, uncertain, vulnerable and exposed you may be feeling this morning, let the Spirit minister into your heart: God cares for me.

Because of God's character
And then finally (verses 3 and 4) we are also confident in God because of His character.

In our church we are exploring the letter to the Hebrews, in which the writer says, 'Man is destined to die once, and after that to face judgment' (Heb. 9:27). Judgement is written into the fabric of the universe and into the finality of eternity. There are two reasons why this is so.

First, *the injustices of this life*. We are aware that in this life the wicked and the scoundrels do sometimes prosper, and the innocent and the Godly do sometimes suffer. We know it. And we know that life, taken by itself, is not always fair or balanced. We feel in our hearts that it could not be right that a Nero and a St Paul, an Adolf Eichmann and an Albert Schweitzer, an Adolf Hitler and a Martin Niemoller, an agnostic and an Augustine, an atheist and an Athanasius, a Judas and a James should all equally be committed in sure and certain hope of the resurrection of the dead unto eternal life through Jesus Christ our Lord. And because we are aware that there are injustices and wrongs in this life, we know that judgement is necessary.

Second, *the justice of God*. He may not send His bills in at the end of every month, but the bills come in. There are judgements to be faced. If God is good, then at the last things must be put right. If we say God is good and just and life is sometimes unfair and unjust, then there must be

---

1. Martin Luther, 'Ein' feste Burg' (c1513). Luther also composed the tune.

beyond death an expression of God's justice—if He is good. And He is! And that's what the psalmist is wrestling with, there at the end part of Psalm 125. Repeatedly in the Bible it says, whatever a man sows in this life he will also reap because God is not mocked. 'The sceptre of the wicked will not remain over the land allotted to the righteous . . .'. 'Do good O LORD, to those who are good, to those who are upright in heart. But those who turn to crooked ways the LORD will banish with the evildoers.'

> Once to every man and nation comes the moment to decide,
> In the strife of Truth with Falsehood, for the good or evil side,
> Some great cause, God's new Messiah offering each the bloom or blight,
> Parts the goats upon the left hand and the sheep upon the right.
> And the choice goes by for ever 'twixt that darkness and that light.[1]

The psalmist is homesick for God, his protector and security. We go out with that confidence today.

> I do not know what lies ahead, the way I cannot see;
> But one stands near to be my guide, He'll show the way to me.
> I know who holds the future, He guides me with His hand;
> With God things don't just happen, everything by Him is planned.
> So as I face my future with its problems large and small,
> I trust the God of miracles, give to Him my all.

Why? Because He's my protector, and He's my security.

---

1. James Russell Lowell (1819–1891), 'The present crisis'.

3: God is my Deliverer
(Psalms 126–128)

Psalm 126: A Godly Hope

In Psalm 126 we find again the note of homesickness in the soul (verse 1). The captives were 'like men who dreamed'; but the dream was to become a reality (verse 2). In the remainder of the psalm the psalmist makes it personal: 'Our mouths were filled with laughter, our tongues with songs of joy ...'

I wanted to try to recapture for you the atmosphere of this magnificent psalm. Then I remembered reading Terry Waite's account of his captivity, *Taken on Trust*. He was captured at the beginning of 1987, and was held captive for 1,763 days. He spent almost four years of that time in solitary confinement. Can you imagine that? What disturbed me about his book was the cruelty of one man towards another. It is incredible that any human being could treat another in such a way. Terry Waite said, 'I did what generations of prisoners have done before me. I stood up, and, bending my head, I began to walk round and round and round and round like an animal.'

At the end of the book he says:

> We landed at RAF Lynham. .... I hobbled across the tarmac, into a car, and we drove to a hangar. I made my speech, hobbled out and climbed into another car. We drove to the far side of the airport. My companions melted away. I stumbled through a glass doorway and stared. Ruth, Clare and Gillian ran towards me.

Frances and a young man I assume was Mark his son stood quietly in the background. They moved forward. We wept and embraced each other. Gillian, my youngest daughter, looked at me.

'Daddy,' she said, 'take all the help they will offer you here.' I nodded my head. . . .

This evening, in the quiet of my room in Cambridge, I recall the words that were discovered written on the wall of a cellar in which a victim of Hitler's persecution hid and died:

I believe in the sun even when it is not shining.
I believe in love where feeling is not.
I believe in God even if he is silent.[1]

'We were like men who dreamed'—something was in their hearts; a longing, a hope, an anticipation, an eagerness. And that's why I call this psalm a 'Godly hope'. It's all there. 'Our mouths were filled with laughter, our tongues with songs of joy.' There was something that was bubbling over and just about to spill out into their lives.

The past
Whether in captivity or in exile, there was something in the hearts of God's people that longed after God and was homesick for Him, ever since the exodus, when God reached out of glory into history and rescued over 2,000,000 of His people. Egypt was the most fortified country that was then known. To its west and south was a desolating desert. To its east and north was a sea that was difficult to negotiate. To the west and to the south as well as to the east, there was a line of fortresses built by the Egyptian authorities. Nobody quite knew whether it was to keep the people in or to prevent an enemy from invading.

A military expert has described the Exodus as 'an amazing expedition'. The route to God's land was through one of the most desolate deserts in the world. He estimated that 900 tons of food a day would have been required; 2,400 tons of firewood; around 2,000,000 gallons of water a day. In a desert! That is the magnificence of what God did as He reached into history and rescued His people.

---

1. Terry Waite, *Taken on Trust* (Hodder & Stoughton, 1993), p. 358.

And, says the psalmist, this is what we remember from the past (verse 2b–3). Notice, 'great things for them ... great things for us'. It is both general and personal.

No wonder the Jewish nation celebrated the Passover with such enthusiasm! There were two major feasts—those of Pentecost and Passover—and many smaller ones; but there's something special about the Feast of the Passover. They taught the details and background and environment of the record of this feast for a month in the schools and the synagogues, so that the Jews would have a clear picture of all that God had done on their behalf. This was God taking the initiative. This was God redeeming them, rescuing them out of slavery into security. This was God fulfilling the promises of His heart, this was God acting in a supernatural way. This was something that could never be explained in human terms. This was a time for national fervour and rejoicing. And the psalmist tries to pick all of this up, 'When the LORD brought back the captives to Zion,' whether in captivity or exile, 'we were like men who dreamed. our mouths were filled with laughter, and our tongues with songs of joy.'

I sense deep within my own spirit that God wants us to pause in the middle of this week just to look back for a moment. We will be doing that on Friday night when we share bread and wine together. We look back with gratitude, we look up with thanksgiving, we look forward with expectation to the return of our Lord Jesus, but Psalm 126 is calling us at this point in the beginning, to look back with gratitude—how God transformed our shame with His glory, transformed our failure with His forgiveness, transformed our captivity with His freedom, transformed our burden with His blessing, our weakness with His strength, our humanity with His divinity, our sin with His salvation, our loneliness with His fellowship, our hardness of heart with a gentleness and softness of His love, our waywardness with His correction, our tears with His joy. How is it possible that the people of God would refuse to sing with joy and gratitude in their hearts? Whatever our circumstances, whatever our pressures, whatever the things that confront us and challenge us and sometimes can make us fearful this morning.

The psalmist at the end of verse three says, 'we are'—as

we look back, as we remember, as we see the hand of God generally but also personally—there's a joy that floods from our hearts.

'Restore our fortunes, O LORD, like streams in the Negev'—in the desert. He's now looking forward to the prospect of the mercy of the God for whom his heart is homesick. God is his deliverer. He brings us out, so that he might bring us in. 'Restore our fortunes, O LORD, like streams in the Negev. Those who sow in tears will reap with songs of joy. He who goes out weeping, carrying seed to sow, will return with songs of joy, carrying sheaves with him.'

My wife and I have been greatly helped by the writings of Oswald Chambers, especially that amazing book, *My Utmost For His Highest*. In it he says,

> It's easier to serve God without a vision, it's easier to work for God without a call, because then you're not bothered with what God requires. Common sense is your guide veneered over with Christian sentiment, but once you receive a commission from Jesus Christ, the memory of what God wants will always come like a goad, and you'll no longer be able to work for Him on the common-sense basis.

The prospect
This is the place of remembrance that brings rejoicing, but it's also the place of vision as we look to the future.

Peter Brierley tells the story of a young boy called Jimmy who was found by his mother sitting by the window, when he should have been in bed. He was looking up at a full moon. 'What are you doing?' she asked him. 'I'm looking at the moon, Mummy,' he replied. 'Well, it's time for you to go to bed now,' she remonstrated. But as one reluctant little boy settled down he said, 'Mummy—you know, one day I'm going to walk on the moon!'

Who could have known that the boy in whom the dream was planted that night would survive a near fatal motorbike crash that broke almost every bone in his body, and would bring his dream to fruition thirty-two years later, when James Irwin stepped on to the moon's surface?

Will you dream big dreams for God this Keswick day? I

believe God is looking for dreamers. Will we allow him to do so?

I dream; I dream of a church throughout this nation that really worships God, that's no longer content with singing hymns and critiquing some of the peripherals of worship, but one that begins to realise that worship affects the mind, the imagination, the emotions, the conscience and the will. I dream of a church throughout this nation, which is learning how to worship God. I dream of a church that takes the word of God seriously, that doesn't simply explore it so that it can discuss it, but explores it so that we would do it, knowing that here God speaks with such clarity and power in the hearts of His people. I dream of a church that wants to pray and has discovered that prayer is not me bringing God into my world to solve my problems, but that prayer is taking me into God's world to serve His purposes; that prayer is neither me getting God to do what I want nor God getting me to do what He wants, but that prayer is me getting God to do what God wants.

I dream of a church that is filled with the Holy Spirit, that is no longer dependent on its own energy and enthusiasm but knows something of the reverberating vibrant reality of the risen life of the Lord Jesus made available to us by the Holy Spirit; the reality that what Jesus made possible for us on the cross of Calvary, the Holy Spirit wants to make actual to us as we walk on the face of the earth. I dream of a church that is Spirit-filled. I dream of a church that is family-oriented, a church that no longer sees young people as the church of tomorrow, but sees them as the church of today; a church that no longer sees elderly people as the church of yesterday, but sees them as the church of today, because we are all one in Christ Jesus our Lord. I dream of a church that is family-oriented. I dream of a church that has evangelism as its highest priority, that has come to terms with the fact that the church is the only organisation in our society that exists primarily for its non-members. I dream of a church that is no longer so in-turned that it can no longer be out-going, under the Lordship of our Lord Jesus Christ. I dream of a church that has a serving heart; one that is no longer concerned with what it can get, but with what it can give.

In the name and the power of the Lord Jesus, that's my dream. Right across this land I dream of a church liberated from the shackles of traditions that are no longer valid. Ladies and gentlemen, we do not honour the past by living in it; we honour the past by learning from it and by going on in the power of the risen Lord Jesus, as a church that's liberated from self-centredness and from the pressure of time, and is now free to serve God and free to serve the world and free to serve one another.

What is your dream this morning?

The psalmist has a Godly hope, because he is aware of the past and because he's anticipating the future that lies ahead. Please, for Jesus' sake, let God put dreams in your hearts, before you go any further. Restore our fortunes, O Lord like streams in the desert. 'Those who sow in tears will reap with songs of joy. He who goes out weeping, carrying seeds to sow, will return with songs of joy, carrying sheaves—harvest, richness, fruitfulness—with him.' What a prospect!

Psalm 127: A Godly Home

As we come to the second psalm, let me share with you an outline of it by Dr Stephen Olford.

> Divinely founded—'Unless the Lord builds the house'—where marriage is authorised and solemnised by God.
>
> Divinely fended—'Unless the Lord watches over the city'—where the throne of God, the word of God and the Spirit of God are all honoured.
>
> Divinely furnished—'In vain you rise up early and stay up late, toiling for food to eat'—a home built not on human possessions but upon the divine presence and peace.
>
> Divinely favoured—'Sons are a heritage from the LORD, children a reward from him'—where the desirability and the responsibility of parenthood are recognised.

God's purpose

Families are in God's purpose. 'Unless the Lord builds the house, its builders labour in vain.' Edith Schaeffer in her

lovely book *What is a Family?* concludes a long description of
the richness and complexity of family life with these words:

> Memories, trust, loyalty, compassion, kindness, in honour
> preferring each other, depending on each other, looking to each
> other for help, giving each other help, picking each other up,
> suffering long with each other's faults, understanding each other
> more and more, hoping all things, enduring all things, never
> failing, continuity. A family knowing always that if a thread wears
> thin and sags there's help to be had from the expert, the Father
> of whom the whole family in heaven and on earth is named.[1]

The Lord builds the house; its builders labour. A Godly
home is in the purpose of God.

God's protection
And we can have God's protection. We'll be looking at this
more closely tomorrow, when we'll be seeing that one of the
great sadnesses of the British church is that we have
concluded that we're living in peace, when in fact we are
living in war. We've concluded that we are civilians, when in
fact we are soldiers, we are in a battle. But the psalmist says,
'Unless the LORD watches over the city, the watchmen stand
guard in vain.'

God's provision
Verse 2: 'In vain you rise early and stay up late, toiling for
food to eat—for he grants sleep to those he loves.' It's not an
encouragement to indolence or carelessness, but an encouragement to a sense of perspective and to trust God in new
ways in the home. I spoke earlier this week about one of my
heroes, C. T. Studd. He came from a very wealthy
background. One day he became aware of the size of his
inheritance, which by the standards of his day was a
magnificent one. And in a single day, under the guidance of
God, he gave almost all of it away. He gave some further
money to the China Inland Mission, leaving himself with

---

1. Edith Schaeffer, *What is a Family?* (Fleming Revell, 1975), p. 255.

£3,400. Just before his wedding, he presented his bride with this money.

She, not to be outdone, said, 'Charlie, what did the Lord tell the rich young man to do? Sell all! Well then, we will start clear with the Lord at our wedding.'

They wrote as follows to General Booth on 3 July 1888:

> My dear General . . . I cannot tell you how many times the Lord has blessed me through reading your and Mrs. Booth's addresses in the *War Cry* and your books. And now we want to enclose a cheque for £1,500. The other £500 has gone to Commissioner Tucker for his wedding present. Besides this I am instructing Messrs Coutts and Co. to sell out our last earthly investment of 1,400 Consols and send what they realize to you. Henceforth our bank is in heaven. You see, we are rather afraid—notwithstanding the great earthly safety of Messrs Coutts and Co. and the Bank of England—that they may both break on the Judgement Day. And this step has been taken not without most definite reference to God's Word, and the command of the Lord Jesus, who said, 'Sell that ye have and give alms. Make for yourselves purses which wax not old.'[1]

That was how God led that couple. I think it echoes the heart of this psalmist.

God's present

And finally verses 3–5: 'Sons are a heritage from the LORD, children a reward from him . . .' Children are not an intrusion, they are not intended to be a burden, they were never meant to be an inconvenience to spoil our lifestyle. It says here that they are God's reward.

The biblical purpose of marriage, I believe, is for partnership and secondly for parenthood—we'll be looking at that biblical pattern tomorrow. It needs to be said: home-making, being a full-time wife and mother is not a destructive drought of usefulness, but an overflowing oasis of opportunity. Homemaking is not a dreary cell to contain

---

1. The story is told in Norman P. Grubb, *C. T. Studd: Cricketer & Pioneer* (Religious Tract Society, 1933), ch. 7.

one's talents and skills, but a brilliant catalyst to channel creativity and energies into meaningful work. It is not a rope for binding one's productivity in the market place but reins for guiding one's posterity in the home. It is not oppressive restraint of intellectual prowess for the community, but a release of wise instruction to your own household. Home-making is not the bitter assignment of inferiority to your person, but the bright assurance of the ingenuity of God's plan for the complementarity of the sexes, especially as worked out in God's plan for marriage. It is neither limitation of gifts available, nor stinginess in distributing the benefits of these gifts, but rather the multiplication of a mother's legacy to the generations to come and the generous bestowal of all God meant a mother to give to those He entrusted to her care.

A home that's Godly is God's purpose. A home that's Godly has God's protection. A home that's Godly has God's provision—sometimes we don't always have what we want, but we have what we need. And a Godly home is the environment to receive and to care for and to nourish and instruct and inspire, what I've called, God's present.

Psalm 128: A Godly Heart

Our third psalm tells us that a Godly heart (verses 1–4) is the result of two things.

Getting our priorities right

'Blessed are all who fear the LORD, who walk in his ways.' One of the things I've missed since I left Scotland where I spent my boyhood and my years as a young man and a young minister, is the singing of the metrical psalms and the paraphrases. One of them went like this:

> Fear Him ye saints and ye shall then
> have nothing else to fear.
> Make but His pleasure your delight,
> your wants shall be His care.

'Blessed are all who fear the LORD, who walk in his ways.

You will eat the fruit of your labour'; there will be fulfilment rather than frustration. 'Blessings and prosperity will be yours'; there will be fruitfulness that will overcome failure. 'Your wife will be like a fruitful vine within your house; your sons will be like olive shoots round your table. Thus is the man blessed who fears the LORD'; family, fellowship and friendship will be your experience rather than loneliness and friendlessness. The psalmist calls us to get our priorities right, to walk in God's ways.

Where do we find the ways of God? We find them in Scripture, we find them displayed in our Lord Jesus Christ. Let me remind you of what the Bible does for us: the Bible strengthens us, purifies us, helps us to find answers to our prayers, brings joy to our hearts. The Bible provides for our spiritual nourishment and growth, gives us wisdom—the ability to see things from God's perspective and point of view. The Bible guides us in our decisions and helps us to be effective and relevant and significant members in the new body of Christ on earth, the church.

And, cries the psalmist, blessed are those who fear the Lord—who live their lives with a sense of awe, that God is God and He is my God. He is a God of revelation. He is not a God who hides Himself, He is a God who wants to reveal His heart—'Blessed are all who fear the LORD and walk in his ways.' This Convention is, among other things, a very clear encouragement to the people of God under the Lordship of Jesus to take God's word seriously; to explore it, to read it, to think it over, to write it down, to pray it in, to live it out, and to pass it on.

When I was a young undergraduate struggling with my theological stance, I was greatly helped by the writings of Dietrich Bonhoeffer. He said, 'Every day in which I do not penetrate more deeply into the knowledge of God's word in Holy Scripture is a lost day for me.' What a statement! 'I can only move forward with certainty upon the firm ground of the Word of God. I cannot expound the Scripture for others if I don't let it speak daily to me. I will misuse the word in my office as a preacher if I do not continue to meditate upon it in prayer.'

Let us take the Scripture and allow God to speak into our

hearts. Let us allow the Spirit to be our teacher, so that we might grasp it, understand it, believe it, put shoes on it and live it day by day.

A Godly heart is a heart whose priorities are right because they are biblical, they are in accord with the ways of God, they are priorities that are recognised under the Lordship of Jesus.

Our peace needs to be restored
But a Godly heart is also where the peace, the *shalom* of God has been or is being restored. God wants to do that this morning; He wants to restore our peace. Jesus said, 'Peace I leave with you; my peace I give you. I do not give to you as the world gives' (John 14:27). Can you hear the cry of His heart to you this morning, as He names you because He knows you? 'Don't let your heart be troubled. I know your circumstances. I know the issues that you're facing. I know the conflict that confronts you. Don't let your heart be troubled. You believe in God, believe also in Me.'

Will you forgive me if I share just one other piece of personal testimony? Some considerable time ago I was going through a very difficult time. A member of our congregation wrote to me. I want to close this morning by reading to you what he wrote, and which I keep in my prayer diary.

> Jesus heard you when you prayed last night; He talked with God about you.
>
> Jesus was there when you fought that fight, He is going to bring you through.
>
> Jesus knew when you shed those tears, but you did not weep alone.
>
> So the burden you thought was too heavy to bear, He made His very own.
>
> Jesus Himself was touched by that trial, which you could not understand.
>
> Jesus stood by as you almost fell, and lovingly grasped your hand.
>
> Jesus cared when you bore that pain, indeed He bore it too.
>
> He felt each pang, each ache in your heart, because of His love for you.
>
> Jesus was grieved when you doubted His love, but He gave you grace to go on.

Jesus rejoiced as you trusted Him, the only trustworthy one.
His presence shall ever be with you, no need to be anxious or fret,
Wonderful Lord! He was there all the time, He has never forsaken you yet.

4: God is my Champion
(Psalms 129–131)

Psalm 129: The Enemy We Face

Perhaps you feel rather remote from Psalm 129, and as you read it you may well feel that this isn't something that you can easily relate to. The psalmist is speaking about opposition, hostility, conflict, the reality of confronting enemy forces. Of course the psalmist is speaking about flesh and blood reality, he is speaking about weapons and battle and military strategy. And we may feel somehow or other that doesn't affect too many of us in this tent.

But it seems to me that one of the tragedies of the church in the West is that we have concluded that we are living in peace-time, when in fact we are living in war-time. We've concluded that we are civilians when in reality we are soldiers. And of course the way that you live in peace-time is quite different from the way that you live in war. Many here this morning will remember at least the Second World War. No doubt there are some who remember the events of the Great War of 1914–18, but many of us remember something of the atmosphere, the restrictions, the fear, the concern for defence and all the other things that marked those years 1939–45.

And what I want to say to you this morning is that we are an embattled people. People don't believe in the devil now as their parents used to do. They have opened the gates wide to let his majesty through.

140

Never a sign of his cloven hoof or the darts of his fiery bow
is seen in all the earth today, for the people have voted it so.
. . . The sceptic says the Devil's dead. Of course what he says is
   true.
But who is doing the awful work that the Devil used to do?
If there isn't a devil whence all the sin and the jarring and
   hideous sounds,
That are heard in Senate and marts and homes, to earth's
   remotest bounds?
It may be true what the scoffer says, that the Devil is dead and
   gone,
But sensible folks would like to know:Who carries His business
   on?

And that's what I intend to confront in this morning's
teaching. I believe that that is the heart of these psalms; that
there is an enemy whom we face, but God is our champion.

Catherine Marshall has written several very helpful books.
Her husband, Len LeSourd, writes:

Catherine and I went through periods when we seemed to be up
against a kind of unexplained opposition. There would be a
series of breakdowns in our household equipment, times when
all the children misbehaved for no apparent reason. Work would
be constantly interrupted and we would feel a heaviness in our
spirits. At first we tried to examine these happenings logically.
And then as we learned more about the dark powers and
principalities that work in the world, we realised that on occasion
we were under a form of satanic attack. When Catherine was
writing *Beyond Ourselves* she reported the spirit of opposition in
her office as being almost palpable. No wonder. This book more
than any other of hers helped people move from unbelief and
uncertainty and into making a commitment to Jesus Christ as
Lord. As we learned more about the enemy and his cohorts we
were able to pray against those dark spirits reducing their
effectiveness. But we were never free from them. In fact as the
years went by we accepted the fact that for all of us engaged in
Christian service there is never ending spiritual warfare.

In the final years of her life as her body weakened from a
series of ailments, Catherine had a daily battle with the dark
forces. Rebuking the enemy in the name of Jesus was the best
weapon for reclaiming the creative atmosphere to do our work,
to minister to others and to protect our home environment.

And he finishes with a very simple sentence: 'But we could never relax our vigilance.'

Psalm 129 draws our attention to the fact that the people of God have always been under pressure. They've always had to confront problems in one form or another. To live under the Lordship of Jesus and in the power of the Holy Spirit inevitably, in one form or another, will lead to persecution. And I'm impressed by the fact that right at the beginning of Jesus' earthly ministry, He was made aware that the real enemy was not the Romans who crucified Him, or the Jews who condemned Him, but rather the Devil who confronted Him. Do you remember Matthew 4, as Jesus moved out of these early years? Undoubtedly He was serving God, without yet entering upon the ministry for which He came, which ultimately would lead to Calvary. Right at the beginning of that public ministry, we are told, the Spirit (and He is the focus of this Bible Reading) led Him into the desert to be tested by the Devil.

And then at the end of Jesus' earthly ministry, on the last night He was on earth in His incarnate body, he was gathered with His disciples. We have in John 14:27–31 the last words that He spoke before leaving the upper room, to move across that vast temple area and down the Kidron Valley and up the Mount of Olives to the Garden of Gethsemane and into these final hours of His life. And in verse 27, He says these remarkable words with which I ended yesterday's Bible Reading, 'Peace I leave with you; my peace I give you. I do not give to you as the world gives. Do not let your hearts be troubled and do not be afraid.' He is saying, 'My peace, that which I am experiencing and enjoying, I want to give to you.' In John 14:27–31 there are three ingredients of that peace.

First (verse 28) He speaks of *His confidence*. He doesn't say, 'I am going to the cross' or 'I am going to suffer pain' or 'I am going to endure unbelievable suffering and an ultimately death'. He says, 'If you loved me, you would be glad that I am going to the Father.' That's the ground of His peace. He is convinced, He is confident where He's going.

Second, He speaks of *His conviction of the purity of His heart*. The devil is a legalist and wants to claim the ground that we give him. But Jesus says, verse 30: 'The prince of this world is coming. He has no hold on me.'.

Third (verse 31), He speaks *of the priority that has controlled Him*. 'I do exactly what my Father has commanded me.' He speaks of the prospect that lies before Him, he speaks unashamedly of the purity of His life and He speaks about the priority that has controlled Him and guided Him through the years.

We have a saying, 'Your wish is my command'. But when we become Christians we change that round. We look into the face of our Heavenly Father and we say, 'Father, Your command is my wish'. We speak so often of Christian vocation in terms of answering the question, 'What are you doing?' But the Bible doesn't.

There are two other questions that need to be asked and answered. First, 'Why are you doing what you are doing?'; and second, 'How are you doing what you are doing?' It doesn't matter if you are at home or abroad, whether your responsibility is 'secular' (I hate that term) or spiritual, it doesn't matter whether we are 'full-time' or 'part-time'—the issue, ladies and gentlemen, is that I am doing what I am doing because this is the will of God for me, and I am doing what I am doing in the power and the demonstration of the Holy Spirit. That's what last night's World View service was about. God was speaking clearly through His servant by His Word. Our hearts were called to examine where we are, why we are where we are, and how we fulfil what we are doing under the Lordship of Jesus.

His continual persistence

I wanted to share the beginning and the end of Jesus' earthly ministry with you this morning, because in both there was an awareness of the enemy He confronted day by day. I wanted to spend some time with you looking at the enemy. And I do not want us to be engrossed in that, but I do want us to be aware of what we are about. When Field Marshall Montgomery was leading the allied troops in the North Africa campaign, he had in his headquarters a photograph of Field Marshall Rommel. Montgomery was very aware of, and respectful, of the enemy that he faced. He knew he faced a great strategist and a great general. He knew that Rommel had a string of victories and accomplishments behind him. And he kept a photograph of him so that he would never forget the real enemy that he was facing.

I wanted to list for you some of the characteristics of the enemy that we face.

He is invisible. Ephesians 6:12—'For our struggle is not against flesh and blood, but against the rulers, against the authorities, against the powers of this dark world and against the spiritual forces of evil in the heavenly realms.' Most of us in the West find that extremely difficult to absorb. Our mind-set says that reality is determined by what we know from our five senses. If I can hear it, see it, smell it, taste it or touch it, I say it's real. We struggle with things that can't be scientifically analysed and identified. They don't have the same problem in the East. And I sense that God wants to bring us to understand the reality of the eternal as well as the historical, of the unseen as well as the seen, of the intangible as well as the tangible. And the Bible declares that the enemy we face is invisible.

He is attractive. 2 Corinthians 11:14—'Satan himself masquerades as an angel of light.' How? By the things he says, the company he keeps, the activities he gets involved in, the people he uses and the Scripture he quotes. And we are misled.

Romans 16:17–18—'I urge you, brothers, to watch out for those who cause divisions.' . . . Watch out for those who upset people's faith, who go against the teaching which you have received. Keep away from them! . . . 'For those who do such things are not serving Christ our Lord but their own appetites. By their fine words and flattering speech they deceive the minds of naive people.' Do you know anything of that?

He is a liar. John 8:43–45: he'll tell lies to you about yourself, so that you miss the wonder of your inheritance in Jesus; you miss what God is saying about you through His word into your heart. He tells lies to you about others, it's one of his frequent strategies. He tells lies to others about you; you wonder what's happened. He tells lies to God about you, it says in the book of Job. And he tells lies to you about God.

He is cunning. Ephesians 6:11—'Put on the full armour of God.' Why? So that you will be able to stand against the Devil's evil tricks. He's not only strong, he's subtle, he's cunning. And we need to be aware of his stealth; the way that he goes about his business is sneaky, underhand and behind your back; it's not straight forward and upfront. He is prepared to deceive.

He is an accuser. Thirteen times in the New Testament he is spoken of as 'the devil'. The word means 'the slanderer'. He wants to slander you—child of God, member of the Royal Family, one who has been redeemed by the blood of Christ and set free by the grace of God. He wants to slander you. He wants to tell you that you are a failure, to insinuate to you that you have wasted your life. How many of you here are labouring under that kind of accusation? He says to some of us, 'God can never un-mess your mess. You have made such a hash of life that even God can't unravel it and make it straightforward and pure once again.' He's the accuser, saying to others that you have mistaken your guidance, that God will never fulfil his promises to you the way He does to others.

And one of his favourite accusations against God is that God will not provide for you and me, that God makes promises He cannot keep. He says to some this morning, 'Your shame is too deep for the cleansing of the precious blood of Christ.' But we have already heard in this Convention about the fountain that is open for sin and uncleanness.[1] I sense that some of you are still carrying guilt and shame deep inside, because the slanderer has said, 'There is not enough for you.'

He is strong. 1 Peter 5:8–9—'Your enemy the devil prowls around like a roaring lion.' He wants to paralyse us with fear, to overwhelm us with guilt, to devastate us with sickness, to

---

1. The address by Rev Keith Weston is included in the present volume, p. 242.

smother us with depression and taunt us with persecution. He is strong.

Do you know the hymn, 'We rest on Thee, our shield and our defender'? Back on 3 January 1956, five young American missionaries were setting out to take the gospel to a newly-discovered tribe. They wanted to take the redeeming love of God in Jesus His Son to the Auca people. Elisabeth Elliot, the wife of one of them, Jim Elliot, writes this:

> At the close of their prayers the five men sang one of their favourite hymns, 'We rest on Thee', to the thrilling tune 'Finlandia'. Jim and Ed had sung this tune since college days and they knew the verses by heart. And on the last verse their voices rang out with deep conviction,
> We rest on Thee our shield and defender!
> Thine is the battle, Thine shall be the praise:
> When passing through the gates of pearly splendour,
> Victors—we rest with Thee through endless days.

God is our champion. Look at Psalm 129. The enemy's work is to oppress (verses 1 and 2), to gain advantage over us, to cause pain (verse 3), to bring us into captivity (verse 4), to hate (verse 5). And so the psalmist speaks in the first three verses of the devil's continual persistence. Do you remember the passage I read to you from William Law? Our enemy never gives up.

Our constant protest
The remainder of the psalm is all taken from Scripture. Verse 4 is from Exodus 9:27; verse 6 is from 2 Kings 19:26; verse 7 is from Deuteronomy 28:58. Thus the enemy that we face is confronted by the word of God.

Let me give you some more scriptures. Ephesians 6:17 —Accept the word of God as the sword which the Spirit gives you. Take it, grasp it, understand it, hide it in your heart, clothe it with your body, use it as the weapon of the Holy Spirit in the spiritual battle in which we are engaged. Colossians 1:13—Learn to use Scripture in the battle. He has rescued me from the power of darkness and brought me safe into the kingdom of His dear Son by whom I have been set free—tell the enemy that! I am no longer in the kingdom of darkness. I've been liberated by the grace of God and by the sacrifice of Jesus. Proverbs 18:10—The Lord is like a strong tower where I can go and be safe; when the battle is fierce and the pressure is great, there is a tower that is our refuge and our strength. Luke 10:17—The disciples returning to Jesus say, 'Lord even the demons obey me when I give them a command in your name.' I have authority, not because of my experience, not because of my spirituality, not because of my training, not because of my position—I have authority because Jesus Christ is Lord. That's what they were discovering! 2 Timothy 1:7—The Spirit that God has given me does not make me timid; instead the Spirit fills me with power, love and self-control. That's our focus this morning. The third person of the Trinity, the Spirit of the living God fills me with power and love and self-control. Declare it. Protest to the devil about his advances to you.

Joshua 1:5–6—'I will always be with you, I will never abandon you.' Tell him: 'God has made a covenant in the blood of His Son with me. We celebrate it with thanksgiving as we break bread and we drink wine together.' Colossian 3:3—'For I have died,' says the apostle. 'Powers of darkness, you need to know that my life is hidden with Christ in God.' Martin Luther, who was very well aware of the devil's blandishments, said this:

> The devil came to the door of my heart and I opened the door and I saw the devil standing there and I said to him, 'Martin Luther does not live here any more because he has died. Jesus Christ lives here now.' And the devil left.

Hebrew 2:14—Jesus himself became like me and shared my human nature. He did this so that through his death he might destroy the devil who has the power over death. The word 'destroy' there doesn't mean 'annihilate', it means 'render powerless'. The devil has no power over me. And finally 1 John 4:4—The Spirit who is within me is more powerful than the spirit in those who belong to the world.

So, while we recognise continual persistence, we need to make our constant protest through the Scriptures of God, that the devil should flee from us. And of course we also

have three other means by which we confront the enemy: the
protection of the cross, the provision of armour, and the
power of the Holy Spirit. 'We sing our songs of triumph,
Our hearts are free from fear'—because God is our
champion.

Psalm 130: The Expectation We Have

From the enemy we face, we turn now to the expectation we
have.

Because of God's grace

And our expectation is based not on a false hope, but first of
all on God's grace. Is that what the psalmist is saying when
he writes, 'Out of the depths I cry to you, O LORD; O LORD,
hear my voice. Let your ears be attentive to my cry for
mercy.'? The Hebrew word would sometimes be translated
in Greek by the word *charis*—'grace'.

'If you, O LORD, kept a record of sins, O LORD, who could
stand? But with you there is forgiveness; therefore you are
feared.' Why? Well it's one of expectation and hope for the
future because of God's grace. A former Principal of my old
college, Trinity College Glasgow, said: 'The essence and
centre of Pauline faith and religion can be summed up in one
brief sentence—all is of grace and grace is for all.' Every
letter of Paul's in the New Testament begins and ends with
grace. Check it: it's a good little Bible study.

For Paul, the essence of the gospel is grace. And in that
word there are two main strands. Let me share them with
you. The word *charis* translated 'grace' originally meant 'a
lovely thing'. It could refer to physical beauty, charm or
attractiveness. There are some religious words that have a
very stern and severe note in them; but not 'grace'. There's a
beauty, an attractiveness, a winsomeness about grace. That's
the first strand of its meaning.

The second strand is that it's undeserved. It speaks of
something that's entirely and completely free. Grace and
merit are mutually exclusive. You cannot earn grace, you can
only humbly and gratefully and adoringly receive it.

The word therefore speaks of the beauty of God and of

the bounty of God. That is why we can face the future with confidence. Grace is the sheer undeserved generosity of the heart of God, and because of that reality I can face the future with confidence.

That's what the psalmist is saying. 'Let your ears be attentive to my cry for mercy'—that is my hope; 'If you, O LORD, kept a record of sins, O LORD, who could stand? But with you there is forgiveness; therefore you are feared.'

Because of our faith
The second part of the psalm speaks of the psalmist's faith. I noted down some definitions of faith. 'Faith is the sixth sense which enables us to grasp the invisible but real spiritual realm.' . . . 'Faith is the open hand by which we take what God is offering us in His grace.' . . . 'Faith is confidence in a God who is absolutely trustworthy and utterly reliable.' . . . 'Faith is willing to accept what it cannot understand.' . . . 'Faith is neither encouraged nor discouraged by circumstances.' . . . 'Faith is ever discovering what God is able to do in face of all opposition and difficulties.' . . . 'The first, chief occupation is obtaining the promises of God.'

And so we have an expectation based on the grace that is made real to us, through faith.

Psalm 131: The Enlightenment We Need

And so to our third psalm. The first thing that we need to see clearly is that our pride can so often get in the way of what God wants to do in us and then through us. By His word today, and through His Spirit, God wants to explore our hearts. It was such a blessing to me some years ago to discover that the Spirit of God doesn't come to condemn me. But He often comes to convict me, because then He can lead me to Jesus, and I can see who Jesus is and what He's done. That's the Spirit's ministry.

Our pride
He wants to show some of us the pride of our hearts. Forgive me for being very personal now. I think of all the things through the years that I've struggled with more than anything

else. It's been a proud heart; I know it's wrong and the Spirit of God has so graciously again and again spoken into my life and shown me that my attitude and my reaction, the position that I've sometimes so stubbornly taken, is because of pride.

I found something in one of George Verwer's books which I wrote at the front of the Bible that I use every day.

Oh Jesus, meek and humble of heart, hear me. Deliver me, Jesus, from the desire of being loved, from the desire of being extolled, from the desire of being honoured, from the desire of being praised, from the desire of being preferred to others. Oh Jesus, please deliver me from the desire of being consulted, from the desire of being approved, from the fear of being humiliated, from the fear of being despised, from the fear of suffering rebuke, from the fear of being forgotten, from the fear of being wronged, from the fear of being suspected. Oh Jesus, deliver me and grant me the grace to desire that others might be loved more than I, that others may be esteemed more than I, that in the opinion of the world others may increase and I may decrease, that others may be chosen and I set aside, that others may be praised and I unnoticed, that others may be preferred to me in everything, that others may become holier than I, provided that I become as holy as I should.

'From heaven you came,' writes Graham Kendrick:

Entered our world, your glory veiled.
Not to be served but to serve
And give your life that we might live.
This is our God, the Servant King
He calls us now to follow Him,
To bring our lives as a daily offering
Of worship to the Servant King.

The final thing that the psalmist says is so beautiful: 'Like a weaned child with its mother, like a weaned child is my soul within me. O Israel, put your hope in the LORD both now and for evermore.'

His peace
We need the enlightenment of our proud hearts, but also His peace. Do you know the hymn by H. G. Spafford:

When peace like a river attendeth my way,
When sorrows like sea-billows roll,
Whatever my lot thou hast taught me to know,
It is well, it is well with my soul.
Though Satan should buffet, though trials should come,
Let this blessed assurance control,
That Christ hath regarded my helpless estate,
And hath shed his own blood for my soul.

'Like a weaned child with its mother is my soul within me.' It is well, it is well with my soul. Hallelujah!

5: God is My Joy
(Psalms 132–135)

It's been a great delight to be here over these days, and I have appreciated the opportunity of sharing rich fellowship with so many and of being asked to study these fifteen Psalms and give some pointers as God has been speaking into our hearts. Thank you for being such a marvellous family as we've shared with you what our Father wanted us to share.

This morning's title is 'God is my joy'. And I'd like you to have your hymnbooks open as well as your Bibles. I would like us to end this Bible Reading at the point where we are able to sing that great hymn by Charles Wesley,

> Rejoice, the Lord is King
> Your Lord and King adore.
> Mortals give thanks and sing
> And triumph evermore.
> Lift up your hearts, lift up your voice,
> Rejoice, again I say rejoice.

That, I hope, is where we will get to as we close these Bible Readings.

A great leader called Dr H. H. Farmer was once in a large rally, seated near the orchestra which happened to be a Salvation Army band. Dr Farmer apparently had very decided musical tastes, and it so happened that by some misfortune he was placed right beside the drummer. He began to become irritated, and asked the drummer to play less loudly. The drummer, a Salvationist, said, 'Lord bless you Sir, since I have been converted I am so happy I could bust the bloomin' drums!'

That's not very biblical language, but I notice that fifteen times in the forty-four verses of these four psalms there is a note of praise. That's why I chose the title I did.

The senior lecturer in New Testament at my old college once remarked, 'The trouble about life is that we get bored and fed up with it. Life loses its interest. Things get stale, flat and unprofitable. We get into a state when we can't be bothered. And when we couldn't care less, work becomes a weariness, pleasure loses its thrill, its taste and tang. There's a kind of vague dissatisfaction in everything. But when Jesus comes into one's life, there comes this new exhilaration like water turning into wine.'

This evening in the communion service we will take ordinary bread and wine. We'll break it and we'll share it, we'll eat and we'll drink it, and in our hearts by faith we'll feed on Christ with thanksgiving. We'll reach beyond the symbol, so that we touch the reality. We are going to crown this Friday with that magnificent opportunity. And I sense that God wants to put into our hearts, whatever our circumstances, a new joy and exhilaration, a new sense of His presence, peace and power, so that we'll go back tonight or tomorrow morning to familiar situations that haven't changed, but we'll go back with a new sense of God reverberating within us.

John Masefield wrote a poem called *The Everlasting Mercy*, about a drunken reprobate, Saul Kane, who encounters the Lord Jesus Christ; his life is absolutely revolutionised. He writes,

> Oh glory of the lighted mind, how deaf I'd been, how dumb, how blind.
> The station brook to my new eyes was bubbling out of Paradise.
> The waters rushing from the rain were singing 'Christ is risen again.'
> I thought all earthly creatures knelt from rapture of the joy I felt,
> The narrow station walls, brick ledge, the wild hop withering on the hedge,

> The lights in huntsman's upper storey, were parts of an eternal
> glory.

Think about it. The context that Saul Kane was living in was
drab and lack-lustre, but something or someone had invaded
his being and transformed all that he was. God wants to do
that. It's very easy in all the busy-ness and pressure of
responsibility to become dry and empty. God has brought us
to this place so that He might renew us and revitalise us and
send us back with a new longing after God in our souls.

'Homesick for God', I called this series of Bible Readings.
God who is my protector, my security, my deliverer, my
champion—and finally, God who is my joy, whatever our
circumstances. You see, peace is joy resting; joy is peace
dancing. That's what God wants to communicate into our
hearts and lives this morning. Peace and joy; because the
ordinary is being touched by His glory and becomes
extraordinary. The things that seem to us common are
touched with His glory, and they become holy. And our
human problems and pressures become shot through with a
divine perspective.

And so the psalmist says, Psalm 132:9—'May your saints
sing for joy', and in verse 16, 'her saints shall ever sing for
joy'. Psalm 134:1—'Praise the LORD, all you servants of the
LORD . . . Lift up your hands in the sanctuary and praise the
LORD.' Psalm 135:1—'Praise the LORD. Praise the name of
the LORD'; verse 3, 'Praise the LORD, for the LORD is good;
sing praise to his name, for that is pleasant.' Then Psalm
135:19—'O house of Israel, praise the LORD . . . Praise be to
the LORD from Zion, to him who dwells in Jerusalem. Praise
the LORD.' I hope you're going to find it difficult to remain
seated as we get towards the end of these Bible Readings!
Well, we'll stand in a little while to sing 'Rejoice, the Lord is
king.'

I remember a number of years ago quoting in a sermon
from C. H. Spurgeon's great book *Lectures to my Students*:
'An individual who has no geniality about him had better be
an undertaker and bury the dead, for he will never succeed
in influencing the living.' Then I looked up and saw one of
our deacons sitting there, and I remembered that he was the

funeral director of the Co-operative Wholesale Society ...
We are still friends.

There is that note of joy and wonder and praise and
thanksgiving and worship about these four psalms.

Psalm 132: The Place Where God Lives

Psalm 132 reminds us of the place where God lives. That
takes us back to 2 Samuel 7:1–2, which is the background to
a great deal of this Psalm. 'After the king was settled in his
palace and the LORD had given him rest from all his enemies
around him, he said to Nathan the prophet, "Here I am,
living in a palace of cedar, while the ark of God remains in a
tent." ' Then God speaks through His prophet Nathan and
gives David the king a revelation through His prophet: "I will
build a house for you" ' (verse 10). The other part of the
revelation was, 'You build a house for Me' (that's in verses
5–7). Then in verses 18–29 we have David's response. So
God reveals what's on his heart, and David makes his
response.

Remember that magnificent fourteenth chapter of John,
where Jesus in the last hours of His earthly life says: 'Let not
your heart be troubled: ye believe in God, believe also in me.
In my Father's house are many mansions. . . . I go to prepare
a place for you. And if I go and prepare a place for you, I will
come again, and receive you unto myself; that where I am,
there ye may be also' (John 14:1–3). That's the Authorised
Version, but that's what I was brought up on.

In the first eleven verses of that chapter Jesus is giving
assurance of the place that He is preparing for His people.
We are not going to be like disembodied spirits floating
around in some kind of vague shadowy existence. We are
going to have new bodies. And that's why Jesus is preparing a
place for us, because bodies need a place to live; and we are
going to have bodies like Jesus' glorious body. When we see
Him we are going to become like Him. It's all there in John
14:1–11.

But in the second half of that chapter Jesus speaks about
the people that He is still preparing, for the place that He is
going to prepare for them. A rough summary of John 14, it

seems to me, would be, 'I will prepare a place for you in eternity as you prepare a place for Me in history, on the face of the earth.'

I was reminded of that as I read to you again 2 Samuel 7. Of course you will know that Solomon, David's son began constructing that place for God to live, in the fourth year of his reign. And the temple was completed seven years later.

The promise that was made

Notice that Psalm 132 has two parts: verses 1–10 and verses 11–18. The first part is about the promise that was made to God. You probably know that the emphasis of the Old Testament is that God dwells in buildings, whereas the emphasis of the New Testament is that God dwells in people. I am persuaded that revival will come to this nation not when God's buildings are filled with people, but when God's people are filled with the Holy Spirit. And that is the heart-cry of God.

Turn to 1 Corinthians 3:16. Hear the cry of the Spirit through His apostle: 'Don't you know that you yourselves are God's temple and that God's Spirit lives in you?' Three chapters later on, 1 Corinthians 6:19: 'Do you not know that your body is a temple of the Holy Spirit, who is in you, whom you have received from God? You are not your own; you were brought at a price. Therefore honour God with your body.'

The cry of God is not that He would be given a place of bricks and mortar to live in on earth now, but that He would be given people whose lives are glad to receive Him, lives that rejoice that He is dwelling within them by His Spirit.

In this last Bible Reading we've come to the most basic aspect of being a Christian, that Jesus gave His life for me on the cross that I might live eternally, beginning now. But the other side to that, is that I need to give my life for His in order that He might live historically.

I have written down a Credo, an 'I believe', so far as Jesus is concerned. It goes like this. 'I believe that a human being called Jesus of Nazareth was consciously alive before He was conceived. He was not then human, but one of three persons, in the Spirit we call God. He has always been there, sharing fully in the making and maintaining of our universe and all life in it. I believe He chose to come into our world by being born as a baby, and all His divine nature was embodied in His flesh.'

It seems to me that that is the bottom line of the Christian faith. Jesus is God made flesh—'Our God contracted to a span, incomprehensibly made man'. When He grew up He did and said things which only God can say and do. He was put to death as a dangerous impostor. His claims to be God the Son were proved when God the Father brought Him back to life with a new body. I believe that He has since returned to the place from which He came, taking with Him His human nature and experience. There's a man in heaven this morning, and His name is Jesus.

That's what we believe. His place on earth has been taken over by the Holy Spirit who has no body, but lives in Christians. One day the Lord Jesus Christ will return to this planet and give all His friends a new body like His, and take them to be with Him for ever and for ever.

What a gospel! And the crux of what I'm saying this morning is that Jesus wants to come and live within us by His Spirit.

A few years ago somebody gave me the following covenant, which I will read to you.

My body is a temple of the Holy Spirit, redeemed, cleansed and sanctified by the blood of Jesus. My members, the parts of my body, are instruments of righteousness, yielded to God for His service and for His glory. The devil has no place in me, no power over me, no unsettled claim against me. All has been settled by the blood of Jesus. I overcome Satan by the blood of the Lamb and by the word of my testimony and love not my life unto death. My body is for the Lord and the Lord is for my body.

'He swore an oath to the LORD, and made a vow to the Mighty One of Jacob; 'I will not enter my house or go to my bed—I will allow no sleep to my eyes, no slumber to my eyelids, till I find a place for the LORD.' What a vow! That is what God calls us to this morning as we recognise that our bodies are temples for the living God. Let's acknowledge Him, recognise Him, and make Him feel comfortable in the place where He wants to live.

The promise that was given
But the second part of the psalm, beginning at verse 11, is the other side of that: the promise that was given by God. I think there's a prophetic edge to this part of this psalm. We know from the books of Kings and Chronicles that the line of David wasn't always one of great honour. One sinner after the other seemed to sit on the throne. There were very few of them who were really kings; only five of them saw revival come to the nation.

I believe that when God was making His oath to His servant in verse 11—'One of your own descendants I will place on your throne'—He was speaking of what would happen a thousand years later, when the Lord Jesus, king David's greater Son, occupied that throne. He says, 'I want to bless you' (verse 15), 'I want to clothe you' (verse 16), 'I want to make . . . to set . . . to crown' (verse 17). And that is consummated and fulfilled in our Lord Jesus Christ. His zeal never degenerated into passion, nor His constancy into obstinacy, nor His benevolence into weakness, nor His tenderness into sentimentality. His unworldliness was free from indifference and unsociability. His dignity was free from pride and presumption, His affectability from undue familiarity, His self-denial from moroseness, His temperance from austerity. He that is Jesus combines child-like innocence with manly strength, absorbing devotion to God with untiring interest in the welfare of man, tender love to the sinner with uncompromising severity against sin. He commended dignity with willing humility, fearless courage with wise caution, unyielding firmness with sweet gentleness. He is our King.

So there is a promise that was made to God, and a promise given by God. He is a covenant-keeping God. And as we have responded through these days, making our new commitments, our new beginnings, our new vows; and as we come to the table of Christ this evening, we come to make our sacrament. The word comes from *sacramentum*, the word once used to describe the Roman soldier's oath to his commanding officer, or a citizen's oath to his emperor. And as we come to the table of Christ to make our sacramentum, and we see the broken bread that reminds us of a body broken and out-poured wine that reminds us of precious blood that was shed, we will be reminded that in His brokenness is our wholeness and in His passion is our hope. And with cleansed lives made whole by His grace, we can acknowledge again that our bodies are temples in which God wants to dwell and our lives are the places over which Jesus wants to reign.

Psalms 132 and 133: The People Whom God Loves

I want to pick up the end of Psalm 132 where God is making promises, giving reassurance to His people (verses 15–18). The concern of God is to turn our mourning into dancing, our sorrow into joy, our tears into laughter, our frustration into fulfilment, our burdens into blessings, our fear into faith and our despair into hope. That is the reassurance that God wants to build into our hearts on this Friday morning.

The reassurance God gives
The precious oil that's spoken of in Psalm 133, as David speaks about the relationships that he is longing for, comes from Exodus 30:23. You can find the recipe there. It is the anointing oil. It brings a fragrance, filling the immediate area with something intangible but real. And God wants not only to give us reassurance this morning, but He wants us to enter into relationships that are worthy of him.

The relationships God wants
Genesis 4 follows quickly on Genesis 3. When man breaks fellowship with God, inevitably he breaks fellowship with men. The cross of Jesus is intended not only to restore our fellowship with God, but our fellowship with one another. I find it a very solemn thing to say: that my vertical relationship, my relationship with God, will always be demonstrated in my horizontal relationships. In fact, the Bible says you can't have one without the other. If I'm out of

sorts, if I'm critical and have animosity and coldness in my
heart towards a brother or a sister, it indicates that however
many great hymns I sing, however often I come to Keswick,
it makes no difference whatsoever if my horizontal relationships are not a demonstration of my vertical relationship.

The Bible is stubbornly real and demandingly practical.
It says, 'How can you love God whom you have not seen,
if you don't love your brother whom you have seen?'
(cf 1 John 4:20). The reality of your vertical relationship is
demonstrated in the reality of your horizontal relationships.
Among us at this Keswick Convention, and without doubt
it's true of past Keswicks, one of the things that some of
us are going to have to do almost immediately we get home
is to repent of a critical spirit, a coldness of heart, an
undermining of a brother or a sister, a way of speaking that
has been destructive, of things said that have not affirmed
but hurt.

I've brought with me another list this morning, and it's one
that I find overwhelming. It's entirely derived from Scripture,
and I call it 'Attitudes in Christian Fellowship'. The list
contains twenty-seven of them.

> Love one another, encourage one another, spur one another on
> towards love and good deeds, bear one another up, admonish
> one another, instruct one another, serve one another, bear with
> one another, forgive one another, be kind to one another, be
> compassionate to one another, be devoted to one another,
> honour one another, live in harmony with one another, be
> sympathetic with one another, be patient with one another,
> accept one another, submit to one another, clothe yourselves
> with humility towards one another, teach one another, live at
> peace with one another, confess your sins to one another, offer
> hospitality to one another, greet one another, have fellowship
> with one another, agree with one another, carry one another's
> burdens.

Ladies and gentlemen, that's the way it's supposed to be! By
the grace of God, as a result of the finished work of Calvary
and as an evidence of the working of the blessed Holy Spirit
within us and among us. And I have compiled another list, of
'Nine prohibitions in Christian fellowship'.

Do not hurt or harm one another, do not irritate one another, do not be jealous of one another, do not hate one another, do not judge one another, do not lie to one another, do not criticise one another, do not complain against one another, do not take legal proceedings against one another.

It's all in the book. It's all Scripture. And the psalmist declares in Psalm 133, 'How good and pleasant it is when brothers live together in unity!' It's a fragrance that not only others can smell, but God can. It delights Him. He enjoys it, His heart is blessed with it. 'It is like precious oil poured on the head, running down on the beard, running down on Aaron's beard, down upon the collar of his robes.'

Psalms 134 and 135: The Praise Which God Receives

'Praise the LORD, all you servants of the LORD who minister by night in the house of the LORD' (Psalm 134:1). It's an invitation to worship, particularly to the priests, the Levites who kept nightly watch in the temple. 'Lift up your hands in the sanctuary and praise the LORD.'

The invitation to worship

At the end of last night's meeting I went over to the young people's meeting—high energy, high volume, eardrum-bleeding stuff! I tell you, God was there. A young woman came on to the stage at one point to take one of the lovely worship songs. And I found such a blessing simply in the way she lifted her hands. There was a quality, a reality, a dignity, a significance about it. It was something that came not only from the heart but from the spirit. And as I stood there, it blessed me. That's what the psalmist is speaking about here. 'Lift up your hands in the sanctuary and praise the LORD.'

In a New Testament passage written by Paul—it's given the title 'Instructions for worship' in the NIV—he says, 'I want men everywhere to lift up holy hands in prayer, without anger or disputing.' (1 Tim. 2:8).

We are not making a point, we are not demonstrating some kind of earthly allegiance or some kind of acknowledgement of some part of some doctrine. That's not what the psalmist is talking about. Psalm 134:2—'Lift up your hands in the sanctuary and praise the LORD. May the LORD, the Maker of heaven and earth, bless you from Zion.' Psalm 135:1–4—'Praise the LORD, praise the name of the LORD; praise him, you servants of the LORD, you who minister in the house of the LORD, in the courts of the house of our God . . . for the LORD is good; sing praise to his name, for that is pleasant. For the LORD has chosen Jacob to be his own, Israel to be his treasured possession.'

I want you to notice not just the invitation to worship, but also,

The implication of worship

Just two things as we close this morning. What is it that makes worship real? It's when we recognise the one that we are worshipping. And the implication of the worship that's described here is, first of all,

God's character is perfect

That is what is said in Psalm 135:3—'Praise the LORD, for the LORD is good; sing praise to his name, for that is pleasant. For the LORD has chosen Jacob to be his own.' I could understand it if it were Abraham, I could understand if it were Joseph, I could understand if it were Daniel. But Jacob? He was a man who cheated his father and deceived and defrauded his brother. 'The Lord has chosen Jacob to be his own.' God is in the business of mending broken things, of cleaning dirty things, of correcting wayward people and bringing them back into the warmth and security of His love. The implication of worship is that the character of God is perfect. That's the God whom we worship.

But finally, in the last part of Psalm 135, the implication of worship is,

God's conduct is powerful

'I know that the LORD is great,' says the Psalmist (135:5–14). Someone sent me a cutting from *The Times*. This is what it said,

The biggest known black hole in the universe has been discovered by the Hubble space telescope. The object, which is an estimated one thousand million million times more massive than the earth, ten thousand million miles across, is believed to be swallowing up billions of stars. The telescope found it in a galaxy called M87, fifty-two million light years away in the constellation of Virgo, which through earthbound telescopes appears as faint blob. But the orbiting telescope with its tremendous resolution has revealed that the heart of this galaxy, a gaseous region some five hundred light years across, is spinning rapidly as it swirls around an unseen super-massive object.

And a NASA scientist is quoted saying, 'I've been a sceptic about black holes but I believe this evidence is definitive.'

This discovery is the most significant made so far by the telescope. A black hole is an object with such strong gravity that nothing, not even light can escape from it and must therefore be invisible. Such objects are predicted by Einstein's 1916 general Theory of Relativity, which states that light possesses weight and can be trapped by a sufficiently strong gravitational field. Many galaxies including our Milky Way are believed to have black holes, but they are thought to be comparatively tiny objects.

My first thought was—'Wow!' And then I thought to myself, 'My Father is in charge of it all! And so often, Father, I have diminished You by my lack of faith, by the doubts that sometimes have arisen in my heart, by the fear that has gripped me because I felt so small and weak and human and inadequate and inept. But You are the One who put the stars in space, and You are the One who upholds them and controls them, light years and black holes and millions upon millions and thousands of millions and gravitational power and all that kind of stuff is in Your hands. And I worship You, because you are not only my God, Your Son taught me to call You Father.'

That is the implication of worship: the worship that God receives. 'Idols,' says the psalmist, 'are powerless.' But, dear Father, Your character is perfect, and Your conduct is powerful.

Rejoice, the Lord is king;
Your Lord and king adore;
Mortals give thanks and sing,
And triumph evermore.
Lift up your hearts, lift up your voice.
Rejoice, again I say, rejoice!

—Because God is your protector. God is your security. God is your deliverer. God is your champion. And God is your joy.

THE ADDRESSES

'The Temple of the Holy Spirit'

by Rev Tony Baker

1 Corinthians 6:9–20

Medical statistics are absolutely fascinating—did you know that there are over 600 named muscles in the human body, and 206 bones? Well, you know now! Yet there's an infinitely more significant statistic contained in our passage tonight: 'Do you not know that your body is a temple of the Holy Spirit, who is in you, whom you have received from God? You are not your own, you were bought at a price. Therefore honour God with your body.'

Before we come to that passage and its immediate context, let me remind you of certain facts concerning the Old Testament temple, built of course as the permanent successor to the tabernacle, the building in which God's name was to be honoured.

More than once in the Old Testament God says, 'The temple is the place for the honour of My Name.' It was a building in which God's presence was to be manifested. Even the builder of that Old Testament temple was significant, for David wanted to build it, but he was not allowed to because God said, 'You have shed much blood and you have fought many wars' (1 Chron. 22:8). The temple was to represent the peace between God and sinners that can be established only through God's grace; God's presence again coming among His people through His grace. So it wasn't appropriate that David, who had shed much blood, should build it.

But when it was built by Solomon, the heart of the temple was the Most Holy Place, the Holy of Holies, with those sculptured cherubim. You can read about it in 2 Chronicles 5:7—'The priests then brought the ark of the LORD's covenant to its place in the inner sanctuary of the temple, the Most Holy Place, and put it beneath the wings of the cherubim. The cherubim spread their wings over the place of the ark and covered the ark and its carrying poles.' Now, note very carefully verse 10: 'There was nothing in the ark except the two tablets that Moses had placed in it at Horeb, where the LORD made a covenant with the Israelites after they came out of Egypt.'

In the covenant box called the ark, right in the centre of the Most Holy Place, were the Ten Commandments, the truth of God written with the finger of God on Mount Sinai. And we told that when the temple was completed, there God manifested His glory. Glance further down in 2 Chronicles 5:13—'They ... sang: "He is good; his love endures for ever." Then the temple of the LORD was filled with a cloud, and the priests could not perform their service because of the cloud, for the glory of the LORD filled the temple of God.'

There was God manifesting something of Himself when that temple was dedicated. And after Solomon had prayed, the glory came again and indeed the fire fell (7:1–3); a marvellous picture of the Old Testament temple of God.

Bear that in mind and come back to 1 Corinthians. Not quite yet chapter 6, but by way of chapter 3, because here in 1 Corinthians Paul sets in motion two gigantic earthquake shocks which in a sense demolish part of the Old Testament order—which does not mean that the Old Testament is anything other than God's word, but that aspects of it are fulfilled in the coming of the Lord Jesus Christ. And so in 3:16 Paul, addressing the Corinthian church, says of them together, 'Don't you know that you yourselves are God's temple and that God's Spirit lives in you?' These Christians

together in Christ are now the temple of God. Maximum
rating on the spiritual Richter scale!

This is such a dramatic, radical truth that as with quite a
lot of other dramatic, radical New Testament truths we
sometimes find it convenient to live almost forgetting it. It's
much less demanding to try to pretend that in some way
ecclesiastical buildings are still the temple of God, rather
than we, the people of God together; so when you've got over
the first shock of the earthquake you rebuild the building just
as it was. And still, very often, when people talk about a local
church they mean the building rather than the people.
It's much easier to make a building the temple of God
than to make a congregation the temple of God with all
the implications of that. It's much more comfortable that
way.

But then (and now we are back to where we started) comes
earthquake number two. Here we are again: 1 Corinthians
6:19—'Do you not know that your body'—your individual
body—'is a temple of the Holy Spirit, who is in you, whom
you have received from God?' So each Christian individually
is now called to be what the Old Testament temple of God
was; not just the congregation, but each individual believer.
This is a statement. It's not, 'You might become that, if you
become very holy, if you come to Keswick every year, or
whatever.' It's not a question of entering one of those
competitions with these fabulous prizes. Have you met
anyone who has won any of those prizes, the £100,000 a
week for life or even the new Metro? Has anyone here ever
won one?

Here is a statement, not a remote hope. 'Do you not know
that your body is a temple of the Holy Spirit, who is in you,
whom you have received from God?' This is one of the
highest privileges of every believer in Christ. We are not only
justified by God the Son, we are not only a child of God the
Father, we are a temple, each one of us; if we are believers,
we are a temple of God the Spirit. Let's say it again: what the
temple of God was in the Old Testament, each Christian is
now called to be.

Now I think it's possible to bring these verses into very
sharp focus. There are three focal points.

Focus on Your Body

You may say, 'I'd rather not focus on my body.' You may be young and beautiful, but you may not be. You may reckon you bulge in all the wrong places; you may be developing varicose veins; perhaps you're not quite what you were, but even now you're quite sure what you will be as the years go by.

I'm told that when John Laird, who was once General Secretary of Scripture Union, got up in the morning, he not only talked to the Lord but he talked to himself. As he looked at himself in the shaving mirror he used to say, 'Come on, old chap, you've got to live with yourself today.'

Nevertheless, like it or not, focus on your body. Every one is still 'fearfully and wonderfully made' (Psa. 139:14). It doesn't say, 'focus on your soul' in verse 19. It says, 'focus on your body', because each of us is a whole person; the body stands for the whole person. Without the body being active and responsive, all our dedication to God and our being spiritual fade into nothing. It's one thing to sing songs at a Convention meeting, but the real test is what we do with our bodies.

When the Lord Jesus Christ became incarnate and took human nature, He took a body. He didn't just float around. And that's why in Romans 12 our response to the gospel of His grace, which involved His offering up of Himself on the cross, is to offer our bodies: 'Therefore, I urge you, brothers, in view of God's mercy, to offer your bodies as living sacrifices, holy and pleasing to God—this is your spiritual act of worship. Do not conform any longer to the pattern of this world, but be transformed by the renewing of your mind' (Rom. 12:1–2). We can only be living sacrifices if we are ready to present our bodies.

Never think that it doesn't matter what we do with our bodies. The ancient Stoics have infiltrated the Christian church from the start. One was called Epictetus. He said, 'I am a poor soul shackled to a corpse.' He meant, 'I don't like my body, I want to get away from it, it's not me.' He was 100% wrong. The body stands for the whole person. We

shall not be complete until we have our resurrection body.
And it is our body which is the temple of the Holy Spirit.

Focus on the Holy Spirit

Our second focal point is the Holy Spirit who, we are told, is
in you, whom you have received from God. When we are
born again by the Spirit, the Holy Spirit comes within us in
His fullness.

It does not matter, brothers and sisters, whether you know
the date when you were born again. As a young believer I
was quite often asked, by those who expected me to know,
when I was born again, but I didn't know. But what matters
is not that we know when, but that we know we are believing
now. And whenever that was, the Holy Spirit came in in His
fullness.

Of course for many of us it happened before we were
really conscious of how much or how little we believed the
Holy Spirit was at work. I cannot honestly say as I look back
that I can ever think of myself, having had a Christian home,
as being an unbeliever. (I think, incidentally, that it's a
reminder not to put pressure on youngsters in Christian
homes to 'make a decision' but rather to reckon that the Holy
Spirit is at work, and to regard them as within the family of
God unless they opt out, and to regard them as having the
Holy Spirit within them.)

It is the Holy Spirit who makes each Christian a temple of
the Spirit. What that building was in the Old Testament, you
and I individually, as well as in local churches, are called to
be now. Now this earthquake of a truth becomes the more
violent the nearer we get to the centre, which is very
characteristic of earthquakes. The word for 'temple' is not
the common word for 'temple'; here, as in 3:16, it is the
word for 'shrine'—that is, the word used for 'the Holy of
Holies'. So take this on board! It's the work of the Spirit to
make us not just a temple of God in general, but the Most
Holy Place in particular. This is amazing and awesome.

Near where I live in Sussex is a Tudor house in which
Queen Elizabeth I once slept. Her room is quite interesting
and the royal connection is one of the main 'selling points' of

the house. But I will tell you one thing for sure. Queen Elizabeth is not sleeping there now. She has been, and she has gone. But the Spirit, once within the individual believer, is always there. There is no question about it, your body is the temple of the Holy Spirit, who is in you, whom you have received from God. When did you last realise that we are the New Testament parallel to the Old Testament temple?

And here is where the link-up comes so incredibly. What was in that Most Holy Place, inside the covenant box, the ark? The words of God written by the finger of God. Now in the New Testament, according to Jesus, the Holy Spirit comes within us, the temple of God, as the Spirit of truth (cf John 15:26). So He is now within us to write, deep within us, in our minds and hearts, all the truth that has now been given in completeness in the Scriptures. Ezekiel makes this precise point prophetically, 'I will give you a new heart and put a new spirit in you; I will remove from you your heart of stone and give you a heart of flesh. And I will put my Spirit in you and move you to follow my decrees and be careful to keep my laws' (Ezek. 36:26–27).

If we would be worthy temples of God, we must be ready for the Spirit of God to write within us the fullness of God's written revelation. How open are we? We might use the analogy of a tattoo; once it's there, it's there for ever. And God's word written within is to be there for keeps.

How big is your Bible? I don't mean, do you have one of those Bibles that are so enormous you have to wheel them around, but: How big is your Bible in the way you actually use it? Do you think it's possible that though you have been a Christian some years, there are parts of the Bible you've never read? And if you've never read it, how can the Spirit of God write it within you as the temple of God? You say, 'When I read it, or when I hear addresses at Keswick or whatever, I can't remember it.' Can't you believe more of the Holy Spirit than that?

I cannot tell when most of the truth of God which has begun to go into my heart over the years, by the grace of God, began to go in. But the Holy Spirit starts writing it, and He is able to continue. And you find when you've been a Christian for a while, when you are taking part in a Bible

Study or, even more, sharing the gospel with somebody else, that there is something written within that you can share, because the Spirit of truth has been writing it within you. But if we are not open to it, how can He?

In the New Testament we are not only told that He is the Spirit of truth, but that He is the Spirit of Christ. 'If anyone does not have the Spirit of Christ, he does not belong to Christ' (Rom. 8:9). He comes within to bring glory to Christ by remaking us like Christ. Of course, to have the Spirit as the Spirit of truth and as the Spirit of Christ is really two sides of the same coin. Our coinage bears the image of the Sovereign, and around the edge it has writing in Latin which explains whose the image is. When the Spirit comes in as the Spirit of truth and the Spirit of Christ, it's all part of the one coin. He is working within us gradually, to make us more like the Lord Jesus Christ, to manifest Christ and to write the word of Christ within us.

Do you remember at that temple how the glory of God was manifested, and the crowd came so that the priest could not minister? The Holy Spirit wants to manifest His glory in us and to us. If our concern is not with the glory of Christ, if our concern is not with growing like Christ and with His honour, we shall grieve the Holy Spirit whose concern is Christ's truth and Christ's glory. We shall be out of step with the Holy Spirit: and Galatians 5:25 reminds us how important it is to keep in step with the Spirit. But sometimes we get out of step with the Holy Spirit because our concerns are not His.

This is the Year of the Family. A major factor in destroying family life is sexual promiscuity, so that if and when two people finally do get married, they can't cope with a life-long committed permanent relationship because they are so unused to it. And the pressures are on Christians, particularly acutely on young Christians but also on all Christians, to trip us up in this area. I put it to you: if we realise we are the temple of the Spirit, that becomes unthinkable.

Look at the context of our text, verses 12–18. It's very clear. The world calls it 'sleeping with someone', 'making love'. The Bible calls it 'sexual immorality' (verse 13), and the old, ugly yet accurate word is 'fornication'. And I have to say, in the light of this passage, that when a Christian sins in this area the shocking, shocking truth—if I read verse 15 aright—is that the Christian is causing Christ to fornicate. And that is shocking, because the Christian is the temple of the Spirit of Christ. Of course in the mercy of God there is full forgiveness, though there may well be consequences, perhaps scars. But it is unthinkable, if we realise that what's happening, that we should cause Christ to fornicate.

Look at the verses that follow our passage. Many Christian marriages are not as strong as they should be, and 7:3–7 gives one reason: if there is not the effort to make the physical side what it should be, then the whole marriage can be weakened. Christians need to face these things from the word of God. It tackles things that sometimes we wish it wouldn't. Those first verses of chapter 7 speak very clearly. In our Christian marriages we are sometimes—to make an analogy with dwellings—semi-attached. And if you are semi-attached, you are semi-detached, and it is not right, where God has called two temples of the Holy Spirit to be together, to hold them apart.

Somewhere in Norfolk there are two church buildings within the same churchyard. They were built by two sisters who had fallen out with one another. It's pathetic, tragic, but I think it serves as a small illustration of the point I'm making.

Focus on a Body on a Cross

'You are not your own; you were bought at a price' (6:19). Christian, you know where and when that happened, don't you? It happened when the body of the Son of God hung on a cross. Remember, it could not have happened if He had not been ready to take our human nature, our human body; and on the cross He bought us at a price. And the price was that He was made sin, as we shall be thinking tomorrow evening. That was the price of buying sinful people like us from judgement and death and hell, at the cost of His own life-blood. He called His body His temple (John 2:19). And He was ready for the temple of His body to be destroyed so that we might have life and in turn become the temple of the Holy Spirit.

There is one thing to which I drew your attention earlier when thinking about the Old Testament temple, to which I haven't come back. Perhaps you scarcely noticed it at the time. After Solomon had prayed, the fire of God fell on the sacrifices at the temple. And when finally the fire of God's just anger fell against sin, it fell on Christ on the cross, the final sacrifice of sin; so that when the fire of God falls on us now by the Spirit, it does not destroy us but it purifies, kindles and burns inside us a burning for Christ.

Isn't it remarkable that the Spirit of God can come upon us and make us the temples of the living God—without our being destroyed? But that happens, because the destructive power of the fire of God burnt itself out on Christ on the cross. He was, as it were, burnt up with our sin, but then emerged as victor the other side. We may now burn with love for Him, because His Spirit is within.

Are we ready to let these earthquake-shocks touch us? We are pretty safe from earthquakes in this country. But there are earthquakes for each of us, when we have believed in Christ and realised that our body is the temple of the Spirit. So focus on our God-given bodies; focus on the Holy Spirit who is in us; and focus on a body on a cross. And 'Therefore,' as 1 Corinthians 6 concludes, 'honour God with your body.'

'As for Me and My House'

by Rev Chua Wee Hian

Joshua 24:1–27

Joshua was a superb general. He had led Israel to victory; under him the Israelites had occupied the land of Canaan. He had a brilliant track record. He was a man of faith, courage, integrity, consistency and vision.

At Shechem Joshua gathered the elders, the leaders and officers of Israel to preach to them his farewell message. And he did so in the presence of God. Every time I teach I'm delighted and excited because the Lord Jesus is here by His Spirit. Even if only a hundred people turn up Jesus is there, we always meet in His presence as we do tonight.

But some of you might be thinking, 'Why are you taking us back to Joshua? It was 3,200 years ago. We are living in 1994, at the threshold of the twenty-first century; what's the relevance of the message that Joshua preached so many years ago?'

I love Lesslie Newbigin's definition of history: 'The continuing conversation between the past and the present about the future.' And I believe that tonight God is going to speak to us from the past, to show us the sins His people committed, to reveal to us also the decisions that we have to make. Our church is in a quandary. It's in a desperate state here in Britain. And I believe the greatest sin that's gripping the church is the sin of idolatry, and that you and I need to confess this sin before God Himself this very evening.

175

So I've chosen for my text tonight Joshua 24:15, the words of that great general: 'As for me and my household, we will serve the LORD.'

The Choice is Real

Joshua was addressing real people of flesh and blood. He wasn't speaking to robots. And God is speaking to you and to me today. We are not divinely pre-programmed. God has not pressed a celestial button so that we will respond with an automatic 'Yes, Sir' or 'Yes, God'. We are able to say yes to God or no to Him. The choice is very real.

The Choice is Critical

Israel was standing at the cross-roads of its history. Under Moses and Joshua she had been able to conquer the land of Canaan. There were still enemies to be overcome, there was still land to be possessed and to be settled in, but the big question was, which god will you serve? In other words, Joshua was asking the people: 'On whom will you rely? Who's going to shape your life and your destiny? Who is going to be your king, your supreme sovereign?'

He told them the choice was critical and vital. 'You have a pantheon of deities to select from. You can have the ancestral gods, the gods that your fathers served beyond the River Euphrates, the gods that Abraham's forefathers worshipped. You can have the gods of Egypt, the land where you were once slaves; those household gods like Osiris who control the rising and the ebbing of the waters of the Nile. Gods like the crocodile, the ass, the snake, these gods that you are familiar with—you can choose them. Or the local gods, those of the Amorites—the Canaanites, the Baals, the god of the grain, the god of the rain, the fertility gods symbolised by the image of a potent bull. If you follow the local gods there is no moral demand or expectation—it's free sex, you can engage in sexual orgies; there's no morality.'

Joshua told his people, this choice is critical: 'Whom will you serve?'

He himself had made a firm decision. 'As for me and my household, my family, we will serve the Lord, that's where we stand. And we are flying this banner and we are not ashamed of it. We will serve the Lord.' The choice is so crucial because God in the Ten Commandments said, 'I am the Lord your God, who brought you out of Egypt ... You shall have no other gods besides me' (Exod. 20:2-3). In other words, God says: 'I am exclusively your God.' The Lord Jesus categorically stated, 'No man can serve two masters.' He went on to say, 'You cannot serve God and mammon.' And mammon is the personification of wealth.

Today many of us would say, 'We don't worship or serve these false gods, idols made of wood, stone or metal. Those belong to the people in the rural areas, in the jungles and uncivilised places.' But brothers and sisters, we have our own idols. We are guilty of idolatry. Bishop John Wescott defined idols thus: 'An idol is anything which occupies the place due to God.' In other words, idols are God-substitutes.

If you think seriously about it, many of us are guilty of idolatry. Our gods are rather sophisticated. Mammon, money, is still a powerful deity. Millions—including some Christians—bow before the shrine of the almighty dollar, the Deutschmark, the Swiss franc and the British pound. We want money so that we can have status, power and control over others. Our eyes light up when we see the word 'Sale'. Someone has said that the new dictum of today is 'I shop therefore I am', or 'I consume therefore I am'. But brothers and sisters, the apostle Paul tells us greed and covetousness is idolatry. That's not my assessment, it's what God's word says. Avarice, greed and covetousness are judged by God as idolatry. We drive ourselves to own and possess things. In the end we are owned and possessed and controlled by things, by these God-substitutes. God is saying to us tonight, 'If you want to serve Me, then you will have to renounce and throw away all these false gods.' Tonight the question comes back to us: 'Who are we really serving; the Lord Yahweh, the Great I am, or other gods?'

The Choice is Rational

When God gives us a challenge to either serve Him or to serve other gods, it's not based on our feelings, our sentiments, or even the faith of our forefathers. He gives us facts. And Joshua presented the children of Israel with data, with plain facts. Why choose God, why serve Him, why follow Him? Joshua gives us the answers.

In verses 2–4 Joshua told his people 'We want to follow God because God chose us, He chose Abraham, Isaac and Jacob. He promised them the land, He promised it to the family of Abraham—all the nations of the earth will be blessed, all the families of the earth will bless themselves.' And God had chosen the patriarchs.

In verses 5–7, he went on to say, 'Look at the history of our people.' God chose them, God rescued them from the powers of the Egyptian army, from Pharaoh himself. And then God fought for them. He drove out the Canaanites before the face of these people the Israelites. He gave them land, a good land flowing with milk and honey. And then (verse 10) God blessed them 'again and again'; even when Balaam was sent to curse them, God turned those curses, the intention of Balak and Balaam, into blessing.

Think of the New Testament. God chose us, as we studied today in the letter of Paul to the Ephesians. He chose us before the foundation of this world, He elected us, He predestined us, He chose us by His grace (cf Eph. 1:4). And then God rescued us, 'from the dominion of darkness and brought us into the kingdom of the Son he loves' (Col. 1:13). He has rescued us, freed us from our sin and shame. And God has also provided for us. He keeps on blessing us, keeping us and sustaining us. He has blessed us, as we read this morning, with 'every spiritual blessing in Christ' (Eph. 1:3). We have true riches.

The people of Israel were asked to reflect on their history. God brought them out of Egypt and He also brought them in, into a new land, and made them a nation. Joshua was saying, think of all these things God has done for you: who do you choose?

Think for a moment. If we don't choose God, if we choose other gods, what will happen? If we choose Mammon, as the materialists do, we will be giving over all our lives and energy to earning money; we'll probably develop ulcers in the process, we'll be acting like sharks, biting other people, hurting other people, trampling on their feelings.

And if we have pleasure as our goddess, what will happen? This bubble which seems to shine and glimmer so beautifully bursts before our face. It's empty, it doesn't last, it's never satisfying. And when we follow other gods, what happens? We are still in slavery; we are still addicted; we find ourselves hooked by drugs and becoming slaves to alcohol. And the end of our journey will be death and hell.

That's why this choice is so rational. Do you want a God who saves, protects and loves you, a Lord who promises to be with you all the time? 'Here are the facts, make up your minds,' said God to His people. And He says the same thing to us this evening.

The Choice is Personal

Choose *for yourselves* this day whom you will have to serve, says Joshua. You will have to make a very, very important personal decision and commitment. You have to respond; you can't be neutral, you cannot be a fence-sitter.

Some years ago, during the Vietnamese war in which the great nation of America was embroiled, my prime minister went to Washington DC. He was asked by reporters, 'Mr Lee, what are you? Are you a hawk or a dove?' ('Hawks' were those who favoured the use of military might to end the war, 'Doves' were those who would sue for peace). He thought for a few moments, then being an astute man replied, 'Neither. I'm an owl.' It was a brilliant political judgement. But you and I cannot be spectators; we cannot be owls. We must make a decision either to follow God, to worship and serve Him ('serve' comes fifteen times in this short passage), to devote all our energies to Him—or we'll have to serve other gods. The choice is very personal. And God is saying to us, 'Who will you really serve?'

The Choice is Corporate

But it is not only personal. It affects our family, our community, our church. The poet John Donne was right when he wrote, 'No man is an island, entire of itself.' The Channel Tunnel visibly reminds us that we are part of Europe, there's no going back. And here Joshua says, 'As for me and my house, we will serve the Lord.' Joshua, the head of his family, did not abdicate his responsibility as a leader. 'I've made a decision and my family will have to live by my decision.'

This is the year of the family. Families in this country are going through a bad time. Families have a bad press. I recently read an article entitled 'Betrayed', by Dr Jonathan Sacks, the Chief Rabbi in Britain. He and his wife were walking along Oxford Street and were mugged by six teenagers. They went to the police who merely commiserated with him and told him they could do nothing. The Rabbi wondered about those six well-dressed children who stole from defenceless people. What were their homes like, who are their parents? Society has all kinds of answers. They are deprived because of their upbringing, probably because of capitalism, and they were marginalised; that's why they resort to crime, to earn money ... Then the Chief Rabbi wrote this:

> We have abdicated the teaching of clear and shared moral rules. We have given our children freedom but not guidance, condoms instead of sexual restraint. When they most need us we are not there. We somehow seem as if we care more about threatened wildlife and rain forests than about our own children, whose human environment has been systematically degraded since the sixties ... Whenever the debate about crime turns to family, the argument is dismissed on the grounds that our times have changed. This is a dangerous fallacy. There are matters of which we as individuals have little control. We cannot single-handed reduce the rate of unemployment, bring peace to Bosnia or save the whale, but we can affect the future of our children. Over their lives we have an influence greater than any politician and a greater responsibility. We have brought them into the world, we must not leave them stranded and alone.

Well said. We must take responsibility for our children, for our families. We must start in the church of Jesus Christ, with our own families. It's no good castigating the world, throwing stones at a world with its broken fragmented families. We must put our own house in order. Brothers and sisters, if Jesus is Lord, if He is central in our lives, then He must be the head of our families and of our homes; we must adopt these values and His concerns and life-style.

When our children were very young two of them had a terrible argument; one vowed he would never speak to his brother again. My wife said to him, 'If you don't make it up with your brother Stephen, then you are not following the Lord. In our house we have the values of love and forgiveness. Do you want to follow Jesus, or do you want to follow the devil?' The quarrel was immediately resolved. We must have Christian values. And when she and I quarrel (we preachers are very ordinary human people, we have our fair share of conflicts and battles) our children see us arguing at night but the following morning we can tell them how by God's grace we have received His forgiveness and have forgiven each other. There is security, there is understanding, there is restoration and healing. We must inject these feelings.

When our youngest son was head boy of his school and student representative on the school board of management, there was a scandal in which a lady teacher was involved. One of the tabloids telephoned my son and offered him £100 if he would give them some juicy material. Stephen slammed the phone down, saying, 'No thank you—I would never do that.' He earned our commendation, because it was the right thing to do. And we need under God to teach our children to be people of integrity, to obey God's law.

But, alas, in many of our homes today things have changed so much. When I was a student in England in the 1950s and visited many Christian homes in England and Scotland, the centre of the living room was the hearth, the fire place. There families and friends would sit and chat together. But today the furnishing is changed. The telly-god is in the centre, the video recorder its high priest. I'm told that every European watches three-and-a-half hours of television programmes or video a day; that parents have communication with their children for only two minutes a day. Our values are set by the media, by the pop stars, the sports idols. This telly-god has also broken up relationships between husbands and wives. Many of us Christians have allowed the television and video to control our values, our time and our lives. And God is saying to us today, 'What is your priority? Is it really me? Am I the centre, the Head of your home?'

Consider too the church, the first family of God. Christ is supposed to be its Head. But those of us who are leaders need to ask ourselves, 'Is Jesus really Lord of my congregation? Does He have all the honour, all the glory? Is our supreme ambition His glory, is it His agenda or ours? Are we teaching, equipping, motivating, mobilising our people to serve Him in today's world?'

I know some of us, and I myself need to repent of this sin, look at some cynical modern bishops in the Church of England, we look at some of our mainline churches today and we say, 'There, but for the grace of God, go I.' Our church is so evangelical, so pure, so independent; and we divorce ourselves from the Church that you and I are members of, the body of Christ. But as I look at the prayers of righteous great men of God like Daniel and Nehemiah, I find that they didn't talk about 'those horrible rebellious Israelites'. They prayed, 'We and our fathers have sinned.' You and I need to confess the sins of our church. We have not let God be God. His glory is not our consuming passion. We have let idolatry infiltrate our ranks, weaken and dilute all our values. And brothers and sisters, God's heart is broken. God is grieving over our idolatry and we must repent of it.

The choice is urgent

'Choose for yourselves this day.' I believe that we are here at the decisive moment of God, the *kairos*, when God demands that we respond to Him. The Scripture always tells us: today. 'Today, if you hear his voice, do not harden your hearts' (Psa. 95:8). Moses heard those words from God; the psalmist recorded it, the writer to the Hebrews penned it (Heb. 3 and 4).

Joshua preached for a verdict and I want to preach for a verdict too. You can't procrastinate. God does not guarantee our tomorrow. We can't adopt the Spanish word *mañana* —'by and by, let it come.' We must make our commitment today.

You might say, 'But didn't I make my commitment to follow Christ and serve Him ten, fifteen, twenty years ago?' We need to renew our commitment to Him. Suppose, those of you who are husbands, that your wife asked you, 'Why do you never tell me that you love me? I love to hear those words.' You might reply, 'Oh, you silly woman, didn't I say I loved you when I proposed to you when I married you? Didn't I tell you then? Let's leave it at that.' But our wives wouldn't hear those tender words of assurance, 'I love you'. And I believe that God wants to hear from our lips tonight, 'Lord I love You, I want to follow You, I want to serve You.' At Shechem Joshua renewed his, and their, covenant promise to God Himself, because God is delighted when we declare our love for Him and our desire to follow Him totally.

The Choice is Binding

When the people of Israel heard these stirring words of Joshua, what was their response? 'Yes we want to serve the Lord, we want to follow Him. We will serve the Lord. We won't serve the gods of the Amorites or the gods in the Ur of the Chaldees, we will follow the Lord Yahweh Himself.'

But Joshua challenged them further. 'Are you true to your confession? Is your declaration absolutely correct, do you mean what you say?' He was saying to them that a commitment to follow God was a serious matter. Serving God means obeying Him, fearing Him, adhering to Him, following His law, His word and allowing Him to control and direct our lives. It is a long-term covenant even beyond life itself. It's an eternal bond between God and us. Joshua wanted His people to renew this covenant tie with God, because the covenant is a permanent contract. That's why Joshua reminded them: 'Look this God that you are dealing with is a holy God.' Verse 19: 'You are not able to serve the LORD. He is a holy God.' He is wholly other, He is transcendent. Don't play with God, because He is a consuming fire; you get burnt, you get hurt, so be careful about your commitment and your decision.

He is also a jealous God. He is concerned for His honour. If He loves you and brings you into union with Him, you cannot lust after and pursue other lovers, because God cannot tolerate other rivals and competitors. He wants all our love, affection, time and energy. Commitment to Him is total. So when we want to respond to this covenant we have to renounce these other gods.

Now, it's relatively easy to say, 'I want to follow Yahweh, I want to follow the Lord.' I've been involved in helping people who have been bound by occultism and by Satanism. They were once enslaved and oppressed, terrorised by oppressive spirits. Sometimes they could confess, 'Jesus is Lord.' But whenever I said to them, 'I want you to renounce Satan, I want you to say "I will no longer serve the demonic forces",' very often they choked, they got stuck, they couldn't do it, because the demonic forces would attack them with great ferocity.

That is why Joshua said, 'You've got to repudiate these gods.' We do it in our baptism service; we renounce the world, the flesh and the devil. Do we mean those words? It means we are going to cut all ties with them, they are not going to dominate us, they are not going to control our lives or shake our value system. Before we can enter into this covenant relationship with God we have to forsake every other god. In the words of William Cowper,

> The dearest idol I have known,
> Whate'er that idol be,
> Help me to tear it from Thy throne
> And worship only Thee.[1]

We have to tear all the idols away from our lives and our hearts. And then we can enter into this loving relationship and covenant with the Lord.

In verse 24 there is the wonderful response of the

---

1. William Cowper, 'O for a close walk with Thee' (1769).

Israelites, 'We will serve the Lord.' Yes Joshua, they said: we have counted the cost, we are willing to pay the price. And then Joshua sealed their words, he made a binding contract with them. He recorded the matter in the Book of the Law, and (verse 26), 'he took a large stone and set it up there under the oak near the holy place of the LORD. "See!" he said to all the people, "This stone will be a witness against us. It has heard all the words the LORD has said to us. It will be a witness against you if you are untrue to your God." '— 'You've resolved to follow the Lord, you've made your choice. Wonderful! But remember; this is a solemn moment and this covenant has been recorded.' The stone was a witness. And earlier in verse 22, ' "Yes, we are witnesses," the people replied.'

I believe tonight that as God is speaking to you and to me, He wants a response. What do we do? What do we write in the Book of the Law? I suggest that if God is speaking to you, if you want to follow the Lord Jesus completely, then write today's date alongside Joshua 24:15 in your Bible. Make that covenant with God. For He is still saying to us, 'Choose you yourself this day whom you will serve.' And can you say, 'As for me and my house we will serve the Lord.'?

'Light for the Darkness'

by Rev Clive Calver

1 Kings 17:1–24

Our subject is 'Light in the Darkness', and I want us to recognise the reality of the darkness in the context of the special theme of 'family' that we have here at the Convention this week. Some of the things that I have to say will inevitably not be pleasant. They are not things that I rejoice in saying or want to say, but they are facts of our society, and therefore are things that we need to recognise so that we may pray, to identify so that we may speak out, to be certain of so that we may be part of God's answer to this world in which we live.

A survey taken two years ago of 500 British brides established that only 4% were virgins on their wedding night. The figure for the men was 1%. Also, 1% of the women had already been unfaithful to their partners before marriage, as had 3% of the men. The average wedding day cost £7,300 and 62% of all the couples had lived together before the ceremony, though 86% had a church wedding.

More than a third of Britons would like a ban on the sale of soft-porn magazines. Thirty-four percent of those surveyed wanted them banned—yet they still the invade the top shelves of the average newsagent. I went once to talk on pornography to a Brethren Assembly, and afterwards the Assembly agreed that they would send the elders to examine the top shelves of the town newsagents. After due prayer they did so and found that out of twenty-five shops, twenty-four stocked soft-porn magazines. The twenty-fifth had declined all financial inducements and refused to degrade women in that way. So the elders went back to the Assembly and encouraged the whole membership to transfer their orders for their daily papers to that one newsagent, who was immensely blessed by the sudden rise in trade, so much so that one of the other newsagents immediately adopted the same policy. Righteousness can be worth it!

But we are living in a society where every year, one in ten of the couples who marry will be divorced before their fifth anniversary. Half of the marriages will break up. There are 160,000 children who are innocent victims of divorce every year. Talking about 'family' is difficult in a nation that has lost its family values. And it's fine for the government to say we need to get 'Back to Basics', but no one is sure to what basics they are referring: Victorian social values, Conservative economic policy or biblical basics.

I want this afternoon to call us back to what Scripture has to say about living in darkness. I want to take us back to the society of the ninth century BC. I want to take us in 1 Kings 17 to the land where Elijah lived.

Things go wrong inside the heart of a nation before external factors bring that nation down. That is the story of every fallen empire. And if you go back to the verses immediately before our passage you will discover that Israel had already fallen from within. The latter verses of 1 Kings 16 say so plainly. Ahab the king of Israel 'did more evil in the eyes of the Lord than any of those before him' (1 Ki. 16:30); again in verse 33. He copied Jeroboam first, who led the revolt against Rehoboam the son of King Solomon, who set up Baals at Dan and Bethel for Israel to worship, who taught the worship of idols and fertility to Israel. But we read that Ahab went further than Jeroboam. He married Jezebel, princess of Sidon. In Sidonian her name means 'primrose' or alternatively 'chaste virgin'; in Hebrew it means 'dunghill' which was far more appropriate, because that's the kind of person she was. She pushed her husband and he led Israel into sin. They worshipped the Baal (16:31) and established fertility cults, with all that meant.

Have you noticed how reluctant people are to admit that

Scripture can be relevant today? That's dreadful, in a society where 50% our twenty-year-olds don't even know what happened on Easter Sunday. The relevance of Scripture has gone. And if you ask people today about 1 Kings 16, they will fail to see any relevance. at all.

I want to establish that relevance to you now, but I'm going to be controversial and I ask you in advance to forgive me. What Ahab and Jezebel taught Israel to do was to worship Baal and Asherah. Said like that it's tolerable. But you have to understand what the Baal and Asherah cults were. They were fertility cults, and you worshipped them at the cult shrines of cult prostitutes. The worship of Baal and Asherah was the worship of the penis and the vagina. And that is exactly what we are taught to worship today. It was the worship of sexual activity; the notion that you didn't worship a transcendent living God out there, a living Jehovah, you worshipped what was far closer to home: sexual practice. And that is exactly what goes on in our society today. Chapter 16 is so relevant. It describes our society, one that has deserted the living God and worships its own sexuality. If you don't believe me, turn on your television at six o'clock and watch *Neighbours*. You'll see what the god of our age is actually like. It's the same situation.

Well, we had to look a little at the darkness, and I apologise for that. But let's move to the heart of what I want to share with you this afternoon, which is seven simple statements. I want us to concentrate not primarily on the darkness, but on the light that God shines into it.

Have you ever been to one of those restaurants where they make sure it's very dark so that you can't read the prices on the menu? My job involves visiting the House of Commons frequently. If you eat in the dining rooms there, they don't let you see the prices. The only person who's allowed to is the MP who's paying the bill—that's one of the delights of the experience! But have you noticed, in restaurants where you can't read the prices, that when they bring the menu so you can order the dessert, suddenly you can see, and you realise what an awful thing you've done?

Our eyes become used to the dark. We don't worry any more. It's possible, as people of God, to get used to the darkness, to accept something and say we can't change it, to become virtually immune.

1 Kings 17 starts in this dramatic way: 'Now Elijah the Tishbite, from Tishbe in Gilead, said to Ahab. . .' What God wants is a people who are prepared to stand out from the crowd and be different. That's what the Greek word *hagios*, 'holy', really means: it means 'being different'. And Elijah was different; he stood out in any crowd. His name branded him as different. The name Elijah is a combination of the two main Hebrew words for God: Elohim and Yahweh. 'Elijah' means, 'I am a man who serves the God whose particular name is Jehovah.' His very name said who he was! He was a Tishbite, and Tishbe meant 'pioneer'. He was from Gilead, and Gilead meant 'a rocky place'. So there you have this pioneer from a rocky place who bears the name of God.

Elijah is Prepared to Stand Out

He storms into the royal court. It's reminiscent of John the Baptist going into the wilderness, looking at the Pharisees and saying, 'You bunch of filthy snakes. You need to repent, for there's one coming after me' (cf Matt. 3:7). And Elijah bursts into the court of the king and he bursts out: he's come with a message and he's prepared to stand out in the crowd, to address the king and through him the nation. He doesn't dress up for the task or accommodate himself to the manners of the court. He serves a higher God, a higher Lord, a higher king than Ahab could ever be. He comes to tell Ahab what God has to say.

Brothers and sisters, I believe in this nation there is no hope for our society in any political party. I believe the only hope for this nation is Jesus. I believe the only hope for this nation is that it will listen to the words of Scripture again. I believe the only hope of this nation is that God's people will speak. And therefore it is too late to accommodate ourselves to the nice-sounding, wishy-washy, mealy-mouthed extravagances of accepted institutional religion. It's time we spoke the word of God.

I was asked on Radio 4 a couple of weeks ago whether

Prince Charles should be allowed to be the head of the Church of England 'after what he's done'. My reply went like this: 'It depends on whether you believe the church should be established. If you do, and you believe that the monarch ought to be the head of the church, then you have a question or two when it comes to Prince Charles. But Christianity is about forgiveness and if Charles, whatever he has done, comes to the foot of the cross to a living God, asking for forgiveness, he will receive it from Jesus. And if he wishes to own that Jesus alone is King of kings and Lord of lords, and acknowledge Him as his King and his Lord, then Jesus will be there. And if he is prepared to own that Christianity as opposed to every other faith alone is the worship of the living God and he wants to head a church that worships that God, then that's fine, as far as I am concerned. But anything less than that would be hypocrisy. And I don't believe Charles is a hypocrite.'

You can't be head of a church if you don't believe that church is distinct and different from any other faith. You can't be head of the church if you are still living in sin and not prepared to receive forgiveness. Yet we have a Lord who wants to give forgiveness.

So Elijah wasn't afraid. He went into the courts of the king and spoke the word of God, because he was prepared to stand out from the crowd. And we need people like that today.

Elijah Announces God's judgements

This is not an arbitrary negative statement. He didn't come and give a woolly hellfire-and-damnation address. He was very logical and specific. Verse 1: 'As the LORD, the God of Israel, lives, whom I serve, there will be neither dew nor rain in the next few years except at my word.'

Have you noticed in Scripture how often God, when He wants to punish His people and make them listen to Him, turns the rain off? It wasn't a hard thing for the Lord who made heaven and earth to do in Israel; if you changed the wind direction, the rain stopped. But in Israel it was a much more serious matter than anywhere else in the ancient Near

East. Up in Mesopotamia they had the Tigris and Euphrates rivers, so agriculture could continue. In Egypt they had the Nile, which is why Israel, when she wasn't depending on God and famine struck, had to go down to Egypt. That's why Jacob sent his sons down to Egypt. You might say, 'Well Israel's got a river too—the Jordan.' If you'd ever seen the Jordan you wouldn't say that: it's a dirty little muddy stream in comparison with the great rivers of Mesopotamia and Egypt.

So why didn't God give Israel a great river? Because He wanted to make Israel dependent on His provision, not on water that was there but on water from heaven. And whenever God didn't want to give that water from heaven He turned the wind round and there was no rain. And when there was no rain, people knew that God was displeased with them.

So Elijah was perfectly logical. 'This is what God says: if you want to act like this, I'm going to stop the rain.'

He was also very specific. 'You are going to suffer from famine, you will have your backs against the wall.' Reject God's instructions, go against what God commands and intends, and it's equivalent to the death sentence.

Let me try to explain it in modern day terms. You know how the Press love to accuse evangelicals of believing that AIDS is the judgement of God. I don't believe it, not the way they say it. What they imply is that we say that AIDS is a nasty arbitrary side-swipe from an invective Deity. I don't believe that. I drive a diesel car. If I go to the garage and fill the tank with petrol, it will stop working. Is that God's judgement on me for buying a Renault? Or has it happened because I ignored the maker's handbook? I have treated my car in a way it was never intended to be treated. Is God being nasty to me, or have I been stupid, ignorant and disobedient?

It's exactly the same with AIDS. God made sexuality for people to practise in a loving committed relationship, in the context of marriage, between two people of opposite sexes till death parted them. He didn't make it for any other purpose other than that, and when you don't live in God's world in God's way you mess it up. When you disobey what God intended and you ignore the Maker's handbook the Bible and the Maker's instructions it contains, then you don't get an arbitrary side-swipe from God, you get the logical result of human sin. In one generation gonorrhoea, in another syphilis, in another herpes, and today it's AIDS.

So I don't believe AIDS is a nasty side-swipe from God, I think it's a logical consequence of human disobedience, rebellion and sin. Should we then write people off who are suffering from AIDS? No, we should love them, care for them, tell them about Jesus and provide for them. And the reason we can talk about it is there are more AIDS beds being run in this country by evangelical Christian than any by other grouping, because we are loving the sinner and hating the sin.

Some will say, 'People have also contracted AIDS through blood transfusions.' But that's the awful thing about sin. When sin spreads in society it affects the innocent in the same way as it affects the guilty. And that is the tragedy that results when you do not announce God's judgements. I am tired of people talking about 'safe sex' and how to do it and not do it. It is time we announced God's way of keeping clear and clean in our world. It's time we announced the tenets of Scripture as they are and applied them.

I do not believe the Bible is written just for Christians. If the One we worship is the living God, this is not a book for Christians only. Our society tries to say it is: 'You have your Bible, Hindus have the Bhagavadgita, Moslems have the Qu'ran—choose your scriptures.' But I believe there is one living God who created all things; I believe that He has revealed His will and purpose in His word, and that that word is not relevant to Christians only, it's relevant to the whole of His created order, to the whole of human-kind. And if you don't live in God's world in God's way, you will get it wrong. You'll damage yourselves, probably irreparably. That's why it's time we took Scripture and proclaimed it, not just in our churches but in the market places, in the streets and to the whole of our society; because until people go back to living in God's world in God's way, this land's never going to change. That's the heart of the Christian message. We've got to get back to a Scripture that is relevant to everyone.

Some will say, 'But you can't live biblically unless you've met Jesus.' Yes, that's right, that's what Scripture says—which is why we must proclaim what Scripture says about how to live and then proclaim what Scripture says about the way to live it, which is by surrendering your life to Jesus.

Elijah came announcing God's judgements, 'You've lived this way, so God will turn the rain off.' Why was it so harsh?

If you look back to 1 Kings 16:34 you will find this: 'In Ahab's time, Hiel of Bethel rebuilt Jericho. He laid its foundations at the cost of his firstborn son Abiram, and he set up its gates at the cost of his youngest son Segub, in accordance with the word of the LORD spoken by Joshua son of Nun.' Hiel rebuilt Jericho. When he laid its foundations his oldest son Abiram died. When he put up its gates his second son Segub died. Why? If you read Joshua 6:26, you'll find that God had actually said it would happen. He had given a very simple message: 'At that time Joshua pronounced this solemn oath: "Cursed before the LORD is the man who undertakes to rebuild this city, Jericho: at the cost of his firstborn son will he lay its foundations; at the cost of his youngest will he set up its gates".'

Brothers and sisters, we need Elijahs today to announce God's judgements on society, because if we are not careful our world is going to uncover, bit by bit, what it means to disobey a living God. We need to announce truth because we believe that our Lord alone reigns, because we believe His word is true. It's therefore not only for us. We need to warn our society of what it's doing, of the perils that lie ahead. Why have the things happened to this nation in the last hundred years that have happened to it? Bad government, bad economy—or rejecting God? Circumstances, the Second World War—or rejecting God? Throughout this century we have rejected God. It's time we warned our world that it's time to turn back to Him. I don't want to go Back to the Basics of economic policy or Victorian social justice. I want to go back to the basics of what God's word says, and I want a society that lives that way.

Elijah stormed into the household of the king and said, 'It's not going to rain, because you disobeyed.' You may think I am making too close a connection between 1 Kings 17 and 16. No, I'm not. There are only three parts of the Bible that I do not believe are inspired of God or infallible. They are the maps at the back, the index and the chapter headings (many of which were put in on a French stage-coach 600 years ago; it must have been a very bumpy ride, because some of the chapter headings completely mess up the meaning).

You've got to read 16:34 like this, 'At the cost of his younger son Segub, in accordance with the word of the LORD spoken by Joshua son of Nun.'

And thus Elijah the Tishbite, from Tishbe in Gilead, said to Ahab, 'The logical result of Israel's rejection of God is the judgement of God.' And that too is the logical result of Britain's rejection of God. What is the judgement of God? Paul announces it in Romans, 'I will give them up, I will take away my restraint.' What happens? Sin escalates faster and faster. A worse society for our kids, more violence, more pain, more hurt, more devastation. Brothers and sisters, it's time to announce God's judgements.

Elijah is Supported by Unlikely Methods

God doesn't desert His people in these situations. In verse 4 Elijah is fleeing for his life, in hiding from Jezebel; he spent half his life running from Jezebel. So what does God do? He supports Elijah by unlikely methods. Ravens are sent (verse 4), a refuge is given (verse 3), a widow's support is reluctantly offered (verse 15). It's interesting that the widow was from Sidon where Jezebel came from: not every Sidonian was wicked. Miracles are provided (verse 14). Elijah is called to trust God, and his faith is fulfilled by God's activities. He is not left alone. He is given a new family (verse 9), with the widow of Zarephath.

I love the way that God sends a man to stand out in the crowd and to announce His judgements, and then supports him by such unlikely methods. When you are going out on a limb with God, when you are standing against the tide, He never leaves you alone. He is there with you in comfort and support and grace.

In the old days God sent a prophet, an individual. Today God sends a people, a many-membered corporate bride, His church. Since the death of Jesus, the resurrection of our Lord Christ, He's come to live in the lives of His people to equip us corporately to go and fulfil that ministry that Elijah fulfilled. And He's promised that He'll support us.

Ruth and I have four children. About three years ago we were burgled at six o'clock in the morning, and Ruth's handbag and money were stolen. Later that day our oldest lad was with one of his friends from church on Clapham Common and they had their bikes stolen at knife-point. When I got home from helping the police to look for the bikes (they were not recovered), Ruth was standing by a hole in the study window. She said, 'I've just been shot at.' An airgun pellet had broken the window but had fortunately missed her. We looked at each other and she grinned and said, 'We must be doing something right somewhere.' You don't often get a burglary, a mugging and a shooting in one day.

The great thing is that God protects you. 'But,' you say, 'what about the children?' Oh, the children are rejoicing! You see, Chris lost his mountain bike. But God never owes you anything. A week later a brand new mountain bike arrived from a factory, much better than the one Chris had before, courtesy of the love and grace of a couple of Christian friends who'd found out about it. The children don't suffer. You've got a God who loves you, protects you, cares for you.

We need to pray for those who are on the front line, whether in medicine, teaching, the Civil Service, politics, business or whatever—it's amazing how broad that front line of ministry has become nowadays. But God has placed His people in strategic positions, to tactfully, cogently and carefully announce His will and purpose and His judgement, standing out in the crowd, not as oddities but lovingly and caringly pronouncing His will and He will support His people and care for us. Do we not believe it? So we need to pray for one another.

Elijah Acts in Total Obedience

This whole chapter is a saga of obedience. Verse 5, 'He did what the Lord had told him.' Verse 10, 'So he went to Zarephath.' Verse 15, 'She went away and did as Elijah had told her.' God has asked for a people who will be obedient to Him.

I gave my daughter Vicky a book. She asked me to write in it for her, so I did. She said, 'Dad, why do you always write the same verse in every book you give me?' The verse was John 2:5, 'Do whatever he tells you', the words that Jesus' mother used to the stewards at the feast. You see, I don't think you can go far wrong when you do that. It doesn't matter how stupid it is, it doesn't matter how risky it is, it doesn't matter how dangerous it is—if you do what He tells you. Yes, it's a good thing to check it with those in spiritual authority, and it's always a great thing to do to check it against Scripture; but do what He tells you. Go out on a limb and be obedient.

That's what our society has forgotten. It's forgotten to do what God says. It's developed the idea that each of us makes our own god and our own purpose, that 'It doesn't matter what you believe just so long as you are sincere about it.' I can be sincerely convinced that putting my hand in the fire won't burn me, but it will. There remains right and wrong, there remains truth and falsehood, there remains purity and impurity; and we need to be obedient to Jesus. We need to do what He says, we need to do what Scripture lays out for us. We need to do it with our lives, with our hearts, with our behaviour, with our habits, we need to do what He tells us.

Elijah knew what obedience meant. The widow of Zarephath was going to learn what it meant too, to 'do whatever He tells you'.

Elijah is Prepared to Accept Responsibility

In verse 19 the widow's only son has died. She's turned on the prophet and said, 'It's your fault! How dare you!' And I love the way Elijah says ... what does he say? 'Well, Scripture says not everything goes right for the people of

God'; and the way he excuses himself: 'It's not my fault, you can't blame me' . . .? No he doesn't. There's nothing like that in the text. Elijah says one thing and one thing only. 'Give me the boy. Yes I'm staying in your household, yes you are feeding me, yes I'm part of the family. I don't abdicate my responsibility, give me the boy' (cf verse 19).

I am part of society. I am part of this land. I live in my street. I can't absolve myself of responsibility. For too long the people of God have gone and hidden in their little tin tabernacles and gothic mausoleums and pretended the rest of the world didn't exist. For most of this century we have excused ourselves from thinking we have any responsibility towards our world. Brothers and sisters, Jesus said you are the salt of the earth and the light of the world. Salt in the Middle East was a detergent and a fertiliser. If you and I aren't going to clean up this world and make righteousness grow, who else is going to? Do you honestly believe that New Age has any answers? Do you believe that Buddhism has any answers, or Islam? Ian Coffey has said that so often evangelical Christians live as if they were closet universalists. We live as if we believe that it's all going to be all right in the end.

I believe there is only one way that things will be all right in this nation, and that's when the people of God rise up on the authority of Scripture and proclaim God's word, live God's life in this world and make a difference. You are the only salt and light that this land has any chance of receiving.

Who do you blame for the fact that this land is in darkness? Do you blame sin for being dark, or the light for not shining? It's time we came out, in the right sense of the word, out of our buildings, out of our cosy fellowships, out of the abundance of meetings that we have generated for ourselves. Sometimes we plan a meeting for every night so that we've not time to live anywhere. We need to move out of our confines and into the world, to make a difference.

I'm not suggesting we neglect meeting together 'as some are in the habit of doing' as the writer to the Hebrews warned against (Heb. 10:25). Nor am I suggesting we should neglect prayer or Bible study, nor that we should fail to proclaim the truth from our pulpits. But I am suggesting that we have a mandate to our street, to our neighbour, to our place of business, to our community, to live for Jesus, to let the light shine out of our lives, to demonstrate by the way we live and the kind of people we are who the Lord is that we love and who we serve. That's what will make a difference.

We've lived with words for too long; we have to live lives out there as well. Elijah says, 'Give me the boy. I will take my responsibility.' There are single parents out there who need love. There are kids who've been abused who need care. There are people who are hungry who need food. There are people who are lonely who need company. You say, 'I don't believe it'? One of the latest surveys in the London urban priority area asked non-Christians 'What do you want the church to do?' Of those polled, 84% said, 'We believe the church could give more support for the lonely'; 77% said the church could give more support to the terminally ill; 72% said the church could give more facilities for the elderly; 64% said the church could make a difference in marriage breakdown situations. Don't we believe it?

'Give me the boy.' You say, 'I can't take all that.' That's right! Elijah only asked for one boy. He didn't take the whole community on his shoulders. He did take the one he was responsible for. Ask God what you're responsible for.

You may say, 'It's all right for you preachers.'

Ruth and I asked the Lord who we were responsible for. I preached on this subject some seven or eight years ago from Jeremiah. A girl arrived at our home couple of days later. She stayed for three years. She'd been abused more often as a child than she could remember. She'd tried to love Jesus and she found she couldn't express her love for Jesus. She just kept wandering off with men. She kept hearing sermons, but it didn't make any difference. So we took her into our home—we didn't know what else to do. We let her just see how we lived and be part of our family. The third or fourth night she was living with us, she came into the lounge and sat down with Ruth and me. Then Ruth went to bed and she was left alone with me. The next morning she said to Ruth, 'I don't understand. I was scared stiff last night. Clive was the first guy apart from my father who's ever not tried to assault me.' She stayed with us until she went away to train as a nursery nurse. She'd discovered that you can see more of Jesus, and understand more, than what you understand just by hearing. And I had the great joy of conducting her marriage service a couple of years ago.

There are people who need a home, friendship, love, companionship, support, help, advice, care, compassion. 'Give me the boy.' Lord, which one is it?

Elijah Believes the Impossible

He takes the boy upstairs. He doesn't hold the burden upon himself; it would have crushed him. So he turns it back to God: 'Lord would You do what I've never seen You do, would You bring life to this boy?' There had never been a resurrection in Scripture up to this point. It was the first.

This generation of evangelicals is quite unusual. David Bebbington, the church historian, says that evangelicals have always been distinguished by four things. They are conversionists—they believe in conversion. They are biblicists —they are consistent to biblical doctrine. They are crucicentristic—the cross is at the heart of everything. And they are socially compassionate—they love people. Go back to the nineteenth century. Evangelicals saw the hours and conditions of work for women changed by parliamentary legislation. They saw the hours and conditions of work for children changed by parliamentary legislation. They saw leper colonies built and they staffed them. People like Muller, Barnardo and Spurgeon built orphanages and ran them. They saw child prostitution taken off the streets of London, out of the fashionable West End clubs, through the work of Bramwell Booth with the co-operation of W. T. Stead, the Pall Mall Gazette and others. They were involved in the first employment exchanges which were started by William Booth. They were at the heart of a whole anti-slavery campaign. And four days before he died, Wilberforce finally heard that the campaign had been won and slavery was gone. Evangelical Christianity has never locked itself away. It's always gone into the highways and by-ways and been the faith of the people, because we've taken the message of Jesus and the way we live and the words we say.

I am not trying to make out a case for the 'social gospel'; I believe that social action without the gospel is little more than sanctified humanism. But the gospel without social action is words without deeds; the two must go together. Elijah prays, 'Lord, do what I've never seen You do.' We have seen God working in generations past; let's believe that it can happen again. As one of the writers in *The Sunday Times* said last year, 'Whatever you may think of them, tomorrow belongs to the evangelicals.' Look at the opportunity we have! Look at the world out there to be reached, just look at our streets and our homes! It's all there for us.

Elijah Starts With the Small Things—and Moves On

And the boy comes to life. Elijah takes him downstairs and hands him to his mother. And the woman says, 'Now I know that you are a man of God and the word of the Lord from your mouth is the truth' (verse 24).

Why is that important? Well, in a few days he's going to stand on Carmel and take on 850 prophets of Baal and Asherah. He's going to stand alone and believe that God will answer by fire. And God's going to do it and He's going to win the greatest victory. Why did he have the courage? Because he stood in that little bedroom. He starts not with the big things but with the little ones. You get to Zarephath before Carmel. God starts in the small what later He'll do in the big.

There's a wonderful beginning. Elijah believed he was the only one of God's prophets left (18:22); God had to remind him later that there are 7,000 others (19:18). God is at work. What is light in the darkness? It's the people standing out in the crowd, living holy lives, loving, caring, sharing. It's the people announcing God's judgement to a world that's beginning to get ready to listen. It's a people supported by their Lord in unlikely ways. It's a people acting in obedience. It's a people accepting responsibility. It's a people believing the impossible. It's a people who start with small things and move on to the big ones.

An elderly evangelist wrote to me once. 'Clive, it's better to light a candle than to grumble about the dark.' What's our light meant to be? It's the way we live, it's the people we are, it's the gospel we preach, it's the Lord we share. Not in the context of our churches, but in the world where God's put us. Israel needed to hear, and Britain needs to hear, because we've come right to the brink and time is short and it's time we started to speak again. Evangelical Christians are growing in every denomination right now, because God's people are coming alive and we need to live the truth and be light in the darkness.

'Let your light shine before men, that they may see your good works and praise your Father in heaven' (Matt. 5:16). I want to be light! And the darkness will never win, because when the light shines, the darkness is expelled. Hallelujah!

'Rivers of Living Water'

by Rev Keith White

John 7:37–39

A member of the church of which I'm rector said to me recently, 'Keith, I feel as if my life as a Christian is going nowhere. I think I've hit a spiritual plateau in my experience of God. If the truth be known, I've got into a rut.'

I guess many of us can identify with that. Maybe we look back to the good old days of our spiritual experience; and if the truth be known, they are days of long ago. 'Where is the blessedness I knew, when first I saw the Lord?' wrote Cowper. 'You were running a good race,' says the apostle Paul, 'who cut in on you?' (Gal. 5:7). Or as the risen and exalted Lord says to the church in Ephesus, 'I hold this against you: you have forsaken your first love'—and that means your best, your chief love (Rev. 2:4).

Maybe we've found a niche in our own Christian life and are quite comfortable there. There are many strengths in our position. We are loyal, we show endurance and doctrinal orthodoxy; yet somehow all these things have obscured the one quality without which all these other things are useless. Do we really love God? Do we really love our neighbour as ourselves? 'A new commandment I give you,' says the Lord Jesus. 'As I have loved you, so must you love one another' (John 13:34).

'I feel I'm in a spiritual rut,' said my friend. I guess he's not alone. Christians can get in a rut just like other people, from which it seems there is no escape. We know we are the children of God, but somehow we can't stop acting as slaves. We are trapped by a sense of guilt, futility, inadequacy or sheer boredom. We know in our heads that when we met Jesus Christ He provided purpose and direction for our lives, but Christians aren't immune from this yawning dissatisfaction with what's going on in our own experience.

Add to our disillusionment a sense of guilt, because we know we should know better. I meet many discouraged Christians who share in the kind of emptiness that the world seems to experience. We share in the typical agony of the affluent twentieth century, an affluence that threatens to make us ten times more miserable than poverty ever did. We have all the gadgets, the video, Hi-Fis, microwaves and everything. We have all sorts of things to entertain us and amuse us, and yet there is this enfeebling lack of direction. It robs us of the incentive to do anything, to be someone for the Lord Jesus Christ.

People react to this feeling in all sorts of ways. It's just like the ancient Romans. They knew the feeling. Some of them were great fatalists, involved in adding things to their religion. They practised fortune-telling: 'You can't escape fate, so at least let's try to anticipate it.' And that mixture of religious belief and superstition has never really gone away. Another way out of the rut for the Romans was the games, the amusements, the sports, the theatre, the arena. 'Let's escape for a few hours, even if it's only in our imagination.' Today there's a whole industry exploiting that longing: alcohol, soap-opera, cheap paperbacks. All trying to run away. A fantasy world that's a little less depressing than the real world.

Others face the spiritual rut like the stoics of old. 'That's what life really is all about. So grin and bear it. Keep a stiff upper lip.' We have become complacent in our expectancy. Other Christians face with the spiritual plateau play games, pretending all is well. Adrian Plass tells of a family dragged to church against its will by a mother and father who have been arguing and don't even speak to each other on the way there. They arrive at church, go through the outer doors into what he calls the 'decompression chamber', in through the inner doors of church. Suddenly everything's fine; blessings on everyone, 'Lovely to see you, praise the Lord!'; they go through with what they've got to do. Then out again at the end of the service, through the decompression chamber again, and a reversion to type. Nothing's changed. We play games. We are very skilled at the whole thing. We can use the right words, we've got the right movements, and yet deep down we feel very empty.

Do you remember what Jesus said to the church at Sardis? According to Him they were a full church, a fashionable church and a dead church (cf Rev. 3:1–3). You say, 'Is that possible? To create an illusion of spiritual vitality and yet in reality be nothing more than a spiritual corpse? Jesus said, yes it is. It was so for the whole church in Sardis. Once a busy programme of activities is created, it's quite possible to keep the whole thing going by good organisation. Once the tradition of a lively and well-attended prayer meeting's established, you can continue it by habit. Worship services, once generated, have no difficulty in maintaining an atmosphere of spiritual effervescence simply by means of theatrical techniques and group psychology. It's possible to build a reputation for being alive with nothing more than clever planning, hallowed traditions and emotional froth. It happened at Sardis, and it can happen to us as individual believers. Others may admire your progress in the Christian life, but see how mechanical it's all become. Driven along by a momentum generated way back in the past.

Roy Clements once remarked, 'You can depend more on the lubrication of the minister's management skills than on the oil of the Holy Spirit.' We grind along sufficiently— effectively, even; but without real life.

It's important that we face up to our condition before God. What are we? Weary and heavy-laden? Many of us have come to the Convention feeling like that. And as good as the ministry has been somehow it hasn't made that journey from the head to the heart, to our whole life's experience and knowledge of the living God. We become seduced by the world and its agenda.

Others of us are simply worn out from the battle to which

we've been called. And there are reminders of the reality of that battle. I believe it was Ernest Shackleton, the Polar explorer, who placed the following advertisement: 'Men wanted for hazardous journey. Small wages, bitter cold, long days in complete darkness, constant danger, safe return doubtful.' You will not be surprised to learn, he wasn't inundated with applicants. How empty our churches might be, if we advertised for converts in similar terms!

Don't worry, we haven't. We've done something with the Christian faith that the early church would have scarcely thought possible: we have made it safe. And yet it's an invitation to the most perilous journey the world has ever known, one which makes a trip to the South Pole seem like a Sunday-School outing by comparison. Remember the words of Jesus, 'If anyone would come after me, he must deny himself and take up his cross daily and follow me' (Luke 9:23).

Of course we tame the language by reinterpretation. Self-denial now means giving up sweets for Lent. Carrying your cross means enduring your rheumatism or wearing your fish badge to work. 'If anyone would come after me'—we evade the challenge by applying these words to the spiritual elite. We canonise such people. They look fine in stained-glass windows. We separate them from us mere ordinary Christians; it enables us to admire them from the distance without ever aspiring to their company. Very convenient! But Christianity without a cross is no Christianity at all.

Now, my brothers and sisters in Christ, where do we stand in all this? Where are we on this journey to which Christ calls us? We identify with the gentleman who came to see me. We're stuck in a rut. And we are too familiar with the escapist entertainment outlets. We play games, we pretend that all is well, and yet really inside we feel very different; maybe we feel shell-shocked, suffering from battle fatigue.

Well, if any of these things apply to us (and I guess that in some way or another we can all identify with some of them), these three verses in John's Gospel have a great deal to say to us all. 'If anyone is thirsty'—Richard Baxter said, 'If the verse had said, "If Richard Baxter is thirsty let him come to me", I would have thought He was talking about a different

Richard Baxter. But the truth is He said "If anyone comes". And I know that I'm included. I am that anyone.'

'On the last and greatest day of the Feast'—it was the Feast of Tabernacles. The whole of John 7 is about that feast: Jesus at first declining the invitation to join His disciples at the feast, and then coming on His own. Mid-way through the feast He was there and teaching in the temple. And, as ever, the people were amazed at His knowledge, wisdom and understanding.

The Feast of the Tabernacles was associated with harvest. It had a variety of meanings. It was associated with the wilderness wanderings of the people of God; it was one of the major pilgrimages to Jerusalem after Passover and Pentecost. And then in autumn came the Feast of Tabernacles. The people made little booths—'tabernacles'—and lived in them for a week. They went to the temple each day to watch the priest making sacrifices. And then each day they'd form a procession behind the priest and go down to the Pool of Siloam. The priest would draw out a quantity of water. They'd process solemnly back to the temple and in an elaborate ceremony the priest would pour out the water on the altar. It was a reminder of the water that was struck from the rock, and those wilderness wanderings, and the provision of God for His people. And it began to be associated with a promise of future blessing, associated with the coming of the Spirit of God.

The festival had been going on for a week. Jesus stood up and cried out, 'If a man is thirsty, let him come to me and drink.' He was saying, 'I am the fulfilment of everything this festival is pointing to.' They were doing all that they had been commanded to. But all the elements of the festival pointed to something beyond themselves. The booths to the rough wilderness life, learning to trust God; the sacrificed animals, to the need for repentance, confession and forgiveness through the shed blood of Christ; the water poured out, to the water from the rock.

They did these things, but they failed to see that they pointed to this spiritual reality, that it was possible for the people of God to be brought out of the deadness and the drabness of a wilderness experience and to be brought into an experience of forgiveness through that blood of Christ, and to experience a quality of life that would overflow from within them. It would be so refreshing that their lives would be no longer like the wilderness but like a promised land, a land of brooks and waters, of depths and rivers—fresh and full and beautiful.

The Lord Jesus came that He may bring this fullness of life. I guess the people in Jerusalem had lots of religion, but not that reality. They were in a religious rut—just like us, sometimes, when we are aware that somehow we often miss out on God's very best for us. The problem for us is often that we can't summon up the energy to do anything about it. These words of Jesus are so important for us, in our experience of living in a fallen and demanding world.

Let's look more closely at these verses.

The Condition

First, there is the condition upon which the promise is based. 'If any man is thirsty'—there's the indispensable condition for knowing our need of God. I rejoiced that the man who came to see me had come to see me, because that was the first step to this fullness of life, to these rivers of living water; to acknowledge that we need a touch of God upon our lives.

The greatest obstacle for anybody getting out of this rut is apathy. I realise that there is a vicious circle here, but we need to be praying so that we're thirsty to be thirsty—if you see what I mean. We need to pray that we will know our need. If we're not interested in a more fulfilling and overflowing life, if we're not thirsty, as Jesus puts it, there's nothing He nor anybody else can do.

A lack of thirst manifests itself in all kinds of ways. As we come to worship we hear the word of God. Where is that basic expectation of meeting with the living God? Or is it just to us a series of religious exercises? 'I didn't like the first reading, or the second hymn, or the third chorus, or the preacher . . .' What about that hunger for the living God and His word? How serious are we? Maybe it's fine while we are at Keswick—but what about next week and the week after? How is it going to be with us then?

Sometimes when we do thirst we thirst for the things that He gives, for the peace and the security that He provides, for the gifts and yet somehow not the giver. We need a thirst for the living God. That's the condition. Do you have that insatiable desire to know God better? During Philip's first Bible Reading on Monday, I was struck that Paul prays that the Ephesians may know God better. That's a great prayer to pray for one another.

One of the major problems in the church today is that we don't address ourselves to this hunger for God. We don't cultivate it and pray for it, its heart-desire for God in one another. The reason that we struggle with the promise of these rivers of living water is that we don't fulfil the first condition very often: a heart for God. Do you remember how Jacob wrestled with God? Until God pulled rank on him and dislocated his hip and Jacob realised that God had broken him for a purpose, he wouldn't let go of God. And instead of the old Jacob with the trickery, deception and self-confidence, there came this great desire to gain the blessing that God wanted to give him by faith. 'Lord, You promised to bless. Do it Your way, but do it. I long to know You better, I long for all that You have for me.' And the beads of perspiration on Jacob's brow are not now because he's trying to escape from God, but because he's absolutely determined to receive from God. If anyone is thirsty, thirst for the word of God.

We fill our lives with so many man-centred substitutes. We try to escape the rut, taking our ease and our comfort, looking for entertainment; but the rivers of living water, that quality of life which Jesus promises to His followers, come in response to this condition: 'If anybody thirsts, if anyone thirsts'.

The Invitation

See how the verse continues: 'Let him come to me and drink.' Aren't they astonishing words? If thirsting has to do with our aspirations, then coming to Jesus has to do with our dedication. And Jesus Himself is the key; He Himself provides the answer.

There are plenty of people around who claim to help those who are in a rut to find their way out. There's the guru, who may offer us some techniques in meditation. There's the course of psychotherapy that may or may not help. But Jesus does not offer a pill or a technique or a course of anything, He offers us Himself : 'Come to Me'. He, personally, is the answer to this spiritual drought. Deliverance is not about taking Jesus' advice, it's about taking His hand. It's not about religious piety, it's about a personal encounter. It's not a new recipe, it's a new relationship.

The closest we ever get to meeting our heart's desire, to finding satisfaction in this world, is in relationships—our friends, our husbands, wives, parent, child, the family relationships. We've been thinking of their importance through this week. And we human beings need ultimately to slake our spiritual thirst in our relationship with Jesus Christ, the greatest relationship of all. I don't wonder that our experience seems like a wilderness, if we are looking everywhere else for an answer except coming to Christ.

Do you remember when John the Baptist was with his disciples and Jesus walked by? John had already been saying, 'Look, the Lamb of God, who takes away the sin of the world!' (John 1:29). Now again he said, 'Look, the Lamb of God!' (verse 35). He was pointing people to Jesus. Last night Clive Calver spoke to us about being sign-posts; being like John the Baptist, pointing people away from ourselves to the Lord Jesus.[1]

We've all got different ways of doing it, of course. You know those car window stickers—I once saw a very flashy car with a window–sticker saying: 'What you need is Jesus.' It was absolutely true, though a little bit blunt. I nearly knocked on his window and said, 'I've already got Jesus, what I need is a car like yours'! We've all got different ways of sharing our faith, of being sign-posts. Some use the blunt, bald approach. For others it's a little more quiet, gentle and subtle. We all play a part in pointing people to Jesus.

Those disciples of John the Baptist saw Jesus walking by,

---

1. Rev Clive Claver's address is included in the present volume, p. 186.

and one look was enough to make them dissatisfied with anybody else. So they left John. It is a very poignant moment as John, so far as we know, sees Jesus for the last time with his earthly eyes, and those disciples see Him with their earthly eyes. One look's enough; they follow Jesus.

And Jesus turns round and says to them, 'What do you want?' It's a great question when it comes from Jesus. What a question—what an offer! Remember, John the Baptist's been saying, 'Behold the Lamb of God that takes away the sin of the world.' So we can expect a very profound answer now from the disciples. 'What do you want?' asks Jesus. They respond, 'Can you tell us where you live?' It's a bit of let-down, isn't it? They should have said, 'We'd like our sins taken away,' but they are honest, and that's wise. Jesus said, 'Come, and see.'

'Come, let's walk together,' He said. He could easily have said, 'Go and see.' He might have said, 'If you want to know where I'm staying it's 38 High Street, Bethany—off you go.' But He said 'Come.' He knew they were far more interested in the person than the place.

'If a man is thirsty, let him come.' It's not 'Let him go,' or 'Let him go to a different church,' or 'Let him change his Bible-reading notes,' or 'Let him go to the latest conference and get hold of a new experience.' These things are helpful in their place, but Jesus says, 'Let him come to me.' Is that arrogant? No, it's Jesus. Others point away from themselves to an answer, Jesus points to Himself. We don't need to use the escapist methods that the world devises to cope with this depressing outlook on life. 'Come to me,' He says. 'If anyone is thirsty let him take early retirement?' No. 'Try two holidays a year to escape the rut ... Tune into the latest technology ... Join that never-ending pursuit of satisfaction'? That's not it at all. 'Let him come to me and drink.'

It's possible that we come solely because we're thirsty. People tell us that we should feel better because we've come, and we go away somehow still feeling rather empty and thirsty. It's like being thirsty and going for a drink—and stopping short of drinking. But you have to do more; you have to take the drink and drink it.

There's aspiration in our thirst, and there's dedication in

our coming to Christ, but there's got to be appropriation as well. We take Jesus to ourselves; we receive from Him, we feed upon Him by faith. Verse 38, 'Whoever believes in me'—by faith, 'whoever goes on believing'. We depend upon Him. And of course our Communion Service tomorrow evening is such a climax to our week together, with that wonderful demonstration of feeding on Jesus by faith. So you take hold of Him to the depths of your being.

So there are four key words here about the condition of this promise and our response to the invitation. Come; drink; believe; go on believing. Faith isn't knowing that God can do it. That's not faith, it's knowledge! Faith is believing that He will do it. It is the expectation that He will do what He has said He will do. We need to get used to the idea of expecting the unexpected. God will do it. And when it happens we will say, 'Oh—there's God again, what a great God! He's done it again. There He goes. Isn't that just like Him?'

The Promise

Verse 38: 'Streams of living water will flow from within him.' They 'will'; and that is a promise. Whenever the condition is fulfilled and we're thirsty, whenever we respond to the invitation by coming to Christ and drinking of Him, we rightly claim the promise of God who claimed us.

I asked a lady once what we ought to do with the promises of God. She replied, 'I underline them in red.' Now, here is the promise you can underline so heavily it will go right through to the maps! It's a great promise, a promise of rivers of living water, a picture of sheer exhilaration, of going out on a limb with Jesus Christ on the basis of a promise like this. It's wonderful. It is possible for me, because I am that 'any' person of verse 37, to fulfil the conditions that He stipulates, to claim the promise which He enunciates, and to experience in my life the outflow of rivers of living water.

Of course to the original hearers water was a very meaningful commodity and a basic necessity. I didn't fully appreciate this until I visited Bulawayo and saw their dependence upon water. The people there didn't need reminding that when Jesus spoke as He did about water, He

was speaking about something absolutely basic and fundamental to their human existence.

But Jesus spoke not just about water, but about 'living
water'. He had a habit of telling people that He'd come to
give them real life in all its abundance. His concept of life
was a fullness, a wholeness and completeness. And Jesus
says, 'It is possible for you to have an overflow from within
your life that will touch everything around you, bringing fruit
and development and blessing to others.' Have you ever
claimed that promise? 'Lord, I want to go into the world and
be the source from which unbelievable blessings and benefits
in terms of this fullness of life become available to other
people'—is that our prayer?

He doesn't just talk about living water, He speaks about
'rivers of living water'. Rivers are probably pretty rare in that
land, but there's something fresh and irresistible about them,
communicating life and the power and well-being. Jesus says,
'You go about things My way, and instead of that cold,
correct, dull orthodoxy, instead of being stuck in a spiritual
rut, you're going to have a living exhilarating power. And
wherever you go you'll bring development and life and
fullness of life that will flow from your life. Out of you will
flow rivers.' Rivers, plural; rivers of living water. It's quite a
promise, isn't it; the vitality of Christian living, purifying,
satisfying, exhilarating. I think that we're allowed to be
excited about our Christian faith, about this life that God has
given to us.

Now, it doesn't mean, and I'm not saying it does, that life
all of a sudden becomes very easy. I'm not saying Jesus is the
instant answer to everything, that He solves all our problems,
heals our rheumatism, reconciles every marriage or makes
every bank balance suddenly look a lot more healthy than it
was. Of course not! But He makes a difference, as we come
to Him thirsty, believing.

And He makes a difference to this inner life. 'Streams of
living water flow from within him.' Literally, from the belly,
the seat of our emotions. We still talk about a 'gut reaction'.
That's where these rivers of living water are. He is promising
His followers a spring, rivers of living water, from deep
within them, delivering them from the rut; not by changing

their outward circumstances, but by transforming their inner lives, their inner resources.

The Explanation

Verse 39: 'By this he meant the Spirit, whom those who believed in him were later to receive.' You may say, 'Mr preacher, I think you've got something wrong tonight, because tonight is Thursday and Thursday night at the Keswick Convention is Holy Spirit night, when we focus on the ministry of the Holy Spirit. And you've hardly mentioned the Holy Spirit so far.' I beg to differ. We've been talking about the ministry of the Holy Spirit from the moment we started. This is the explanation of what we've been talking about. What does the Holy Spirit do, but point us to Jesus and glorify and honour Him? That's the explanation of this kind of life in Christ.

A Christian isn't somebody who goes to church, or says their prayers, or believes in God, or wouldn't hurt anybody. Lots of people think that Christianity is a combination of religious performance and good deeds. Jesus came to bring us not a new prayer book or an improved code of ethics, but a new energy, a new power: 'the Spirit whom those who believed in him were later to receive.' The person who has the Spirit of Christ within them, creating these streams of living water from the core of their inner existence—they can't be bored any more. Guilt no longer should burden them, futility no longer saps their drive and their enthusiasm; life for such a person is no longer a meaningless journey to nowhere. There's no more need for escapism, no more excuse for apathy, because the compass needle of our lives, from swinging aimlessly around, has suddenly located its North Pole. From then on every step has direction, every choice has significance. We are out of the rut and on the highway, with the Spirit of Christ the king of the universe directing and controlling in our hearts; the Spirit of God kindling that new life in our souls.

Jesus is glorified through His death, resurrection and ascension, the necessary prelude to the pouring out of the Holy Spirit on the Day of Pentecost. And see what fruit follows: the conditions were fulfilled, they came thirsty to drink and to believe. And there was the promise of rivers of living water as many became followers of Christ and that ongoing truth. They kept coming, thirsting for more, to know God better; coming to Christ and drinking of Him and believing on Him with that expectant faith and claiming His promise. Rivers of living water!

Where's our life really going? Are we really determined to know God, to receive from Him so that we may be a blessing to others?

Here's the final thought. Do you know that old chorus which goes,

> And whoso drinketh, Jesus says,
> Shall never, never thirst again.
> What? Never thirst again?
> No—never thirst again.

That's only half the story; I'm not interested in a Christianity that is simply directive, and never thirsting again. That's fine, but we need to go on. I'm interested in a Christianity that brings me into a relationship with Jesus Christ, into the family of Jesus, so that such an unbelievable fullness of Him overflows that rivers of living water are the result. 'Out of you will flow rivers of living water, into the lives of those around you'—you would expect verse 38 to say, 'Rivers of living water will flow into him.' But it says out 'from' him. It spills out. The love of Christ is shed abroad in our hearts by the Holy Spirit.

What is the effect of that? It ought to be that it spreads outwards into the lives of those around us. What happened on the Day of Pentecost? The Spirit was poured out; that wonderful experience led to the transformation of lives, the love and reality and significance of Jesus Christ taken out into the world. And the lives of the people of God overflowed into the lives of those around them.

So how's it going with you? How is your own relationship with God? Does it resemble this picture of rivers of living water, or is it like trying to fly a kite on a windless day? You know—we are going flat out, we seem to be getting exhausted and if the truth were known we are not getting very far; we need the wind of God the Spirit.

Someone has said it's not churches full of people that we need, it is people full of the Holy Spirit. Perhaps our daily prayer could be, 'Lord, I thirst for this kind of spiritual reality. Don't let the world seduce me into its monotonous, cramping, aimless kind of life. Bring my wayward passions under the control of the Holy Spirit. Lord, provide that strength and that power for life and ministry today. Lord, as I thirst and as I come and as I drink and as I go on believing, I claim this promise: may my life be so full of Your life that it overflows into the lives of those around me. Amen.'

'Living in the Spirit'

by Rev Alex Ross

Romans 8

When anybody comes to stay in our house, life always changes. The jam tends to appear in a nice bowl instead of in the jam jar, and our conversation is little bit more polite round the meal table. I think the quality of the meals goes up as well, so I always love it when visitors come to stay. Tonight we are going to see some of the changes that God brings to our lives when He comes to live within us. Real changes take place.

Let me give you an introduction to Romans 8. The first four verses are really the summary of the first seven chapters, which are all about what Jesus Christ has done for us; why we are Christians and why it is possible to know God. In verses 5–17 we are told what the Holy Spirit is actually doing in our lives as His people, and the difference it makes. Sometimes we forget what a great privilege it is to have God within. It's an amazing thing, isn't it, that God by His Spirit will come and live in sinful people like you and me.

I'm staying in a room with a wonderful view of the hills. But I know that after a couple of weeks I wouldn't even notice it any more. Life is like that; when we are privileged and have something that is really special, we become blasé and take it for granted. It often happens to us as Christians; we just forget how great it is to be a Christian, how wonderful it is that God will live within us. There was an old

Smarties sweets advert where the Smartie kids used to say, 'What a lot we got!' And as we go through these verses in Romans 8, I think we are going to see 'what a lot we got' as Christians.

I'd like you to notice seven blessings that we have because the Spirit of God lives in our lives; seven new things that God has done for us as Christians.

A New Mindset (verses 5–8)

People talk about having their 'minds set' on things. Some people have their minds set on getting a degree, some have their minds set on a new job, some have their minds set on a new home. Paul in verse 5 talks about two mind-sets in the world: 'Those who live according to the sinful nature have their minds set on what that nature desires; but those who live in accordance with the Spirit have their minds set on what the Spirit desires.' Our minds are either set on the sinful nature, or on the Spirit.

Paul is very negative about the mind that is set on the sinful nature—that is, our lower nature, or the flesh. Verse 6 tells us that the mind set in that direction has no future; verse 7, that the mind that is set in that direction is hostile to God; verse 8, that that person cannot please God. So it's a very depressing, bleak picture for the mind that is set on its own ideas, paths and ambitions. The future is death and hostility with God, and we are displeasing to Him.

Paul is doing this because he wants to contrast it with the mind that is set on the Spirit. Look at the second half of verse 5: 'But those who live in accordance with the Spirit have their minds set on what the Spirit desires.' Paul always sees the importance of the mind. He is going to talk about that later in Romans 12:2. And I think we have a problem today with this part of Paul's teaching, because we live in a society where people judge things far more by what they feel. Philosophers call it an existential society; we feel something is all right, or we feel the meeting's good, or we feel things are not quite right. That's why a lot of Christian books are about experience and about feelings; it's the culture in which we live.

Os Guinness says of the book of Romans that it would be turned down by most Christian publishers today, because it's too intellectual. He goes on to say that 'most Christians would rather die than think, and in fact most do.' But the person who is filled with the Holy Spirit is someone who thinks. That's what the second half of verse 5 means. The person filled with the Spirit is thinking 'What does the Holy Spirit desire?' This is the principle of the Spirit-filled Christian.

It's not that Paul is against feelings. He talks a lot about them; love and joy and peace, these are the fruit of the Spirit. But, he says, set our minds on the Spirit, not our feelings. And as we set our minds on the desires of the Spirit, so our feelings are altered. That seems to be how Paul is thinking. Let me illustrate this.

A doctor was on his ward round, and he came to a patient who was also a doctor. He asked him, 'And how are you feeling today?' The patient replied, 'I know this may cause offence—but it's not my job to tell you how I feel, it's your job to tell me how I am.' So the doctor checked the patient's chart and saw that temperature, heart, and appetite were all fine. So he said, 'By the look of this, you're doing well.' The patient said, 'Thanks very much. I feel fine.'

That is what Paul is trying to tell us here about the Holy Spirit. When we have our minds set on the Holy Spirit, and when we see what the Spirit desires, we begin to feel fine. How do we know what the Holy Spirit desires? Well, it's all in the Bible, and when we start reading the Bible we start to feel fine, don't we? Because it begins to explain about life, it begins to show us why things have gone wrong, it begins to show us that God loves us, that Jesus Christ died for us, that Jesus Christ rose again, that Jesus Christ is going to return, that God gives us the Holy Spirit in our lives. Once we hear those things we begin to feel very well, and we begin to know peace and joy. So this is the first great blessing of having the Spirit of God in our lives: we have our minds set on the Spirit. This is what the Holy Spirit does. He sets us on His desires.

A New Person in Control (verses 9–11)

You may think this is a rather presumptuous title, but isn't this what Paul is saying in verse 9? 'You, however, are controlled not by the sinful nature but by the Spirit, if the Spirit of God lives in you. And if anyone does not have the Spirit of Christ, he does not belong to Christ.'

If we're honest, for much of the time we don't feel as if we are controlled by the Spirit. So what does Paul mean in verse 9? Were these Christians in Rome an outstanding lot, in a class of their own? Well—if you look again in verse 9 you'll see there that Paul says that all Christians have the Holy Spirit, and if anyone does not have the Spirit of Christ he does not belong to Christ. So there are no first-class and second-class Christians in regard to the Spirit. All who belong to Jesus have the Spirit.

Notice too how the Holy Spirit is described in verse 9. He's referred to as the Spirit, the Spirit of God, the Spirit of Christ; three different titles, all interchangeable, all referring to different members of the Trinity. So it's not surprising, when you consider the titles of the Spirit here, that Paul says we are under the control of the Spirit. The Spirit of God, the Spirit who created the universe, these marvellous mountains, lives within us. The Spirit who led Israel through the desert is within us. And the Spirit of Christ, Christ who fed the five thousand, who brought people back from the dead, who died on the cross and came back to life three days later—this is the Spirit within us. You'd expect Him to be in control, wouldn't you! It would be very odd if He weren't.

Notice that the Spirit doesn't take us over and possess us. That's what happens with the occult; evil spirits possess people. So what does Paul mean here? He means that the process of salvation is begun, not completed. But a definite and decisive transfer has taken place. There is now a new allegiance, we have a new owner, we have God living in our lives. That's the difference. We haven't arrived yet, we are in that in-between stage—but we are under the control of the Spirit.

There are two consequences for us. Verse 10: 'But if Christ is in you, your body is dead because of sin, yet your spirit is alive because of righteousness.' So our bodies haven't changed, we've still got the old problems, we've still got arthritis and we still can't see properly or hear properly. But your spirit has become alive because the Holy Spirit has given us new life, we've been born again.

Then in verse 11, 'And if the Spirit of him who raised Jesus from the dead is living in you, he who raised Christ from the dead will also give life to your mortal bodies through his Spirit, who lives in you.' So even if we die, even though our bodies are dead, we've got new bodies on the way; we are going to have resurrection bodies. And this is not just a nice religious idea, for what does Paul do in verse 11? He points us back to the resurrection of Jesus Christ. He says the Spirit of Jesus, who was brought back to life again, is the Spirit who lives within us. And because we also have the Spirit, the same thing is going to happen to us.

It isn't a pious or religious idea; it happened in history. That's why the historical resurrection is so important. It shows that one day we are going to have resurrection bodies. If Jesus hasn't been brought back from the dead, how can we be sure we're going to be? But the Holy Spirit who brought Christ back is the same Spirit who lives within us. The change has begun, we are under new ownership.

I suppose it's a little like the day after a general election, when a new government has been brought into power. If the Tories had won you wouldn't suddenly find next day that all the buses had been painted blue, or that after every news bulletin we had 'Land of Hope and Glory'. The changes happen slowly. And so it is with the Holy Spirit. We have a new government, a new control in our lives, the Spirit of God: but we haven't arrived. William Temple put it like this:

> It's no good giving me a play like Hamlet or King Lear and telling me to write a play like that. Shakespeare could do it, I can't. And it is no good showing me a life like the life of Jesus and telling me to live a life like that. Jesus could do it, I can't. But if the genius of Shakespeare could come and live in me then I could write plays like that, and if the Spirit of Jesus could come and live in me, I could live a life like that.

Isn't that what verse 10 is saying? That actually we have the

Spirit of God living within us, and so we can begin to live righteous lives? God is in charge.

A New Obligation (verses 12–13)

If God has taken control of our lives, these next verses make a lot of sense. Paul does not presume that automatically we are living by the Spirit. He knows we are not like that. The Bible is always realistic, it recognises that we are fundamentally flawed. We are rebels in our hearts, we are proud, disobedient and dishonest. That's why Paul says in verse 13, 'If by the Spirit you put to death the misdeeds of the body, you will live.' If you want the technical word, it's 'mortification', a putting to death by the Spirit of the evil things in our lives. It's a ruthless rejection of all that is wrong, a daily repentance, a turning from our sins.

Now Jesus was very straight about this; He talked about the same kind of thing. 'If your right eye causes you to sin, gouge it out and throw it away. . . . If your right hand causes you to sin, cut it off and throw it away' (Matt. 5:29–30). As Christians we have an obligation not to play around with sin in our lives. If we belong to Jesus, if God is living in our lives, we are holy people and sin must not be allowed. We have to be hard with ourselves. But how do we do it? Verse 13 tells us: 'But if by the Spirit you put to death the misdeeds of the body, you will live.' We are not doing this in our own strength, gritting our teeth and saying 'Yes I am going to be a better person.' It is by the power of the Spirit, it is God living within our lives. It's not some kind of external law, it's not conforming to some particular tradition, not trying to live a better life. All that happens when we try to do that is we acquire some veneer of respectability. And that's been a curse of the church through history, when people have tried to be outwardly good.

No. Paul is saying, 'It's something that happens internally, in our hearts by the Holy Spirit.' Martin Luther warned against trying to do it externally. 'Worldly reform is like a drunken peasant trying to get on a donkey. He climbs up on one side and falls off the other.' It never works. There has to be something going on in our hearts.

In the back garden of our new house there's a rather nice vine on the back wall. We haven't been there long enough to see what kind of grapes it produces, so we're looking forward to autumn. But I can walk round this vine, I can dig it, I can talk to it, I can even lay hands on it. It's not going to have any real effect on the grapes in the autumn unless something's happening inside. That is always the Christian way. It is always inside out. The great danger in the church is that actually we have it outside-in. That was the problem with the Pharisees—they were white-washed walls, God hadn't affected their hearts. We have an obligation to live by the Spirit, but it's an internal change, it's as we open ourselves to God that the change happens.

Billy Graham tells the story of a fisherman who used to come into town up in Alaska every week with a black dog and a white one. They would fight to order, and people placed bets on which would win. The only person who always won was the fisherman. Eventually his friends asked, 'How on earth do you predict which dog is going to win?' He replied, 'In the week before, if I feed the white one, that will win because it's stronger; but if I starve the white one it'll lose, because it's weaker.'

That is what Paul is talking about. He's talking about weakening the sinful nature, not allowing it to have any strength, denying it access, denying it any kind of food. So by the Spirit we need to learn to get rid of things that are wrong. Maybe something on the television corrupts us; we need, by the Spirit's power, to switch that little knob off. We need to watch what we are reading. Relationships—they can corrupt as well; by the power of the Spirit you must get rid of those relationships. This is what Paul is talking about; putting to death things that are wrong. With God's help we can do it. We have an obligation to. If God is in our lives we need to do it, we want to do it. It's a marvellous obligation to have; to start dealing with sin.

A New Family (verses 14–15)

Now Paul here is negative and positive. Negatively, he is saying, 'You did not receive a Spirit that makes you a slave again to fear.' What fear is Paul talking about? I think he's talking about the fear that some people have about their relationship with their family. Do my family really love me? Am I really appreciated? Am I really accepted? Are my parents really pleased with me? Is the family going to survive?

Some of you may have fears like that about your family. You may have no real security, no real acceptance. You may have been badly let down by your families. Rose Tremaine put it like this: 'The people who are precious to us can suddenly vanish from our lives, they can die, they can leave us.' I think many of us know that kind of fear, the way our families let us down either through death or through casting us aside.

These are some of the fears that Paul is talking about. Interestingly, they are the same kind of fears as those of man-made religion. Can I please God? Am I good enough for God? Can I pray enough? Will I get to heaven? Will I survive as a Christian? What do other people think? Paul says, the Christian family isn't like that. Christianity isn't like that. Verse 14: 'Because those who are led by the Spirit of God are sons of God'; verse 15: 'But you received the Spirit of sonship.' That's where we are as Christians.

The footnote in the NIV refers to the Spirit of adoption. We have been brought into a new family, we have been adopted. This is a completely new family, so if we've been let down in our earthly families, don't worry. That was the old family, you now have a new one. Adoption was a very serious issue in the first century, because if you were adopted you were brought into this new family, and as far as your new father was concerned you never came of age, you lost all the rights of the old family, you became an equal heir with all the other children, you became a new person, all your debts were wiped out. You became absolutely a child of your new father. This law was so binding in the Roman world that the senate had to alter it because the Emperor Claudius had adopted Nero and he wanted him to succeed as emperor. But Nero wanted to marry Octavius, who was also his sister because of his adoption. They weren't related biologically, but they couldn't marry, so the Roman senate had to re-write the law.

This is what Paul has in mind. We really are securely in

the family of God. We are not second-rate, we are not second-best, we have all the security of what it means to be totally and completely in God's family.

John Wesley put it like this: 'I have exchanged the faith of a servant for the faith of a son.' That's great news for us, living in a society where family life is disintegrating. Now we come into the family of God; there's no spirit of fear here, we really are the children of God, totally secure.

A New Intimacy (verse 15)

Another privilege of being in God's family is that we can talk to God in this personal way. A Jew told me that they still use the Aramaic word Abba in Hebrew-speaking families. And just as in the first century, it is considered very impudent and irreverent to talk to God like that. You know, of course, that there is in some churches a debate about whether we can describe God as 'Father' any more, or whether that is cultural conditioning and perhaps God should be called 'Mother'. But it was so shocking for the New Testament writers to see Jesus calling God Abba, 'Father', that they didn't even translate it. This wasn't something that was culturally relevant at all; it was a completely new idea, that you could call God in such an intimate way. It does sound cheeky, but this is what Jesus was able to do. And because Jesus was able to do it, we can do it as well. The nearest we've got in our language is the word 'Daddy'. To call the God of the universe 'Daddy, Father'! We wouldn't dare to write verse 15, it sounds over-familiar. But it's there, and it's there for us to enjoy.

C. S. Lewis said,

> To put ourselves thus on a personal footing with God could, in itself and without warrant, be nothing but presumption . . . but we are taught it is not, that it is God who gives us that footing.

You see, we are not claiming it for ourselves. This was something Jesus did and something that is given to us through the Holy Spirit; it is part of the privilege of being in the family of God. So it doesn't matter what experience you've had of your own father; when you come into the family of God suddenly it's very different.

Martin Luther was a man who suffered. He put it like this:

Although I be oppressed with anguish and terror on every side and seem to be forsaken and utterly cast away from your presence, yet I am your child and you are my Father.

And isn't that little word Abba one of the greatest privileges we can ever have this side of heaven? To be able to go to bed at night and say, 'Abba, Father' to the God of the farthest galaxy, to the God who has all power and authority, yet we in this very intimate way can come and call Him 'Abba, Father'. That's the privilege of having the Spirit of God in our lives, of having God within.

A New Certainty (verse 16)

Sometimes Christians are accused of being dogmatic, arrogant and too confident. People can't understand why it is we are so sure of what it is we believe and what it is we are saying. How can we be so confident? Verse 16 gives us the answer: it is the Spirit of God witnessing with our spirit, this quiet assurance.

Doesn't it happen when we pray? The early morning prayer meetings have been one of the great joys for me over these last few days, because there has been the certainty that here we are talking to the God who is in charge of history and what's going on around our world, and that He actually hears and listens to us.

Why can we believe such a thing? It's very strange for over a hundred people to be sitting talking into thin air, but I don't think there's the slightest thought in the minds of any of us that what we are doing is crazy. Why? It's the Holy Spirit inside, witnessing with our Spirit that we actually are talking to God, that we really are talking to our Heavenly Father. That's what Paul is saying. This certainty of prayer, the certainty of believing that our sins are forgiven—this inner witness is one of the best things in the world.

I went to see the D-Day exhibition on the Isle of Wight, where I learned about the PLUTO project—the Pipeline Under the Ocean. It had never crossed my mind that when the British landed in Northern France they would need fuel to keep them going. A million gallons a day went through those pipelines to sustain the British army.

And that is what the Holy Spirit is in our lives. He enables us to feel secure in an alien world, to be able to stand firm in hostile territory. This is God's supply line, so that we know with certainty. We know where we've come from, we know who we are talking to and we know where we are going. That's true, we believe those things. We believe God is the Creator, we look back to the cross and we believe God died for us in His Son Jesus Christ; we look up and we believe Jesus Christ is Lord, and we look ahead to the final day when Jesus Christ is coming again. Why do we believe that? It's nothing to do with us. We haven't worked it out naturally, it's God's Spirit within us, giving us that inner witness that this is true.

Isn't that what keeps us going as Christians? It's not the church or our energy that keeps us going. These things will let us down. The reason we survive as Christians is this truth, that we believe that Jesus Christ is Lord, that He's given us His Spirit, that He's coming back to receive us.

A New Inheritance (verse 17)

We now see the full extent of our privileges of being in the family of God. Not only are we His children, we are actually 'co-heirs with Christ'. All that belongs to Jesus belongs to us; that's the only way I understand 'co-heir'. And what belongs to Christ? Everything. In Christ, everything belongs to us.

A friend of mine was in central London with a very rich young man who said to him, 'You see that tower block over there? My father owns that.'

My Christian friend replied, 'You see the Tower of London there, and you see Canary Wharf over there, you see your father's tower block? In fact everything you can see? My Father owns the whole lot.' That's true! We are co-heirs with Christ. God owns the whole lot. I really do believe that.

I believe that's where we're moving to. That, ladies and gentlemen, is totally true for all Christians.

That's what verse 17 tells us: we are going to share in the future glory; when this world is handed back to its Creator, we will be there with the Lord, because we are co-heirs with Christ.

But Paul does give us an important reminder in the second half of verse 17: '. . . if indeed we share in his sufferings in order that we may also share in his glory.' And Paul goes on in the rest of the chapter to talk about the suffering and the pain of living in this world. We are not on a Rolls-Royce trip to heaven. The King's kids don't go first class. Jesus never lived a life like that, the early church never experienced that, Christians around the world don't experience that. Christians have been some of the most poor and insignificant people.

I read a profile on Romario, the Brazilian footballer. This is how he was described.

> You're held up in Rio de Janeiro traffic. Suddenly he's all over your bonnet. The windscreen is a blur. Then you see his face, the face of a street urchin who isn't going to go away with his sponge until you pay. To him and his family this is no street game, it is the bread of life. Many years later you meet again, only this time Romario . . . is a millionaire who could buy all the bakeries, indeed all the homes, he likes.

That's where we are at the moment. We are the urchins of this world, but with Christ we have a fantastic future. We are heirs of God and co-heirs with Christ.

Now, as you've listened to these verses tonight and seen these seven great blessings we have because the Holy Spirit is within our lives, you may think, 'I don't feel as if I'm in Romans yet. I don't feel as if these blessings are a part of me. I don't have the intimacy of God the Father that I'd like to have. I don't sense that I'm a co-heir. I don't have that inner certainty that Jesus Christ is Lord. And I don't feel I'm under the control of the Holy Spirit.'

But I may say that over these last few days I've loved living in Romans 8. I've found it really hard work and difficult, but it's given me a great joy and a great sense of peace. As these truths have soaked into my mind and into my life, I've sensed that there's some great healthy food here. And what I want to suggest to you is that you take time out and regularly through the day go and read Romans 8:5–17. Pray about those seven blessings and make them a reality in your own life, because this is what we have in Christ, this is what we have when we have the Holy Spirit in our lives.

It's a fantastic thing, isn't it, that God will live in me? And not only will God live in me, He'll change me. And He's changing all of us, and He's going to make us all ready for that great and final day, when we are caught up with Christ in that moment of glory.

'The Lord ... and no other'

by Mr Dick Dowsett

Isaiah 45:18–25
(World View Meeting)

You know of course that the favourite missionary text from
Isaiah is chapter 6. That was really the beginning of it all for
Isaiah, when he learned what it was to bow before the Lord
in all His glory, when he saw Him for what He was in His
utter majesty; when he saw himself in all his messiness and
all his inability to contribute anything to his own salvation, or
for that matter to anybody else's—he was a person whose
conversation showed that he knew of his lostness before the
Lord. It was the time when Isaiah knew what it was to offer
himself to God to be mobilised—'Here am I, please may I
go' (cf 6:8). And it was the time when he learnt to submit,
not simply to give it a go as a bit of a hobby 'as long as they
welcome me', but to submit to God's job description, to go to
a stubborn and unresponsive people and stick at it as God
required, until there were no more people left in the houses.

In our passage tonight Isaiah conveys a message to God's
people to bring them to be what the people of God have
always been meant to be: a source of blessing for the nations,
from that first of the elect, Abraham: 'through your offspring
all nations on earth will be blessed' (Gen. 22:18). And it
remains in Isaiah the calling of the people of God, and it
remains today the calling of the people of God.

229

There are five great facts in this passage that call for our submission, if we take seriously those opening words, 'For this is what the LORD says'. It is not told us as an interesting discussion topic. It is put over as the viewpoint of the only One who really knows what He's talking about, the One who has the claim on our lives, our thinking, our ambitions and our goals.

God is the Creator of the Heavens and the Earth

Verse 18 shows us something of the beautiful world-wide witness of creation. God created the heavens, He fashioned and made the earth. It's not a fluke. It is such a beautiful evening this evening; you can look at the hills and the sky and the way the light strikes things and think, 'I could stay here for ever . . .' Then somebody whispers in your ear, 'Isn't it an extraordinary fluke, that it happened like this?' And you reply, 'Pull the other one! Everything shouts out that it's made by a lovely, beautiful Designer and Creator!'

It doesn't matter where you are. I live in Glasgow which is not the most beautiful place on earth, but there are so many things that you can see there at which you look and think, 'Just by chance? No!' I went to Manila; that's not the most beautiful place on earth either. I will never forget my little two-year-old son running to the window and calling out 'Mummy, come quickly! The Lord Jesus is painting a beautiful sky!' You could say that it's nothing to do with the Lord Jesus, that it's caused by the pollution there is in Manila. But it isn't, is it? And I remember years ago, when I was a student, hearing about a Russian sculptor. Everybody was telling him, 'It's all a fluke, there's nobody there.' He just looked at his thumb for a long time and then he said, 'No, it isn't just a fluke. There's an amazing Designer.'

We need to understand this. When Paul went to Athens they had gods by the dozen, they even had altars to gods of whose existence they had no knowledge, but it was best to make sure. And what did the apostle Paul proclaim to them? That there is a Creator in whom everything makes sense, for, 'The God who made the world and everything in it is the Lord of heaven and earth.' Then he turned to these pagan polytheistic Athenians and said, 'In him we live and move and have our being' (Acts 17:24,28). We see the beautiful witness of creation all over the world, we proclaim it.

But Isaiah also tells us that people are an integral part of God's plan; they are not an accident. 'He did not create [the earth] to be empty, but formed it to be inhabited.' And Paul said to the Athenians, 'From one person he made every nation of men, that they should inhabit the whole earth; and he determined the time set for them and the exact places where they should live. God did this so that men would seek him and perhaps reach out for him and find him' (Acts 17:26–27).

What an amazing thing to say to the Athenians! 'You're in Athens because God the Creator wanted you here, not because He's just dotting people around on a draughts board, but because wherever He sets people in those places, His longing is that they should reach out to Him and find Him.' I found it so moving preaching that verse in a Japanese city, and some of the Japanese Christians saying to me afterwards, 'That's amazing—God is involved in Japanese cities.' God wants, and made, those Japanese people. And God longs that 120,000,000 of them who don't know Him might feel after Him and find Him. God neither wanted nor made an empty world. He didn't want a void. He made this place because He wanted people. And because our God is a people-oriented God, He cries out in verse 22, 'Turn to me and be saved, all you ends of the earth.' He wants people.

There is only one who makes sense of our world and of human life, says Isaiah: the Lord. 'I am the Lord, there is no other,' he says. Once I was flying into Tokyo and watching the video they were showing on the plane. Suddenly I heard the throw-away line, 'Japan's eight million gods are never far from the minds of her people.' No, says Isaiah, they are not remotely going in the same direction as us, as so many British people high and low seem to believe. There is One who makes sense of it all. There is one Creator and He holds it all together.

Have you noticed how important this is? People will say to you today, 'This missionary concept, taking the gospel to all sorts of people, is an unwarranted intrusion.' Did you see the television programme about Papua New Guinea and the people there who practised the most frightening form of sodomy and child abuse? Then the presenter said, 'Missionaries came; a Western intrusion.' Since then, they said cynically, they have had a case where a fellow raped a girl. But what they are really saying is: 'These missionaries—what right have they got to intrude?'

Now look at what Isaiah says: there is only one Creator. In Colossians 1 you find these beautiful words: 'For by him all things were created: things in heaven and on earth, visible and invisible, whether thrones or powers or rulers or authorities; all things were created by him and for him. He is before all things, and in him all things hold together' (Col. 1:16–17). There is only one Creator, and when we read Colossians we know his name: it is Jesus in whom everything holds together, who is involved in creation, and it is all for Him. People say to you and me, 'What right do you have to interfere?' Our answer is, 'I have no right whatsoever, but He does; and He has the right to send messengers.'

God Has Spoken and It Makes Sense

In verse 19 we are told that God has spoken and it makes sense. Look at the lovely thing he says here: there is a reliable and a clear word from the Creator. 'I, the LORD, speak the truth; I declare what is right.' It really means, 'I declare what's plain as a pike-staff'; God says, 'I give you truth that's plain.'

In India once I met a man who in his search for a god had committed himself to snake-worship; and he was getting nowhere. He'd wondered if the Christian Bible might have an answer. He couldn't find one Bible but eventually he found some extracts from the Bible in a Hindu tract opposing Christianity. 'They must have a Bible in the temple,' he realised. He went there and found a Bible and began reading at Genesis 1. Does that make your heart sink? It needn't. He told me, 'I started to read Genesis and I knew it was the word of God and it made sense to me.'

I know that there are difficult passages in the Bible. But you can go to this book and find answers in it that are plain and clear for those who will go to it. I remember a bright medic in our church saying, 'I have just discovered something absolutely wonderful! I want you to read it for yourself. It's in John chapter 3 and verse 16.' It's plain, isn't it? It's beautiful, it's wonderfully clear.

So, God says, His answers are not hidden away. Ours is not a God of hide-and-seek. He doesn't say, 'Well, I'm here somewhere, and good luck to you if you find Me out.' He says, 'I have not spoken in secret, from somewhere in a land of darkness' (verse 19). Perhaps Isaiah was thinking—or God was thinking through Isaiah—of the darkness and the secrecy of so many initiation rights, and so-called revelations through spirit powers and so on. But He says quite clearly here, 'I'm not playing hide-and-seek with human kind.'

It's very important to see what He is and isn't saying here. He is not saying that anybody can see God's answers anywhere. He is saying something rather different: 'I have not said to Jacob's descendants, "Seek me in vain." '. In other words this passage makes it clear that God's truth was mediated to all the ends of the earth through Jacob's descendants. To translate that into modern terms: if you want to find the plain right answers about the God who longs for all the world to come to Him, you've got to look in a plainly stated Jewish book; and I have it here in my hand and you have it in yours. God says, 'That is where I revealed Myself for a lost world.'

But I want you to see also in verse 19 that God spoke plainly because He wanted people to find Him. It is not His purpose that people should search in a futile way. His purpose, as we have already seen in Acts 17:27, was that people might seek Him and perhaps reach out for Him and find Him. Our God is a seeking God, as the Lord Jesus said to that mixed-up Samaritan woman in John 4. He is actively on the look-out for worshippers, He is moving out and wanting them. And so it says here, 'I have not said to Jacob's descendants "Seek me in vain." '.

I have a problem here that I can't answer. There is a people group with whom some friends of mine are working in the Philippines. Three hundred years ago they had a prophecy that someone was going to come with the right answer. Three hundred years later somebody came. Why did it take so long? It's a problem to me. But as I look at these verses I seem to hear God saying, 'Don't blame Me. I didn't hide it.' But it was hidden.

Without God's Truth People are Hopelessly Ignorant

Verse 20 is a frightening verse. I want you to see first of all how it teaches us—and it follows on from chapter 44—that man-made religion can't save: 'Ignorant are those who carry about idols of wood, who pray to gods that cannot save.'

I shall never forget some Christian friends of mine in Korea taking me to see a temple. There was a cordoned-off area with a sign in Korean which my friends translated: 'Keep out, we are making some gods.' It isn't funny, it's tragic—that even in a country like that, where so many turned to the Lord in the 1970s and continue to do so, all that is still going on as well.

But He talks about what I call man-made religion here, and gods are not necessarily made of wood or of stone. There was a Western book published some years ago called *The God That I Want*. None of them were made of wood or stone, but they were just as much figments of the imagination. But the problem of such gods as described in verse 20 is that they carry them about. It's most beautifully contrasted in 46:1—'The images that are carried about are burdensome, a burden for the weary. They stoop and bow down together; unable to rescue the burden, they themselves go off into captivity.'

Then God turns round to His people and says, 'Listen to me, O house of Jacob, all you who remain of the house of Israel, you whom I have upheld since you were conceived, and have carried since your birth' (46:3). And that's the contrast; that man-made religion will give you as much help as you've already got, because you carry it. But the God Who is There (if I may borrow Francis Schaeffer's phrase) carries His people.

There's an extraordinary description in verse 2. It says they carry them, and then they leave them behind. When Cambodia fell, people fled to Thailand leaving their gods behind. The gods hadn't worked in the catastrophe. And that's why a handful of Khmer Christians could lead thousands and thousands of Cambodians to Christ, because they realised that they'd been carrying a god and they needed a God to carry them.

Do you see what it says in 45:20? It says, they pray to gods. In the Hebrew it actually says, 'they pray to a god'. The word is *el*, which means 'him'. You might say, 'Oh, but they believe in God, they are serious about God, they pray and they pray and they pray to God.' And it is the same word. But just look at verse 20. They pray and they pray and they pray and they pray (it says in the Hebrew)—to a god who cannot save. Oh, what a tragic religious world we live in. So much endless, futile prayer. And the question is not, 'Do they have a lot of truth because they know that there's a God, and they pray, and they know it's important and they know that they've got to be saved?'—though that's all there in that verse. It is not 'Are they heading in the right direction, because they certainly want to be saved?' Nor is it 'Are they sincere and regular in their religion?' The question is: 'Does it save, does it really rescue?'

And the awful thing, it says verse 20, is that people can't see it. You explain the gospel to a Thai Buddhist who deals with spirits, you make as clear as you possibly can the wonder of the gospel of grace; and he turns round and says, 'Oh yes, that's just what we believe.' You say, 'Why can't he see?'

You find exactly the same if you talk to folk in the bar and explain eternal issues to them, about a judgement and their sinfulness and their need of a Saviour and these absolutely crucial things that grip our soul—and they turn round and say, 'As a matter of fact I can manage perfectly well without that.' And you say to yourself, 'How ignorant can you get?'

You go into a coffee bar in Japan and say the same things and they turn round and say, 'You're wasting your time; we Japanese achieve things, we can save ourselves.' Well—they can in some ways, economically, but that isn't the question, is it?

Now what is Isaiah saying here? He is saying, 'Because of these awesome facts God wants people to be called to

compare what He says with what they are actually trusting.'
Look at verse 20: 'Gather together and come; assemble, you
fugitives from the nations.' Verse 21: 'Declare what is to be,
present it.' Alec Motyer says the next line should really read,
'By all means let them take council together.' Encourage
them, God is saying, to come and discuss and think through
these things, because you see, our God is a God who wants
to engage the minds of the people of the world. He is not
afraid of their philosophies. And the questions that are being
asked are important ones, in verses 20–21.

His first question is, 'Where else do you find reliable
prophecy; where else do you find answers that really work
with human lives all over the world?' And the second
question is, 'Where else can you find the God who is a
Saviour? There is no other god apart from Me, a righteous
God and a saviour.'

So often when I debate with Moslems, that's the thing that
really strikes them. So many things that they affirm, we are
glad that they affirm: that Jesus is the word of God, that
Jesus was born of a virgin, that Jesus did miracles, that Jesus
brought the gospel, that Jesus will come again as judge. And
then you say, 'And He died for your sins, didn't He.' Then
they'll say, 'God would never allow His holy prophet to
suffer like that.' The Saviour is missing.

But I want you to see that what God is saying is, 'I am not
interested in dumping the gospel on people, I want to engage
their minds and all that is within their minds.' Brothers and
sisters, we must beware, in our hasty generation, of global
gospel inoculation. A Hungarian friend from a lovely
charismatic church in Budapest said to me sadly, 'A bunch of
Westerners came and they did a quick hit-and-run business;
they gave us 400 people who'd made decisions for Christ.
And after all the work of one congregation following that up,
we found that one was converted.' One was converted. Praise
the Lord that one was converted, but we are not called to
give people the gospel and never mind what they think—'Just
make a decision . . .'

We are called to get people to think it through, to engage
with what is in their minds already; because, brothers and
sisters, the gospel is not like make-up to give you a new look.

It is to penetrate, so that you may be a new you, a new creation. And God says, 'To that end, I long that My truth should be interacting with the minds of the world.'

The Message Calls us to be Fugitives From the Nations

Some commentators think the beginning of verse 20 refers to the Jews who are exiled around the different nations, the Jews of the dispersion. I don't think that's right, because the context is God's longing that the ends of the earth should be saved; and that in that sense, Israel should fulfil its role as the light to the nations.

Rahab was not one of the best citizens of Jericho. She realised that going along with Jericho made her a loser. She heard of the living God who was in the midst of His people, and she was determined to belong with the living God and the people of the living God. So she became a fugitive from Jericho, no longer belonging there but belonging in the people of God.

Everyone comes to Christ as a refugee, for our message is, 'You people have had it. Flee to Christ. You people in Nineveh have forty days left. Flee to the Lord.' That is the message, wherever you go. God longs for those who will flee to be saved.

There is in This World No Alternative

We need to stand with Isaiah and understand that there is in this world no alternative to the message of the Bible, the message of our God and Saviour. See how he expresses this fact.

Firstly, in verses 21, 22 and 24, he says that there's no-one else to go to. There is no other God, there is no other saviour, there is no other source of righteousness. When Jesus turned to the disciples and said, 'Are you going to quit too?' Peter said, 'Well—where on earth else can we go? You have the words of eternal life and we have come to believe in You' (cf John 6:67–68). Where else can people go, to get right? He is the only source of righteousness, the only source of strength, for He is the one who says, 'You shall receive power when the Holy Spirit has come upon you.' I once talked with a British Moslem doctor about his faith. He said, 'When I talk about having a relationship with God I don't mean what my Christian friends mean. I have a relationship, as it were, with God's book. My Christian friends have got so much more than that.' There is no other source of righteousness and strength.

Secondly notice that in this matter of alternatives, there's no other future. Verse 23: 'By myself I have sworn, my mouth has uttered in all integrity a word that will not be revoked.'

'I'm not going to eat this word,' He says. And what is this word? 'Before Me every knee will bow; by Me every tongue will swear.' See how this is developed in Philippians: 'Every tongue [will] confess that Jesus Christ is Lord, to the glory of God the Father' (Phil. 2:11). It doesn't say that every tongue and every person behind that tongue will be saved; but they'll all be bowing. Verse 24 shows us that some will bow in awful shame. Verse 25 shows us that others will exult in glory because they have been found righteous. Who are they? The descendants of Israel. It's the people of God, as Galatians 6 makes clear. Who are the true Israel? Those who glory in the cross. They are those who are found righteous. There is no real alternative.

This is where the Lord has a passionate burden, expressed in verse 22: 'Turn to me and be saved, all you ends of the earth.' Do you see what it tells us? It tells us that people need to turn. They are not heading in the same direction as us, they need, as we have needed, to turn from the way they are going. They need to be changed, they need to be saved. They are not all right as they are. The call that goes out, the same that went to Athens ('Now he commands all people everywhere to repent', Acts 17:31), is a call that is to go out to all the ends of the earth.

Many of you will believe that you are called to Britain. If that's God's will, that's fine. But please don't tell me that Britain is one of the least evangelised nations on earth. If you say that to me I will say what George Verwer has said on this platform some years ago: if you think that, it's time you switched your brain on. It's certainly time you bought *Operation World*.[1] But God is saying in Isaiah, people all over need to be saved. He wants them to hear and respond. He doesn't say that there are all sorts of different back doors. People need to hear. They need to turn from the direction they are going, they need to let God work upon them. There has to be change if there's going to be salvation. I love the way that Alec Motyer in his brilliant new commentary on Isaiah translates this: 'Turn to me and your salvation will be certain beyond doubt.' If that's true, praise the Lord! That is the invitation that needs to go to the end of the earth.

That's what God wants. Do you want what God wants? Is verse 22 your longing? If it is, how does it show? For Jesus says, 'All this Lord, Lord, talk on Wednesday nights is wonderful—but do you do what I want?'

This morning we were invited to dream dreams. Let me tell you some of my dreams. The first, I had at the check-out in the supermarket as I was seeing how much food I could buy so I could qualify for £40 worth of free food. Yet there are many places in the world where we are cutting back the numbers of those who will share the gospel so that the ends of the earth may be saved—because there isn't enough money. The call tonight is a call to the Lordship of Christ, to taking the low seat before the Lord. As you gentlemen will know, one of the problems about a low seat is that it empties your pockets. I remember a fellow-elder of mine in a church I used to belong to, who said to me: 'I have just realised that I am spending more on ice-cream and chocolate than I am on getting people to know Jesus as Saviour. I have got to sit down and re-do my budget.' If God's ambition is that the ends of the earth shall be saved, isn't that worth one supermarket trolley loaded with food each week? Or am I being ridiculously over the top?

At the end there's going to be an appeal related to service. You won't be asked to do it, but some of you must do it—you

---

1. Mr Dowsett is referring to Patrick Johnstone, *Operation World* (O M Publishing, 5th edn 1993). This and its associated products form a major information resource on world mission.

must resolve tonight that you are going to go home and completely revise your budget, so that it will show in your pocket that your ambitions fit with God's.

There's a second dream that I had when I was in South Thailand and saw how years and years of missionary work by Spirit-filled people had resulted, if you make the most generous assessment, in perhaps a hundred very fragile, vulnerable, weak believers. I met with missionary after missionary who stood there and cried, and said, 'Why is it so pathetic?' And my dream this time is for people whom Paul called for in Romans 15:30: people who will join the struggle by praying to God on their behalf; people who will stop saying, 'Lord, here's my shopping list, bless me, bless me, bless me, I will not let You go unless You bless me,' and will start praying the New Testament Spirit-filled prayer, 'I will not let You go unless you bless them.'

Some of you are already committed in prayer. But maybe some of you are just playing around. You say, 'Jesus is Lord, Jesus is Lord, praise Him with hallelujahs—but if His ambitions are in this direction, well I simply haven't got time, I'm a busy man, I'm a frantic mum'—or dad, depending on which of you brings up your children in the fear and nurture of the Lord. But the call to sacrifice is to us all. Will you take that low seat which changes your ambition, which makes ambition futile? Will you covenant perhaps to pray for somebody, to pray and to pray and to pray—for a particular people group? 'I will not let You go unless You bless them.'

My final dream is a dream for workers who will be mobilised.

I'm frightened to make an appeal in this respect, because some years ago I made an appeal here and a couple stood up over there. She was later murdered as she prepared a birthday cake for the sixth birthday of her second child. There are many tears in going out. But the seed needs to be sown for the sake of the harvest.

And therefore my dream is that British churches will stop pussy-footing around and playing missionary tourism, and that people will be prepared to take their professions to where those professions are keys to open doors, and to take the gospel of Jesus with them. Or to leave their professions, and transfer and plant churches where churches are thin on the ground.

The call is to take a low seat to fit in with the Lord's ambitions. Can you budget a new, regular, day-by-day commitment to somebody to wrestle in prayer for them? Are you—not just young people—willing to go? I know a lady of fifty-eight who left and planted six churches in Japan. I know a lady of sixty-eight who's teaching English in China. Not all oldies can do that, not all youngies can either; but God can mobilise, and we need to be aware.

Could it be that God has put His hand on you, that tonight it has crystallised in your mind that He is pushing you out, maybe to stay in your job but to change your location for the sake of the gospel—like Aquila and Priscilla in Acts 18? Or you believe God has His hand on you to call you out of your job and switch you into something else, so that you may make disciples somewhere else? Or you may know that God has His hand on you, you can't answer all the questions but you now believe that it's time for you to do what Paul did in Acts 16. You are going to try to go.

I am not just going to ask whether you are willing to go anywhere if God calls you, because I would hope that you'd all stand up for that. But maybe you have come to the point where you know God has His hand on you and now you have to act; to go to that Christian service centre, to get that information, because you believe God wants you to change your location and to move out for Him.

If God has spoken to you and you know that you've got to settle it, and really align yourself with this ambition of God that the ends of the earth should turn to Him, will you stand up as we sing, and we'll pray for you? We're all in full-time service, we're all called to serve the Lord. And if the Lord is especially asking you to move out for Him and for a lost world, stand up so that we can help you and so wc that can pray for you.

'A Fountain Opened'

by Canon Keith Weston

Zechariah 13:1; John 1

I want to look with you at 1 John 1 tonight, despite the fact that my title is taken from the words of Zechariah: 'A fountain opened' (Zech. 13:1).

Those words form a wonderful climax to Zechariah's prophecy. He was a poet, a visionary; his words paint wonderful prophetic pictures. His contemporary prophet, Haggai, was the practical man of the pair. He stirred up the hearts of the people to get on with the task of rebuilding the temple in Jerusalem after the long years of exile. Both men dated their prophecies, which is very convenient for us as we know exactly when they spoke God's word. In Zechariah 1:7 the date is given (you have to translate it into our system) 15 February 519 BC; and roughly a year later, in 7:1, it's dated 7 December.

Urged on by Haggai the people build the temple, while Zechariah lifts their eyes to greater things to come. Of course Haggai does it too: they work in tandem. It's Haggai who says that lovely verse which I'm so glad the NIV has restored to Scripture, the Revised Version doesn't have it—'The desire of all nations will come, and [I] will fill this house with glory' (Hag. 2:7, NIV). He's referring to the very day when Jesus Himself would walk on those paved floors that those builders were laying, and the inference is, 'So don't despise your building because it's so much smaller than the one that was destroyed; don't despise the work you're doing; do it to the best of your ability. This temple is going to be far more glorious than the previous one destroyed by those invading armies.' And we know why. It was in that very temple that Jesus walked and talked and healed.

Now Zechariah's prophetic eye takes the theme further. In the wonderful and strange way God uses prophecy, the outlines for the future that lay ahead in that day 500 years before Christ begin dimly to appear every now and then with shafts of brilliant light. 'Lo, your king comes to you; triumphant and victorious is he, humble and riding on an ass, on a colt the foal of an ass' (Zech. 9:9, RV). But the king's shepherd is rejected: 'Awake, O sword, against my shepherd, against the man who is close to me! ... "Strike the shepherd, and the sheep will be scattered" ' (13:7, NIV). 'They will look on [him], the one they have pierced, and mourn for [him] as one grieves for an only child ... a first-born son' (12:10). He suffers wounds received 'at the house of my friends' (13:6).

All those verses are quoted in the New Testament, when what Zechariah saw with a prophetic eye is clearly seen. Jesus Himself is the person who quotes Zechariah: 'It is written, "I will strike the shepherd ..." ' (Mark 14:27), on the very night when they sang that hymn in the upper room and went out into the dark and into Gethsemane.

Zechariah states—what a beautiful climax!—'On that day a fountain will be opened ... to cleanse ... from sin and impurity.' I don't think he could have seen the whole significance of what he was saying. The prophets searched for the truth that was to come and longed see it themselves. But, says the New Testament (1 Pet. 1:12), it was for us they prophesied it, and we see how those prophecies are gloriously fulfilled.

Zechariah's words are very significant: sin and impurity. Scripture doesn't pile words on top of each other just for rhetoric. 'Sin', in the language in which Zechariah wrote, is the general word for human waywardness that rebels against God. A fountain is to be opened to cleanse from that. And 'impurity' is a Hebrew word that normally has a sexual connotation, which includes all that going after other gods that the prophet so often denounced: 'other gods which are no gods at all'. The old version uses the graphic expression 'a whoring after other gods'. The result is the desperate defilement of the soul; it is the pollution and the filth which Scripture says is a stench in the nostrils of God.

Scripture speaks plainly. All of us have become like someone who is dirty; 'all our righteous acts are like filthy rags' in His sight (Isa. 64:6). The analogy is so stark and brutally unpleasant that no translator nowadays dare risk the offence of translating it straight into English. Christian, how seriously do you regard the sins you so lightly commit, if this is what it does to your Heavenly Father, if it's what it did to Christ His Son? But how merciful is our God, like a human parent whose child has wandered into the mud and is covered from head to foot—so God holds out His holy arms, and pulls us to Himself because He loves us, to make us clean.

Isaiah puts it beautifully, ' "Come now, let us reason together," says the Lord. "Though your sins are like scarlet, they shall be as white as snow; though they are red like crimson, they shall be like wool. If you are willing and obedient . . ." ' (Isa. 1:18). The words He uses are of indelible stains that you think you will never get out; yet He's prepared to clean you and me like that.

'Wash and make yourselves clean. Take your evil deeds out of my sight! Stop doing wrong, learn to do right!' (Isa. 1:16–17). But how? Here is the title for today in the Keswick programme: 'How can a young man [a young woman] keep his [her] way pure?' (Psa. 119:9). Zechariah tells us: 'A fountain is opened for all sin and impurity'.

William Cowper's beautiful hymn was considered by the compilers of the hymn-book Songs of Praise to be rather too brutal for modern singing:

> There is a fountain filled with blood,
> Drawn from Immanuel's veins
> And sinners plunged beneath that flood
> Lose all their guilty stains.

It's a revolting picture. But it means that the finished work of

Christ upon the cross, when that blood flowed like a fountain, is the only place where you can find full cleansing from all your sin and impurity.

> The dying thief rejoiced to see
> That fountain in his day;
> And there may I though vile as he,
> Wash all my sins away.

Turn now to 1 John, where John beautifully expounds this theme. 'This is the message we have heard from him and declare to you... ' (1 John 1:5). It's a message about how a man or a woman can be made clean. Verse 7: 'purifies us from every sin'. What purifies? The blood of Jesus His Son, of course. What an amazing statement!

I often wish that I could read these statements in Scripture as if I had never heard them before, or known them all my life. What does it say to you, 'The blood of Jesus his Son cleanses us from all sin'? It leads you to Calvary, doesn't it, where that blood was shed at such tremendous cost. 'A fountain opened' ... 'And sinners plunged beneath that flood, Lose all their guilty stains.'

Look at 1:9: 'He is faithful and just and will forgive us our sins and purify us from all unrighteousness.' The same thought is in 2:2–3—'Jesus Christ, the Righteous One. He is the atoning sacrifice for our sins, and not only for ours but also for the sins of the whole world.' Look at those superlatives: 'all sins'; 'all unrighteousness'; 'the whole world'. Now, brothers and sisters; does that include you? Of course it does. He couldn't have put it more emphatically. All sins, throughout the whole world, are cleansed through the blood of Jesus alone. Your sins; every one of them. My sins; every one of them. The gross sins of which you are heartily ashamed, or the 'little' sins. Of course no sin is little. But even the sins that we and the world sometimes think of as petty, though they are not so in God's sight and are deadly—all unrighteousness, the sins of the whole world, are cleansed in the blood of Jesus.

Three words are repeated several times in this passage: 'if we claim' (verses 6, 8, 10). Each is a vain profession: 'No need, thank you, of God's cleansing.' John is writing to

Christians. This is not an evangelistic letter, to those who
know nothing of trusting in Christ for the first time for the
forgiveness of their sins. If 'we' claim—we who profess and
call ourselves Christians—if we claim effectively that we have
no need of the cleansing and the blood of Christ, what a
tragic situation we are in! We deceive, we 'make [God] a
liar', he says (1:10).

Sheer Hypocrisy (verse 6)

The first 'if we claim' amounts to the sin of sheer hypocrisy
in the Christian. If we profess and call ourselves Christians
but indulge in secret sins—in our thought life, perhaps, in
harboured resentment or jealousy, hatred, hardened prejudi-
ces—if we say we are Christians and yet walk in darkness, we
are liars and we do not live by the truth.

I know my own heart well enough and I can't help
observing other Christians. When that kind of horrid sin
disrupts church life or disrupts family life, we make God out
to be a liar. We make a big profession of being Christians, we
have big Bibles and probably know them from cover to cover,
we're at every church meeting. But the Bible says that God is
the God who searches the heart, and sometime hearts which
carry big Bibles hide the most horrid sins. You know that, I
know it. If we say we are Christians and walk in darkness, we
are liars and we don't live by the truth. If we profess to be
Christians and indulge in open sins, like resorting to
lying—white lies of course, or just a bit of extravagant over-
statement, or being less than honest with others—if we have
relationships, especially with the other sex, which we know to
be wrong yet somehow we go on doing it—if we foster
undercurrents in our church life which destroy the unity and
make the evangelism of that church totally ineffective—if we
make convincing profession of being a Christian but inwardly
know our lives are living lies, then we are liars not living by
the truth.

But, says Scripture, but there's a fountain open. 'Turn
round,' says John, 'from straying in the dark.' Verse 7: 'If we
walk in the light, as he is in the light . . .' Will you let the
Holy Spirit speak to you if you are in that first category? You

are in great danger. Sins kill, and Jesus died on the cross to cleanse you from your sin. And He reveals to you what is hidden tonight. Oh I plead with you, brother, sister, get right with God and do it tonight. The fountain is open for all sin and impurity, and the blood of Jesus His Son—at such cost—purifies us, goes on purifying us from all sin.

Sheer Pride (verse 8)

The second 'if we claim' amounts to sheer pride. If we claim to be without sin, we can then of course criticise others, in what we think is righteous indignation: but our claim not to have the same faults shouts from the way we talk. Aren't we good at niggling and carping at how other Christians behave? And we become such insensitive and unpleasant people to live with, because in effect we're saying, 'I am not like that.'

'I'm so glad I'm not like that sinner' said the Pharisee, thinking he was so religious. It's pride that makes those claims. 'Don't try to pull the speck out of someone else's eye when there's a tree trunk sticking out of your own,' said Jesus (cf Matt. 7:4–5). What price any concept of perfectionism? John is writing to Christians, and if we claim to be without sin then we are making absolute nonsense claims. There's no truth in it at all and we are poor deceived people.

Are there any poor deceived people in this tent tonight, claiming that you don't have the sins other people have, that you don't act so stupidly as some people obviously do—and you condemn them; that you could do the speaker's job much better? I'm sure you could, dear brother, but beware of the sin of pride that says 'I know all about that and nobody else does.'

But how can a person be pure? Because pride is such an insidious thing, it stains so indelibly. Zechariah comes back : there's a fountain opened. 'And if,' says John, 'we confess our sins'—and that can be very costly indeed, it will mean getting down on your knees, it means getting down low before God and saying, 'Oh God, be merciful to me the sinner.' Perhaps part of that confession will be writing a letter to someone to whom you owe an apology. It can be very costly indeed. It may mean that some husband here has to go home and say, 'I'm sorry' to his wife, or vice versa. It may mean you've got to own up to this, that or the other, and it will be a public and costly confession. Don't write off that little phrase, 'if we confess our sins'. But confess them to God first, and He'll tell you what to do.

But look! 'If we confess our sins, [God] is faithful and just and will forgive us our sins and purify us from all unrighteousness.' Those sins will simply wash off us and we'll be free, as the hymn tells us. What a glorious truth that is! What release to be free from the wretched burden of things we know we shouldn't have done, when we confess our sins. God is faithful, that means He is utterly trustworthy, because He tells us in the Scriptures that if we believe in Jesus and His finished work on the cross at Calvary, then that cross will meet all our needs and purify us from all our sins—however deadly and horrible they are, however hard it may be to put them right.

He is not only trustworthy to His promise, but He's absolutely just. Why? Because, Christian, Jesus went to the cross to bear the punishment that was due to you. He went there to have all that load of your sins laid on Him: 'the Lord hath laid on him the iniquity of us all' (Isa. 53:6, AV). So there's nothing on us to be condemned any more. It's gone, it's been washed away in the blood of Jesus. God removes our sins as far as the east is from the west (cf Psa. 103:12). And therefore He is just to keep to His promise. Though Satan may say to you 'You are still guilty', you can reply 'No condemnation now I dread.'

Why? Simply because of Christ's finished work on the cross of Calvary, where He took all that load of sin, guilt and penalty: all the punishment. Praise be to God, I am free!—if we confess our sins, He is faithful to His promise, and He is just, because the punishment has been borne by another. Tell that to Satan when he tempts you and tells you you are still guilty!

Sheer Unbelief (verse 10)

The third 'if we claim' amounts to sheer unbelief. Can that be true of the Christian? Well, it's possible for Christians to behave like unbelievers, when we make this claim. And if we do, it says—and how striking it is—we make God a liar. We are liars ourselves, but by implication we say that God is a liar too, and His word, says John, has no place in our lives.

Our society says adultery is acceptable; God says it's unacceptable. Does that make Him a liar? God says that homosexual practices are an abomination; society says no, it's acceptable. Do you make Him a liar? Our society says that what you want is the best guidance for behaviour. But God gives us laws in His love, and controls our behaviour for our good and for the good of society. Who is right—you or God? Do you make Him a liar? Do we want to make God out to be unfaithful to His word because we reject that word, because it doesn't suit us at some point? Does God's word really have so little a place in our lives? I wonder how often I have by implication called God a liar because I haven't really believed what He says. I wonder how often you've done it. This is written to Christians. How can a man, a woman, be pure? There's a fountain opened.

John says, 'My dear children, I write this to you so that you will not sin. But if anybody does sin, we have one who speaks to the Father in our defence—Jesus Christ the Righteous One. He is the atoning sacrifice for our sins, and not only for ours but also for the sins of the whole world' (2:1). He is the atoning sacrifice. The original word is 'propitiation'—the NIV weakens it in translation. You propitiate an angry god. That's a problem for some theologians. But God is angry about sin, because that's what the Bible says. Do you believe God, or do you want to make Him a liar?

The wrath of God is not a pleasant thought. But Paul says it is 'revealed from heaven against all the godlessness and wickedness of men who suppress the truth by their wickedness' (Rom. 1:18). Propitiation is what stops that wrath being poured out. People don't like that idea these days.

Interestingly, the word is that used for the Mercy Seat in the Tabernacle with the angel figures over it, where the high priest went on the Day of Atonement and which he sprinkled with the shed blood. The high priest and nobody else took that blood for the sins of the people, and it was poured out on the Mercy Seat.

That's the word used here. The people knew forgiveness through the blood that was shed. He is the atoning sacrifice, the blood that was shed on the place where mercy is shown to undeserving sinners.

In my last job I was Director of Ordinands in the Diocese of Norwich, which meant that men and women used to come to me looking for full-time service. On the day before his ordination a candidate is usually interviewed by the bishop, who will talk to the man and encourage him and pray with him before the great day when he is ordained, in the cathedral the next morning. One ordination candidate said to the bishop, 'Bishop, if you knew how unworthy I am to be ordained by you, you would never lay hands on me.' And that dear bishop replied, 'If you knew how unworthy I am, you wouldn't let me do it.'

Isn't that lovely? We've got to recognise that in the sight of God we are simply unworthy sinners, and we need to come again and again to the cross of Christ and to know the continual cleansing. These are 'present continuous' tenses in the Greek, which means that the translation is, 'Goes on cleansing us from all sin.'

And whoever came to God for any service and said, 'I am worthy Lord'? God have mercy upon us if that's our attitude. No, get down low and say, 'God be merciful to me the sinner.' Paul the apostle himself said, 'Christ Jesus came into the world to save sinners.' And it doesn't stop there because, he goes on to say, 'of whom I am the worst' (1 Tim. 1:15). And you've got to say that and I've got to say that. But the fountain is opened for continual cleansing. And the blood of Jesus Christ goes on cleansing us from all our sin.

I remember a leader of the Crusader class I attended as a boy. He could never speak about the cross without the tears streaming from his eyes. He was an elderly man, it was wartime, the younger men had gone off to war. And God forgive me, I used to think it rather funny to see this old man crying. Have you ever wept at the thought of what Christ did for you on the cross of Calvary? That His blood shed for you might cleanse you and go on cleansing you from all sin? Have you ever weighed the cost it was to Him to save you from your sins?

Many years ago now I was sent as the Keswick speaker, to the great Indian Convention in Kerala in South India. It's a tremendous experience—it's the largest Keswick-type Convention in the world. They are disappointed if they don't get 100,000 people to it. This year they had many more than that. I was preaching on the text that brought me to assurance of faith, Isaiah 53:5–6. As I was preaching on that text to that vast crowd, the Godly priest who was translating for me simply broke down, the tears just flowed down his cheeks at the thought of what Christ has done to redeem worthless sinners like us. And there was a gentle shifting through that vast congregation. I saw the ladies covering their heads with their saris. And another priest told me after the service that he'd seen hundreds weeping.

Have you ever wept out of thankfulness to Christ, what He's done for you?

Oh make me understand it, help me to take it in,
What it meant to Thee the Holy One to bear away my sin.

'A fountain opened' is so easy to say, but it cost God's only Son everything He had. And if you were the only sinner in the whole world, He would have done it for you.

'Walk in the light then,' says John; turn around and go the other way. He's talking to Christians. It may be that there's somebody tonight who ought to turn around and get back into the light, because He is in the light and you can't walk with Him if you are walking in darkness. So have done with that sin, and have done with it tonight. Confess your sins, humble yourselves before the Lord, and He will lift you up. And as God reveals to us in His love and mercy what those sins are which grieve Him, come to the fountain. He shed His blood for you; He bore all our penalties, all our guilt. 'And the blood of Jesus Christ God's Son will cleanse you from all your sin.' That's what it says in the Bible. God is faithful. He is just. And He will forgive you.

Nothing in my hand I bring,
Simply to Thy cross I cling.
Foul I to the fountain fly,
Wash me, Saviour, or I die.

KESWICK 1994 TAPES AND VIDEOS

Tapes and Videos

Here is a list of the tape numbers for each of the addresses included in this volume, followed in each case by the video numbers:

Morning Bible Readings

Rev Philip Hacking	(T)	KESW1, KESW2, KESW3, KESW4, KESW5
	(V)	KES94/05, KES94/08, KES94/11, KESW94/14, KES94/17
Rev Jim Graham	(T)	KESW6, KESW7, KESW8, KESW9, KESW10
	(V)	KES94/21, KES94/23, KES94/25, KES94/27, KES94/29

Addresses

	Tape	Video
Rev Tony Baker	KESW14	KES94/06
Rev Chua Wee Hian	KESW8	KES94/07
Rev Clive Calver	KESW15	KES94/09
Rev Keith White	KESW11	KES94/16
Rev Alex Ross	KESW36	KES94/28
Mr Dick Dowsett	KESW35	KES94/26
Canon Keith Weston	KESW34	KES94/24

Tapes cost £3.00 per cassette plus postage, calculated according to number of cassettes ordered: 1—60p, 2—75p, 3—95p, 4—£1.10, 5—£1.30, 6—£1.50, 7—£1.70, 8–10 cassettes £1.95, 11–20 cassettes £2.95. These rates are for UK only, other rates on application.

Tape orders should be sent to:

ICC (International Christian Communications)
Silverdale Road
Eastbourne
East Sussex BN20 7AB.

A leaflet listing all the ministry recordings made at Keswick 1994, plus details of Keswick music recordings and song-books, is obtainable from the same address, from where you can also obtain information about availability of previous years' recordings.

Videos cost £11.99 per video. Postage is calculated at £1 per video (UK); £2 per video (EEC); and other countries £7 per video. Purchasers should note, however, that the VHS/PAL standard is used. This is the most popular format in the UK but for use in the USA and certain other countries a different format will need to be specially ordered.

Video orders should be sent to:

Mr Dave Armstrong
STV Videos
Box 299
Bromley, Kent BR2 9XB.

Cheques should be made payable to 'STV Videos'

Books

All annual Keswick volumes since 1978 have been published by STL Books (now O M Publishing), the publishing wing of Send the Light Ltd. A major warehouse fire destroyed stocks of many of those years' volumes, but your bookseller will be able to tell you which of the most recent ones are still in print. The anthology *Keswick Gold*, edited by David Porter (O M Publishing 1990), contains a selection of 22 addresses from the 1978–1989 volumes. In case of difficulty, enquiries may be made directly to the publishers (address on reverse of title page of this volume).

KESWICK 1995

The annual Keswick Convention takes place each July at the heart of England's beautiful Lake District. The two separate weeks of the Convention offer an unparalleled opportunity for listening to gifted Bible exposition, experiencing Christian fellowship with believers from all over the world, and enjoying something of the unspoilt grandeur of God's creation.

Each of the two weeks has a series of five morning Bible Readings, followed by other addresses throughout the rest of the day. The programme in the second week is a little less intensive, and it is often referred to as 'Holiday Week'. There are also regular meetings throughout the fortnight for young people, and a Children's Holiday Club.

The date for the 1995 Keswick Convention are 15–22 July (Convention Week) and 22–29 July (Holiday Week). The Bible Reading speakers are Rev Alec Motyer and Dr Roy Clements respectively. Other speakers during the fortnight are Rev Robert Amess, Rev Ian Coffey, Rev Philip Hacking, Mr Nigel Lee, Mr Jonathan Lamb and Mr David Burke.

For further information, write to:
The Administrator
Keswick Convention Centre
Skiddaw Street
Cumbria CA12 4BY
Telephone: 07687 72589